# McGRAW-
# Language Arts

## Preparation and Practice
### for the
### ITBS, SAT-9, and TerraNova

## Grade 3

## Teacher's Edition

McGraw-Hill
School Division

The Princeton Review

## The Princeton Review

This booklet was written by The Princeton Review, the nation's leader in test preparation. The Princeton Review helps millions of students every year prepare for standardized assessments of all kinds. Through its association with McGraw-Hill, The Princeton Review offers the best way to help students excel on the ITBS, SAT-9, and TerraNova tests.

The Princeton Review is not affiliated with Princeton University or Educational Testing Service.

**McGraw-Hill School Division**

*A Division of The McGraw·Hill Companies*

Copyright © McGraw-Hill School Division, a Division of the Educational and Professional Publishing Group of The McGraw-Hill Companies, Inc.

McGraw-Hill School Division
Two Penn Plaza
New York, New York 10121

Printed in the United States of America

ISBN: 0-02-244943-4

5 6 7 8 9 047 04

# ITBS

# SAT-9

# TERRANOVA

# ITBS

# TEACHER
# INTRODUCTION

# WHY *PREPARATION AND PRACTICE FOR THE ITBS* IS THE BEST PREPARATION FOR STUDENTS

Welcome to the Teacher Edition of *Preparation and Practice for the ITBS* for grade 3!

By completing each section of this book, students will:

- Increase their knowledge and understanding of language arts skills
- Become familiar with the types of questions that will be asked on the test
- Become aware of and experience first-hand the amount of time they will have to complete the test
- Become accustomed to the style of the test
- Become better writers and speakers
- Learn test-taking techniques and tips that are specifically designed to help students do their best on the ITBS
- Feel comfortable on the day of the exam

# Parts of This Book

There are eight sections of this Teachers' Edition:

## Teacher Introduction

The Teacher Introduction familiarizes you with the purpose and format of *Preparation and Practice for the ITBS.* It also describes the ITBS sections and questions on the test that pertain to language arts skills.

## Student and Class Diagnostic Charts

This section consists of two charts. A student and a class diagnostic chart are included for the Warm-Up Test. These charts may be used to gauge student performance and to determine the skills with which students will need the most practice as they prepare for the ITBS.

## Student Introduction

This section contains some tips and explanations for students as they begin their preparation for the ITBS. Extra annotations are included for teacher to help you further explain what is expected of students and to encourage them as they begin their test preparation.

## Warm-Up Test

This diagnostic test reveals students' strengths and weaknesses so that you may customize your test preparation accordingly. The skill tested in each question of the Warm-Up Test directly correlates to a skill reviewed in one of the 30 On Your Mark! Get Set! Go! practice exercises.

## On Your Mark! Get Set! Go!

This section consists of 30 practice exercises. Each exercise focuses on a specific language arts skill or test-taking strategy. On Your Mark! introduces and explains the skill. Get Set! provides an example question that tests the skill. (You should go over the question as a class. Get Set! is designed to bridge the gap between On Your Mark! and the test-like questions in Go!) Go! contains questions—similar to ITBS questions—that test the skills introduced in the exercise. Have students complete these questions on their own.

## Practice Test

The Practice Test is an exact replica of the actual ITBS in style and format. The Mini-Practice Test contains the exact number of questions that will appear on the actual test so that students are given a realistic test-taking experience. The Practice Test includes questions from each section: spelling, capitalization, punctuation, and usage and expression.

## On Your Mark! Get Set! Go! Review

This review section is an overview of the skills contained in On Your Mark! Get Set! Go! Similar skills are grouped together and the On Your Mark! Get Set! Go! exercises to which the skills correspond are noted.

## Index

The index is a brief listing of where you can look to find exercises about specific skills.

# How to Use This Book

This book has been designed so that you may customize your ITBS test preparation according to your class's needs and time frame. However, we recommend that you begin your test preparation as early in the school year as possible. This book will yield your students' best ITBS scores if you diagnose your students' strengths and weaknesses early and work toward helping them achieve their best performance. Please note that preparing students for a test such as the ITBS is a process. As much of their preparation as possible should take place in the classroom and be discussed as a class.

## Warm-Up Test

Have students complete the Warm-Up Test in class. It should be administered as early in the school year as possible. By doing so, students will gain familiarity with the types of questions and the specific skills tested on the ITBS *before* they begin working through the skill-specific exercises in this book. Use the student and class diagnostic charts to grade the tests. The results of the Warm-Up Test reveal students' strengths and weaknesses and allow you to focus your test preparation accordingly.

## On Your Mark! Get Set! Go!

We recommend that you review an On Your Mark! Get Set! Go! exercise after completing each chapter in your McGraw-Hill language arts textbook. It is best to go through the On Your Mark! Get Set! Go! section throughout the year so that students can digest the material properly. Consider reviewing On Your Mark! and Get Set! as a class. The Go! section may be assigned as homework or completed by students individually in class. Having students complete Go! individually will provide the best simulated preparation for the ITBS. After students have completed the Go! exercises, go over the correct answers as a class. The Princeton Review's research and experience shows this in-class work to be an essential element in effective test preparation.

## Practice Test

The Practice Test should be administered in the weeks prior to the actual exam. Testing conditions should be simulated. For example, no two desks should be placed directly next to each other, students should have two pencils at their disposal, the room should be quiet, and so on.

## On Your Mark! Get Set! Go! Review

Use this review in the few days leading up to the actual exam. Its purpose is to solidify the On Your Mark! Get Set! Go! skills students have learned throughout the school year. Answer any questions students might have and go over the specific exercises and skills with which students are the most concerned. You might want students to read over the section as homework and bring in a list of their questions to class the next day. Address as many of the students concerns as possible before the actual exam. If students need additional review, consult the On Your Mark! Get Set! Go! exercises that correlate to the skills.

# About the Teacher Pages

Each page of the Pupil Edition is reproduced in this Teacher Edition, either reduced or full-size. Each reduced Pupil Edition page has teacher wrap. Teacher wrap consists of a **column** and a **box**.

- The column serves as a guide for you as you present the material on the Pupil Edition page in an interactive way. Guiding prompts and notes are included to ensure that information pivotal to the exercise is covered.

- The box includes teaching tips and extra activities. The extra activities are often fun, game-like activities for your class. These activities give students the opportunity to learn or apply ITBS-related skills in a variety of ways.

Teacher wrap pages are punctuated with five icon types that help guide you through the Pupil Edition.

 This icon correlates the teacher wrap to the information in the On Your Mark! section of the Pupil Edition page.

 This icon reminds you to go over the example question in the Get Set! section of the Pupil Edition page.

 This icon reminds you to go over each question on the Go! pages of the Pupil Edition.

 This icon provides a point of emphasis for you to make concerning the exercise on the Pupil Edition page.

 This icon identifies an extra activity.

# About the Annotated Pages

Some pages in the Teacher Edition include full-size Pupil Edition pages. These occur in the Student Introduction, the Warm-Up Test section, and the Practice Test section.

All of these full-size reproductions are highlighted with teacher annotations. These annotations, which appear in magenta ink, provide the following:

- **Correct Answers**

The correct answer to each question is circled in magenta ink.

- **Question Analyses**

Sometimes an annotation offers further explanation of a specific question.

- **Extra Tips**

Certain annotations provide you with extra teaching tips specific to the skill tested on the Pupil Edition page.

- **Hints**

Some annotations offer hints that you can give to your students when they are working through the questions in the exercise or test sections.

# Introduction to the ITBS

ITBS stands for Iowa Test of Basic Skills. The ITBS is a standardized test taken every year by students throughout the country. Talk to your school's test administrator to get the exact testing date for this school year.

The ITBS is a multiple-choice test that assesses students' skills in reading, language arts, mathematics, social studies, science, and information sources. This book covers the language arts section of the ITBS, which consists of four parts:

- **Spelling**
- **Capitalization**
- **Punctuation**
- **Usage and Expression**

The specific number of questions for each skill discussed above is broken down as follows on the actual ITBS:

| Skill | Spelling | Capitalization | Punctuation | Usage and Expression |
|---|---|---|---|---|
| **Number of Items** | 31 | 27 | 27 | 36 |

# Timing

The ITBS is a timed test. Students are given one hour to complete all four parts of the language arts section.

# How Language Arts Skills Are Tested

## Spelling

Students are asked to determine which of the provided words, if any, are spelled incorrectly.

EXAMPLE

**A** kone

**B** cool

**C** wear

**D** play

**E** *(No mistakes)*

This question tests students' ability to recognize a misspelled word. Students will circle the answer choice containing the misspelled word. If there are no misspelled words, students will circle the last answer choice.

## Capitalization

Students are asked to identify the sentence, or section of a sentence, which contains an error in capitalization.

EXAMPLE

**J** Rick and Nancy both have

**K** the same birthday. They were

**L** both born on july 2nd.

**M** *(No mistakes)*

This question tests students' knowledge of the capitalization rules for months of the year. Other capitalization questions will ask students to identify incorrect capitalization usage for proper nouns (both people and places), abbreviations (such as Mr. or Dr.) that precede proper nouns, days of the week, addresses, letter greetings and closings, and quotations.

© McGraw-Hill School Division

## Punctuation

Students are asked to identify a wide variety of punctuation errors.

EXAMPLE

**A** At three oclock, my

**B** babysitter picks me up.

**C** Then we go home.

**D** (*No mistakes*)

This question tests students' ability to pick out the missing apostrophe. Other punctuation questions will address punctuation rules for commas, quotations, question marks, abbreviations, initials, and possessive nouns. There will also be questions about correct punctuation usage for letter greetings and closings, addresses, and dates.

## Usage and Expression

Students are asked to identify a variety of mistakes in sentence and paragraph constructions. They are required to recognize many different examples of incorrect or awkward usage and expression, such as run-on sentences, incorrect verb tenses, and improper sentence structures.

EXAMPLE

**The captain is making the soldiers march yesterday.**

**A** make

**B** will make

**C** made

**D** (*No change*)

For this question, students must pick out the answer choice that uses the correct verb tense.

EXAMPLE

**A** Jean walked down to the basketball court, hoping to play a game.

**B** Walking down to the basketball court, a game Jean hoped to play.

**C** To play a game, down to the basketball court Jean walked.

**D** Down to the basketball court, hoping, Jean walked to play a game.

For this question, students must choose the answer choice that best expresses the idea in the sentence.

# STUDENT AND CLASS DIAGNOSTIC CHARTS

# How to Use the Student Diagnostic Chart

The Student Diagnostic Chart on page T15 should be used to score the Warm-Up Test in this book. The chart is designed to help you and your individual students determine the areas in which they need the most practice as they begin their preparation for the ITBS. You will need to make enough copies of the chart for each of your students.

There are two ways to use the Student Diagnostic Chart:

- You can collect the finished Warm-Up Tests from each student and fill out one chart for each student as you grade the tests.

- You can give one copy of the Student Diagnostic Chart to each student and have each student grade their own test as you read aloud the correct answer choices.

*Note: Correct answer choices are marked in the Warm-Up Test of this Teacher Edition.*

## How to Fill Out the Student Diagnostic Chart

For each question number, there is a blank column labeled "Right or Wrong." An "R" or a "W" should be placed in that column for each question on the Warm-Up Test. By looking at the chart upon completion, students will understand which questions they answered incorrectly and to which skills these incorrect answers corresponded. The exercise from the On Your Mark! Get Set! Go! section that teaches the skill is also noted. You should encourage students to spend extra time going over the corresponding exercises covering the skills with which they had the most trouble. The charts will also help you determine which students need the most practice and what skills gave the majority of the students trouble. This way, you can plan your students' ITBS preparation schedule accordingly.

# How to Use the Class Diagnostic Chart

The Class Diagnostic Chart on page T16 should be used to record your class's performance on the Warm-Up test in this book. The chart is designed to help you determine what areas your class needs to practice most as you begin the preparation for the ITBS. The Class Diagnostic Chart is strictly for your own use. You should not share it with students.

## How to Fill Out the Class Diagnostic Chart

Under the "Name" column, you should write the names of each of your students. Then you should use the completed Student Diagnostic Charts to help you fill out the Class Diagnostic Chart. Fill out one row for each student.

For each question on the Warm-Up Test, there is a corresponding row in the Class Diagnostic Chart. The row is labeled with the question number and the exercise number of the correlating On Your Mark! Get Set! Go! exercise. If a student gets a question wrong, you should mark an "X" in the box underneath that question number. After completing a column for one student, add up all of the "Xs" and put a total for that student in the "Total" row on the top of the page. When you have filled out a column for each student, you should total up the "Xs" for each question. Put the totals in the "Total" column on the right-hand side of the page. Assessing both "Total" columns will help you determine two things: 1) which students are having the most trouble individually, and 2) which questions are giving the class as a whole the most trouble.

You should use the information gathered in the Class Diagnostic Chart to determine which skills to spend the most time reviewing and what students need the most individual practice and guidance.

# Student Diagnostic Chart

| Question # | Correct Answer | Right or Wrong | Exercise # | Skill |
|------------|----------------|----------------|------------|-------|
| **Spelling** | | | | |
| 1 | B | | 1 | Adding -ing |
| 2 | L | | 2 | Words with Silent Letters |
| 3 | A | | 3 | Letters Pronounced More than One Way |
| 4 | M | | 4 | Letter Combination Sounds |
| 5 | A | | 5 | Tricky Words |
| **Capitalization** | | | | |
| 1 | C | | 8 | Proper Nouns: Places |
| 2 | J | | 9 | Proper Nouns: People |
| 3 | D | | 10 | Proper Nouns: Dates |
| 4. | L | | 8 | Common Nouns |
| 5 | A | | 9 | Proper Nouns: People |
| **Punctuation** | | | | |
| 1 | B | | 13 | Quotations |
| 2 | J | | 14 | End Marks |
| 3 | C | | 15 | Possessive Nouns |
| 4 | K | | 16 | Contractions |
| 5 | C | | 17 | Abbreviations |
| 6 | L | | 18 | Dates and Addresses |
| **Expression** | | | | |
| 1 | C | | 20 | Verb Tense Agreement |
| 2 | L | | 22 | Sentence Clarity |
| 3 | D | | 22 | Sentence Clarity |
| 4 | J | | 23 | Topic Sentences |
| 5 | C | | 24 | Sentence Order |
| 7 | A | | 26 | Double Negatives |
| 8 | K | | 27 | Pronouns |
| 9 | A | | 28 | Subject-Verb Agreement |
| 10 | K | | 20 | Verb Tense Agreement |

# Class Diagnostic Chart

| Name | | | | | | | | | | | | | | | | | | | | Total |
|------|--|--|--|--|--|--|--|--|--|--|--|--|--|--|--|--|--|--|--|-------|

**Spelling**
- Q1–Ex. 1
- Q2–Ex. 2
- Q3–Ex. 3
- Q4–Ex. 4
- Q5–Ex. 5

**Capitalization**
- Q1–Ex. 8
- Q2–Ex. 9
- Q3–Ex. 10
- Q4–Ex. 8
- Q5–Ex. 9

**Punctuation**
- Q1–Ex. 13
- Q2–Ex. 14
- Q3–Ex. 15
- Q4–Ex. 16
- Q5–Ex. 17
- Q6–Ex. 18

**Usage and Expression**
- Q1–Ex. 20
- Q2–Ex. 22
- Q3–Ex. 22
- Q4–Ex. 23
- Q6–Ex. 24
- Q7–Ex. 26
- Q8–Ex. 27
- Q9–Ex. 28
- Q10–Ex. 20

Total

# Practice Test Answer Sheet

Name: _____     Date: _____

## SPELLING

| | | | | | | | | | | | | | | | |
|---|---|---|---|---|---|---|---|---|---|---|---|---|---|---|---|
| S1 | Ⓐ Ⓑ Ⓒ Ⓓ Ⓔ | | 7 | Ⓐ Ⓑ Ⓒ Ⓓ Ⓔ | | 15 | Ⓐ Ⓑ Ⓒ Ⓓ Ⓔ | | 23 | Ⓐ Ⓑ Ⓒ Ⓓ Ⓔ |
| S2 | Ⓙ Ⓚ Ⓛ Ⓜ Ⓝ | | 8 | Ⓙ Ⓚ Ⓛ Ⓜ Ⓝ | | 16 | Ⓙ Ⓚ Ⓛ Ⓜ Ⓝ | | 24 | Ⓙ Ⓚ Ⓛ Ⓜ Ⓝ |
| 1 | Ⓐ Ⓑ Ⓒ Ⓓ Ⓔ | | 9 | Ⓐ Ⓑ Ⓒ Ⓓ Ⓔ | | 17 | Ⓐ Ⓑ Ⓒ Ⓓ Ⓔ | | 25 | Ⓐ Ⓑ Ⓒ Ⓓ Ⓔ |
| 2 | Ⓙ Ⓚ Ⓛ Ⓜ Ⓝ | | 10 | Ⓙ Ⓚ Ⓛ Ⓜ Ⓝ | | 18 | Ⓙ Ⓚ Ⓛ Ⓜ Ⓝ | | 26 | Ⓙ Ⓚ Ⓛ Ⓜ Ⓝ |
| 3 | Ⓐ Ⓑ Ⓒ Ⓓ Ⓔ | | 11 | Ⓐ Ⓑ Ⓒ Ⓓ Ⓔ | | 19 | Ⓐ Ⓑ Ⓒ Ⓓ Ⓔ | | 27 | Ⓐ Ⓑ Ⓒ Ⓓ Ⓔ |
| 4 | Ⓙ Ⓚ Ⓛ Ⓜ Ⓝ | | 12 | Ⓙ Ⓚ Ⓛ Ⓜ Ⓝ | | 20 | Ⓙ Ⓚ Ⓛ Ⓜ Ⓝ | | |
| 5 | Ⓐ Ⓑ Ⓒ Ⓓ Ⓔ | | 13 | Ⓐ Ⓑ Ⓒ Ⓓ Ⓔ | | 21 | Ⓐ Ⓑ Ⓒ Ⓓ Ⓔ | | |
| 6 | Ⓙ Ⓚ Ⓛ Ⓜ Ⓝ | | 14 | Ⓙ Ⓚ Ⓛ Ⓜ Ⓝ | | 22 | Ⓙ Ⓚ Ⓛ Ⓜ Ⓝ | | |

## CAPITALIZATION

| | | | | | | | | | | | |
|---|---|---|---|---|---|---|---|---|---|---|---|
| S1 | Ⓐ Ⓑ Ⓒ Ⓓ | 5 | Ⓐ Ⓑ Ⓒ Ⓓ | 12 | Ⓙ Ⓚ Ⓛ Ⓜ | 19 | Ⓐ Ⓑ Ⓒ Ⓓ |
| S2 | Ⓙ Ⓚ Ⓛ Ⓜ | 6 | Ⓙ Ⓚ Ⓛ Ⓜ | 13 | Ⓐ Ⓑ Ⓒ Ⓓ | 20 | Ⓙ Ⓚ Ⓛ Ⓜ |
| S3 | Ⓐ Ⓑ Ⓒ Ⓓ | 7 | Ⓐ Ⓑ Ⓒ Ⓓ | 14 | Ⓙ Ⓚ Ⓛ Ⓜ | 21 | Ⓐ Ⓑ Ⓒ Ⓓ |
| 1 | Ⓐ Ⓑ Ⓒ Ⓓ | 8 | Ⓙ Ⓚ Ⓛ Ⓜ | 15 | Ⓐ Ⓑ Ⓒ Ⓓ | 22 | Ⓙ Ⓚ Ⓛ Ⓜ |
| 2 | Ⓙ Ⓚ Ⓛ Ⓜ | 9 | Ⓐ Ⓑ Ⓒ Ⓓ | 16 | Ⓙ Ⓙ Ⓛ Ⓜ | 23 | Ⓐ Ⓑ Ⓒ Ⓓ |
| 3 | Ⓐ Ⓑ Ⓒ Ⓓ | 10 | Ⓙ Ⓚ Ⓛ Ⓜ | 17 | Ⓐ Ⓑ Ⓒ Ⓓ | 24 | Ⓙ Ⓚ Ⓛ Ⓜ |
| 4 | Ⓙ Ⓚ Ⓛ Ⓜ | 11 | Ⓐ Ⓑ Ⓒ Ⓓ | 18 | Ⓙ Ⓚ Ⓛ Ⓜ | | |

## PUNCTUATION

| | | | | | | | | | | | |
|---|---|---|---|---|---|---|---|---|---|---|---|
| S1 | Ⓐ Ⓑ Ⓒ Ⓓ | 5 | Ⓐ Ⓑ Ⓒ Ⓓ | 12 | Ⓙ Ⓚ Ⓛ Ⓜ | 19 | Ⓐ Ⓑ Ⓒ Ⓓ |
| S2 | Ⓙ Ⓚ Ⓛ Ⓜ | 6 | Ⓙ Ⓚ Ⓛ Ⓜ | 13 | Ⓐ Ⓑ Ⓒ Ⓓ | 20 | Ⓙ Ⓚ Ⓛ Ⓜ |
| S3 | Ⓐ Ⓑ Ⓒ Ⓓ | 7 | Ⓐ Ⓑ Ⓒ Ⓓ | 14 | Ⓙ Ⓚ Ⓛ Ⓜ | 21 | Ⓐ Ⓑ Ⓒ Ⓓ |
| 1 | Ⓐ Ⓑ Ⓒ Ⓓ | 8 | Ⓙ Ⓚ Ⓛ Ⓜ | 15 | Ⓐ Ⓑ Ⓒ Ⓓ | 22 | Ⓙ Ⓚ Ⓛ Ⓜ |
| 2 | Ⓙ Ⓚ Ⓛ Ⓜ | 9 | Ⓐ Ⓑ Ⓒ Ⓓ | 16 | Ⓙ Ⓙ Ⓛ Ⓜ | 23 | Ⓐ Ⓑ Ⓒ Ⓓ |
| 3 | Ⓐ Ⓑ Ⓒ Ⓓ | 10 | Ⓙ Ⓚ Ⓛ Ⓜ | 17 | Ⓐ Ⓑ Ⓒ Ⓓ | 24 | Ⓙ Ⓚ Ⓛ Ⓜ |
| 4 | Ⓙ Ⓚ Ⓛ Ⓜ | 11 | Ⓐ Ⓑ Ⓒ Ⓓ | 18 | Ⓙ Ⓚ Ⓛ Ⓜ | | |

# Practice Test Answer Sheet

Name: _____    Date: _____

## USAGE AND EXPRESSION

| | | | | | | | |
|---|---|---|---|---|---|---|---|
| **S1** ⒶⒷⒸⒹ | **7** ⒶⒷⒸⒹ | **15** ⒶⒷⒸⒹ | **23** ⒶⒷⒸⒹ |
| **S2** ⒻⒼⒽⒿ | **8** ⒿⓀⓁⓂ | **16** ⒿⓀⓁⓂ | **24** ⒿⓀⓁⓂ |
| **1** ⒶⒷⒸⒹ | **9** ⒶⒷⒸⒹ | **17** ⒶⒷⒸⒹ | **25** ⒶⒷⒸⒹ |
| **2** ⒿⓀⓁⓂ | **10** ⒿⓀⓁⓂ | **18** ⒿⓀⓁⓂ | **26** ⒿⓀⓁⓂ |
| **3** ⒶⒷⒸⒹ | **11** ⒶⒷⒸⒹ | **19** ⒶⒷⒸⒹ | **27** ⒶⒷⒸⒹ |
| **4** ⒿⓀⓁⓂ | **12** ⒿⓀⓁⓂ | **20** ⒿⓀⓁⓂ | **28** ⒿⓀⓁⓂ |
| **5** ⒶⒷⒸⒹ | **13** ⒶⒷⒸⒹ | **21** ⒶⒷⒸⒹ | **29** ⒶⒷⒸⒹ |
| **6** ⒿⓀⓁⓂ | **14** ⒿⓀⓁⓂ | **22** ⒿⓀⓁⓂ | **30** ⒿⓀⓁⓂ |
| | | | **31** ⒶⒷⒸⒹ |

# STUDENT INTRODUCTION

# INTRODUCTION TO THE ITBS

## What is the ITBS?

The Iowa Test of Basic Skills (ITBS) is a multiple-choice test that helps you and your teacher find out how much you have learned in school so far. Now's your chance to show off all that you learned about reading and writing this year!

## Does the ITBS measure how smart I am?

No, not at all. The ITBS only tests how well you can use the skills you've learned in class so far.

## How can I prepare for the ITBS?

You can use this book to practice the types of questions you will see on the test. You can also use this book to learn some simple test-taking tips that will help you do your best. Just like riding a bike or playing the piano, studying for the ITBS takes practice. The more you practice, the better you will do and the more confident you'll feel on the day of the test!

It's important to tell students that the ITBS measures the skills that they are learning in school. It's not a test of their intelligence. Therefore, the best way for them to prepare for the ITBS is by using this book to familiarize themselves with the types of questions that will appear on the test, review skills they have already been practicing in school, and learn several test-taking strategies.

# There are four parts in this book.

1. **Warm-Up Test**—This test is shorter than the real ITBS, but it will show you what you know—and what you need to practice.

2. **On Your Mark! Get Set! Go!**—Here's where you really get to roll up your sleeves! First, you will learn the skills that you'll need to know for the test. Then you will practice what you've learned on questions that are just like the ones on the real ITBS. Trust us, this is the best part of the book!

3. **Practice Test**—This test is just like the real ITBS.

4. **On Your Mark! Get Set! Go! Review**—This is a list of all the important things that you will learn in this book. Go back to this part when you need to review or study what you've learned.

> You may want to write a timeline on the board to show students how much time you will spend using each part of this book and preparing for the test. This will keep students from feeling overwhelmed and help them maintain a positive attitude about the ITBS.

# USING THIS BOOK

Here's what you can do to help yourself while you use this book:

### Work carefully.

Completing this book is not a race. Now is the time to work slowly and carefully and to really learn what you need to know. We'll teach you how to go faster later in the book, so you'll be ready to take the real ITBS in the time your teacher will give you.

### Pay attention to the directions.

Read all the directions carefully. The directions tell you how to answer the questions. Always make sure you understand the directions before starting a new set of questions. Pretend you are driving a car, and the directions are the road signs that tell you what's ahead.

### Read the questions and answer choices carefully.

Always read the entire question and all of the answer choices slowly and carefully. Make sure you've read through all of the answer choices before you make your choice, even if you think you have already found the correct answer. There might be a better one!

Emphasize to students the importance of reading all test materials carefully. The directions will often provide valuable information about how to approach the questions.

# Get Rid of the Wrong Answer Choices

This book prepares you for the multiple-choice questions on the ITBS. On a multiple-choice question, you are given four or five answer choices to choose from. Only one of these choices is the best answer. Here's how to make sure you find it:

1. Read each answer choice, one by one.

2. Decide whether you think each answer choice is right or wrong.

3. Get rid of the answer choices you know are wrong.

4. Save the answer choices that might be right or that you aren't sure about.

5. Choose the best answer from the choices you think might be right.

6. If you don't know the answer, take your best guess.

> Getting rid of wrong answer choices, even only one, makes your chances of picking the correct answer choice a lot better!
>
> **So remember:**
> ✔ Get rid of what you can.
> ✔ See what you have left over.
> ✔ If you don't know the answer, take your best guess and move on.

© McGraw-Hill School Division

Process of elimination is one of the most important strategies students can use to improve their success on standardized tests. You may want to illustrate this concept by playing some sort of guessing game with your students. For example, write down four things (e.g., flavors of ice cream) on index cards. Share the items with students, and then have one student choose a card. Ask the rest of the class to guess the chosen card. Keep track of the number of guesses. Repeat the game with three cards, two cards, and, finally, one card. This should illustrate to students how the chances of guessing correctly increase as the number of choices decreases.

# Pace Yourself

The ITBS is a timed test. This means that your teacher is only allowed to let you work on it for a certain amount of time. While you take the test, remember to use your time wisely. Here's how:

### Don't spend too much time on one question.

Some questions on the ITBS are harder than others. Don't get stuck on any questions you don't know the answer to. Just take your best guess and move on. You want to be sure that you will have enough time to answer the easier questions that come later.

### But don't rush, either!

Going too fast is not good—you will only make silly mistakes. If you don't waste time on difficult questions, you will have enough time to finish the test without rushing.

### Find your own steady pace.

Everyone works at a different pace. Don't compare yourself with others. Just try to answer as many of the questions as you can. Work carefully through each of them. Pick the best answer, and then move on to the next question. When the teacher says time is up, put your pencil down and feel good about all the hard work you have done.

Pacing is an important aspect of taking tests. Tell students that they need to strike a balance between working carefully and progressing efficiently through the questions.

# MARK YOUR ANSWER CHOICES CORRECTLY

When you take the ITBS, you will be given the test and an answer sheet. The answer sheet is where you mark your answer choices. Marking your answers is very simple. Here's how you should answer a question:

1. Read the question.

2. Decide which answer choice is correct. Each answer choice has a letter next to it. Remember the letter that is next to the answer you picked.

3. Find the question number on your answer sheet that is the same as the number of the question you are answering.

4. Fill in the bubble that has the same letter as your answer choice.

## Always make sure that you fill in the answer bubbles completely.

 Do NOT fill in half of the bubble. This is wrong.

 Do NOT put a checkmark over the bubble. This is wrong.

 Do NOT scribble inside the bubble. This is wrong.

 DO fill in the bubble completely. This is correct!

Then go on to the next question until you are done with the test. It's that easy!

Explain to students that it's important to fill in the bubbles correctly because a machine scores the test. If their bubbles are not filled in completely, students may not get credit for questions that they have answered correctly.

# Practice, Practice, Practice!

The more you practice, the more prepared you'll be for the actual test. Remember, the ITBS tests what you already know. What you should practice is how to use what you know on the test. The more you practice, the more comfortable you will feel taking the test!

To help students understand the value of practice, lead a discussion about how practicing leads to improvements. For example, ask students to name several activities (e.g., sports, music, art) in which they participate. Then ask them to discuss how they practice for these activities. Has practice helped them improve their skills? How? In what ways can they see their progress?

# GETTING READY FOR THE ITBS

You can practice for the ITBS even when you're *not* using this book! Here's how:

**Read as much as you can.** Read everything and anything you can get your hands on. Of course, in class, you should read everything your teacher tells you to read. But outside of class, you get to choose what to read. Read comic books, magazines, and cereal boxes. Read signs as you pass by them. Read stories aloud. Listen to others read stories aloud to you. All reading is good reading.

**Play the word game.** When you come across a word you don't understand, play a game: Try to figure out what the word could mean. Ask yourself, "If I had to guess, what do I think the definition of that word would be?"

1. Write down your best guess.

2. Look the word up in a dictionary, or if you're not near a dictionary, ask an adult.

3. Write the word and its correct definition down on an index card. This will help you remember it.

4. Later, go back and read your index cards to see how good your memory is.

Remind students how important it is to practice reading. Reading is exercise for the brain, and the more they exercise their brains—by reading all types of materials—the greater the improvement they'll see in their overall reading skills and in their performance on the ITBS.

**Pay attention in class.** Not only will you learn cool things, but you'll also spend less time wrestling with tricky homework after school and more time playing with your friends!

**Ask questions.** Ask your teacher if you don't understand why an answer is wrong. Other students probably have the same question.

**Learn from your mistakes.** Notice the questions you have trouble with. Find out why you answered them incorrectly. Ask your teacher to review the skills you need to brush up on.

**Pat yourself on the back.** Congratulate yourself on the things you know well, and keep up the good work!

Answering questions incorrectly can be as valuable as answering questions correctly when preparing for a standardized test. Make sure students understand that it is okay to make mistakes. The important thing is to learn from the mistakes.

As students work through the tests and exercises in this book, provide them with positive feedback and encourage them with congratulations as they improve their skills. Allowing students to celebrate their progress will help them approach the ITBS with confidence and a positive attitude.

# Warm-Up Test

## SPELLING

## DIRECTIONS

Find the misspelled word. If there is none, select the last answer choice, *(No mistakes)*.

**1**  **A** paper
  **B** biteing
  **C** bulb
  **D** frame
  **E** *(No mistakes)*
  biting

**2**  **J** flower
  **K** tree
  **L** hiv
  **M** ladder
  **N** *(No mistakes)*
  hive

**3**  **A** krash
  **B** pool
  **C** tear
  **D** hay
  **E** *(No mistakes)*
  crash

**4**  **J** please
  **K** answer
  **L** over
  **M** brume
  **N** *(No mistakes)*
  broom

**5**  **A** bete
  **B** rug
  **C** fall
  **D** deck
  **E** *(No mistakes)*
  beat

GO ON

## CAPITALIZATION

## DIRECTIONS

Find the capitalization mistake. If there is none, mark the last answer choice,
*(No mistakes)*.

1   A   This is where the new
    B   school is going to be built. The
    **C**   old one was on Hill Cove road.
    D   *(No mistakes)*

2   **J**   While john was on vacation,
    K   Grandma Spadafora came
    L   to stay with us for two weeks.
    M   *(No mistakes)*

3   A   Mrs. Li is having a
    B   party for her son's birthday.
    C   The party is on April 10th.
    **D**   *(No mistakes)*

4   J   Bob and Carol needed
    K   milk and eggs so they went to
    **L**   the local Grocery Store.
    M   *(No mistakes)*

5   **A**   Dear mr. Bowden,
    B   Thank you for sending
    C   me a copy of the newspaper.
    D   *(No mistakes)*

For question 4, *grocery store* is not a proper noun because it does not actually mention the name of a specific store.

For question 1, remind students that *all* of the major words in a proper noun, such as a street name, must be capitalized.

For question 2, remind students that a person's name is always capitalized.

© McGraw-Hill School Division

# PUNCTUATION

## DIRECTIONS

Find the punctuation error. If there is none, mark the last answer choice, *(No mistakes)*.

**1**
  **A** Betty looked at the
  **(B)** dog. "Nice puppy" she said.
  **C** The dog wagged its tail.
  **D** *(No mistakes)*
> A comma is required after *puppy.*

**2**
  **(J)** Yesterday I questioned?
  **K** my friends about whether they
  **L** wanted to go see a movie with me.
  **M** *(No mistakes)*
> No question mark is needed.

**3**
  **A** I told everyone
  **B** who asked that the
  **(C)** costume is her's.
  **D** *(No mistakes)*
> The correct form is *hers.*

**4**
  **J** What's going on?
  **(K)** Theyve only got six players,
  **L** while we have got eleven.
  **M** *(No mistakes)*
> An apostrophe is required in a contraction.

**5**
  **A** Next month my sister
  **B** will marry Ian. She may change
  **(C)** change her name to Mrs Sipple.
  **D** *(No mistakes)*
> A period always follows an abbreviation.

**6**
  **J** 11 Happy Hound Lane
  **K** Willis, MO 00033
  **(L)** September 9 1999
  **M** *(No mistakes)*
> A comma always comes after the day and before the year in a date.

**GO ON ➡**

## DIRECTIONS

Choose the best way to write the underlined part of the sentence.

**1** **The prince is taking the carriage to town yesterday.**

   **A** take

   **B** will take

   **C** took

   **D** *(No change)*

> The word *yesterday* should help students realize that the verb in the sentence must be in the past tense.

## DIRECTIONS

In questions 2 and 3, choose the best way to express the idea.

**2** **J** On a hot summer day there is nothing better. Than going swimming.

   **K** Better than going swimming there, on a hot summer day is nothing.

   **L** There is nothing better than going swimming on a hot summer day.

   **M** Better than going swimming on a hot summer day there is nothing.

**3** **A** At the theater a good movie there is tonight.

   **B** A good movie, at the theater, tonight there is.

   **C** Tonight there is, at the theater, a good movie.

   **D** There is a good movie at the theater tonight.

## USAGE & EXPRESSION

---

## DIRECTIONS

Use this to answer questions 4 and 5.

> [1] She plays an acoustic guitar. [2] It has six strings. [3] Sometimes she uses a guitar pick to strum the strings. [4] She paints her fingernails pink. [5] Other times she just uses her fingers. [6] I love it when she plays "America the Beautiful." [7] I always sing along with her.

**4**  **Choose the best first sentence to add to this paragraph.**

**J** My sister is a terrific guitar player.

**K** Our class went to the music class last week.

**L** There is an instrument shop in our town.

**M** My sister talks to me all the time.

Question 4 is a topic sentence question.

**5**  **Which sentence should be left out of this paragraph?**

**A** Sentence 1

**B** Sentence 2

**C** Sentence 4

**D** Sentence 7

Question 5 is a supporting details question.

**GO ON ➡**

## DIRECTIONS

Find the mistake. If there is none, mark the last answer choice, *(No mistakes)*.

**7**
**Ⓐ** Samantha didn't not want no
**B** pizza yesterday. She ate a
**C** hamburger for lunch instead.
**D** *(No mistakes)*

> Double negative

**8**
**J** Shareen is the happiest girl
**Ⓚ** I know. At school her always has
**L** a nice smile for everyone she sees.
**M** *(No mistakes)*

> *Her* should be *she.*

**9**
**Ⓐ** Rhonda live in town
**B** with her mother and father.
**C** She is an only child.
**D** *(No mistakes)*

> *Live* should be *lives.*

**10**
**J** Annie made me a pie
**Ⓚ** yesterday. Next week I bake
**L** her some oatmeal cookies.
**M** *(No mistakes)*

> Clue: *next week*
> *Bake* should be *will bake.*

**STOP**

# On Your Mark,
# Get Set, Go!

## Exercise 1
# SPELLING

## Adding *-ing, -ly, -s*

 **Review the information at the top of the Pupil Edition page with the class.**

Prepare a list of words for the class and demonstrate how to correctly add suffixes to the words. Make sure that you have words ending in *e*, words ending in a consonant followed by *y*, and words ending in a consonant after a vowel (such as *run*). Some examples you might use are:

- *ride (-ing)*
- *hit (-ing)*
- *quick (-ly)*
- *short (-ly)*
- *try (-s) (-ing)*

Add some new words to the list, and have students add the suffixes on their own. Then go over the correct spellings as a class.

 **Go over the example question as a class.** Have students cover the answer and discuss the choices with them before revealing the correct answer.

---

### Exercise 1

# ON YOUR MARK!
## Spelling: Adding *-ing, -ly, -s*

Sometimes letters are added to the end of a word in order to change the meaning of that word. These are called **suffixes.** When letters are added, there are certain spelling rules that must be followed.

When words end in a silent *e*, drop the *e* when adding an ending that begins with a vowel.

Example: *prove* becomes *proving*.

When a one-syllable word ends in one vowel followed by one consonant, double the consonant before adding an ending that begins with a vowel.

Example: *sit* becomes *sitting*

When adding an ending that begins with a consonant, keep the silent *e*.

Example: *love* becomes *lovely*

When a base word ends with a consonant followed by *y*, change the *y* to *i* when adding any ending except endings that begin with *i*.

Example: *fly* becomes *flies* or *flying*

 # GET SET!
Let's look at an example.

**Find the spelling error.**
(A) diveing
B washing
C singing
D lacing
E *(No mistakes)*

(A) is **correct** because the word *diving* should not have an *e* in it.

---

⭐ ## EXTRA ACTIVITY

Separate the class into three groups. Assign each group one of the three suffixes (*-ly, -ing, -s*) and have the groups list as many words as possible that can use that suffix. Go over the lists in class, and check the spelling of each one.

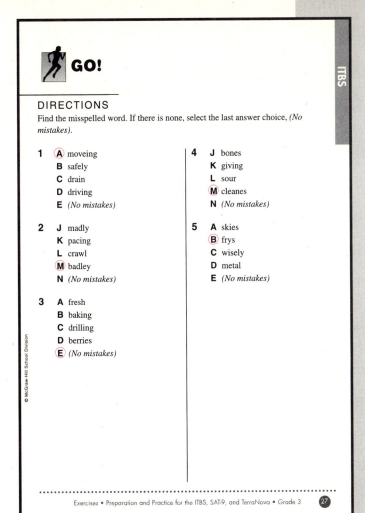

### DIRECTIONS

Find the misspelled word. If there is none, select the last answer choice, *(No mistakes)*.

1  (A) moveing
   B  safely
   C  drain
   D  driving
   E  *(No mistakes)*

2  J  madly
   K  pacing
   L  crawl
   (M) badley
   N  *(No mistakes)*

3  A  fresh
   B  baking
   C  drilling
   D  berries
   (E) *(No mistakes)*

4  J  bones
   K  giving
   L  sour
   (M) cleanes
   N  *(No mistakes)*

5  A  skies
   (B) frys
   C  wisely
   D  metal
   E  *(No mistakes)*

---

 **Go over each question on this page as a class.**

## Questions 1, 2, and 4

These all have mistakes revolving around the letter *e*. Students should know that the *e* needs to be dropped when adding suffixes to these words.

## Question 1

moving

## Question 2

badly

## Question 4

cleans

## Question 5

fries

None of these questions illustrates words such as *run*, which need to have the last consonant doubled when adding *-ing*. Provide the class with an example question of this type.

# SPELLING

## Words with Silent Letters

 **Go over the idea of silent letters with the class.**

Prepare a list of words that use silent letters to supplement the words provided on the Pupil Edition page. Some examples you might use are:

- *know*
- *wrap*
- *tore*
- *often*
- *dumb*
- *taught*

Remind students to pay special attention to the tip provided on this page.

Spend time going over tricky words with the class, such as *climb* and *limb.* Explain to students that although the words are spelled similarly, the /i/ is pronounced differently. Point out that these types of words must be memorized.

 **Go over the example question as a class.** Have students sound out each word slowly before choosing the correct answer.

---

 **Exercise 2**

## ON YOUR MARK!

### Spelling Words With Silent Letters

The words below have silent letters in them. The underlined letters don't make a sound when you say the word.

| | |
|---|---|
| lam**b** \'lam\ | sto**r**e \'stoŕ\ |
| **k**not \'nät\ | **g**host \'gost\ |
| peo**p**le \'pe̅-pəl\ | cau**gh**t \'kawt\ |
| dum**b** \'dəm\ | mus**c**le \'mə-səl\ |
| sof**t**en \'so-fən\ | **k**nit \'nit\ |

> **TIP:** When you spell tricky words, try changing the way you normally say them to yourself. Sound out every letter in your head—even the silent ones. For example, to remember that the word knot begins with a *k*, say /**kuh not**/ to yourself. It may sound funny, but this trick will help you remember when a silent letter is needed.

 **GET SET!**

Let's look at some examples.

**Find the spelling error.**

- Ⓐ clim
- **B** paint
- **C** sting
- **D** blame
- **E** *(No mistakes)*

(A) is **correct!** The word *climb* is misspelled. It should have a *b* at the end.

---

## EXTRA ACTIVITY

Have students group into pairs, and give them five minutes to come up with as many words as they can that include *silent letters*. The pair that comes up with the most in the time allotted wins the game.

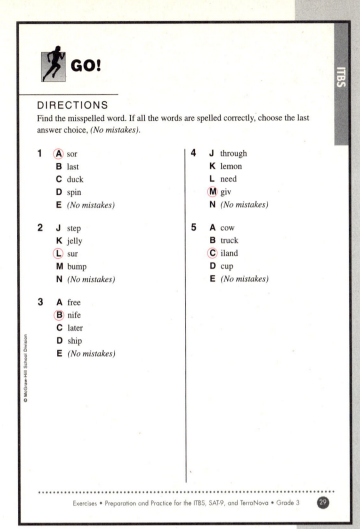

### GO!

**DIRECTIONS**

Find the misspelled word. If all the words are spelled correctly, choose the last answer choice, *(No mistakes)*.

1  A sor
   B last
   C duck
   D spin
   E *(No mistakes)*

2  J step
   K jelly
   L sur
   M bump
   N *(No mistakes)*

3  A free
   B nife
   C later
   D ship
   E *(No mistakes)*

4  J through
   K lemon
   L need
   M giv
   N *(No mistakes)*

5  A cow
   B truck
   C iland
   D cup
   E *(No mistakes)*

 **Go over each question on this page as a class.**

**ITBS**

## Questions 1, 2, and 4

The incorrectly spelled words all require a silent /e/ at the end of the word.

### Question 1

sore

### Question 2

sure

### Question 3

knife

### Question 4

give

### Question 5

island

After answering these questions, have students provide the correct spellings to the misspelled words.

# SPELLING

## Letters Pronounced More Than One Way

 **Explain how certain letters can have more than one pronunciation, depending upon the letters around them.**

Make sure students pay special attention to the tip box on the Pupil Edition page. Tell students it is important that they memorize these rules.

Ask students how many other words they know that illustrate this lesson of pronunciation. A good place to start is with names, for example Greg and George, or Cindy and Caroline.

 **Go over the example question as a class.** Remind students that the *c* is pronounced like a /k/ in this example because it is not followed by *e*, *i*, or *y*.

---

### Exercise 3

## ON YOUR MARK!

### Spelling: Letters Pronounced More Than One Way

Some letters can be pronounced two different ways. Some letters may sound one way in one word, and another way in another word.

**strange**—*the* g *sounds like a* j

**get**—*the* g *sounds like the* g *in* gum

**comb**—*the* c *sounds like a* k

**cereal**—*the* c *sounds like the* s *in* see

**disguise**—*the second* s *sounds like a* z

**set**—*the* s *sounds like the* s *in* saw

> **TIP:** When *g* sounds like a *j*, the *g* is always followed by *e*, *i*, or *y*. Examples are *giant*, *geometry*, and *gypsy*. When *c* sounds like an *s*, the *c* is always followed by *e*, *i*, or *y*. Examples are *trace*, *city*, *bicycle*.

## GET SET!

Now let's look at some examples.

**Find the spelling error.**

Ⓐ kapital
**B** blast
**C** falling
**D** case
**E** *(No mistakes)*

(A) is **correct!** This is because in the word *capital*, the *c* is pronounced like a *k*.

© McGraw-Hill School Division

---

## EXTRA ACTIVITY

Make a worksheet of words like the ones discussed on the Pupil Edition page. Pass the worksheet out to students, and pick individual students to pronounce the words on the worksheet. Point out the different pronunciations for the same letters. Some words you might include are:

- *page*
- *peg*
- *cake*
- *cent*
- *rise*
- *send*
- *peace*

© McGraw-Hill School Division

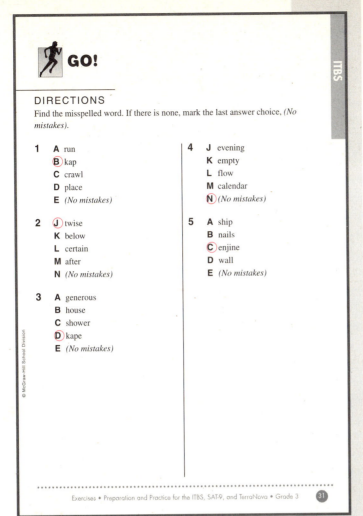

## GO!

### DIRECTIONS

Find the misspelled word. If there is none, mark the last answer choice. *(No mistakes)*.

1  A  run
   **B**  kap
   C  crawl
   D  place
   E  *(No mistakes)*

2  **J**  twise
   K  below
   L  certain
   M  after
   N  *(No mistakes)*

3  A  generous
   B  house
   C  shower
   **D**  kape
   E  *(No mistakes)*

4  J  evening
   K  empty
   L  flow
   M  calendar
   **N**  *(No mistakes)*

5  A  ship
   B  nails
   **C**  enjine
   D  wall
   E  *(No mistakes)*

© McGraw-Hill School Division

 **Go over each question on this page as a class.**

### Question 1

cap

### Question 2

twice

### Question 3

cape

### Question 5

engine

Review the answers with students. Have students explain what rule each word follows—in other words, why the correct spelling is pronounced the way it is.

# Exercise 4
# SPELLING

## Letter Combination Sounds

 **Review the different letter and sound combinations with the class. Have students try to think of other examples on their own.**

Go over the tip listed on the page. Provide the class with other words that follow this rule, such as:

- *quotation*
- *quality*
- *quarry*

 **Go over the example questions as a class.** Have students provide the correct spellings for the answer choices.

---

 ## ON YOUR MARK!

### Spelling: Letter Combination Sounds

Certain letters sound differently when they are next to each other than when they appear separately. For example, the *ch* sound in *choice* sounds different than the *c* sound in *cape* or the *h* sound in *Henry*.

***true***—the ue sounds like oo

***queen***—the qu sounds like kw

***black***—the ck sounds like k

***dream***—the ea sounds like a long e

> **TIP:** The letter *q* is always followed by the letter *u*.

 ## GET SET!

Let's look at some examples.

**Find the spelling error.**

(A) stik
**B** brown
**C** pencil
**D** deal
**E** *(No mistakes)*

(A) is **correct!** This is because in the word *stick* the *ck* is pronounced like a *k*.

**J** radio
**K** barrel
(L) skweak
**M** slack
**N** *(No mistakes)*

(L) is **correct!** This is because the word *squeak* should not be spelled with *kw*, even though that is how it sounds when it is pronounced.

---

## ⭐ EXTRA ACTIVITY

Have students break into teams. Set a stopwatch for five minutes. Have students list as many words as they can that contain the letter combinations on the Pupil Edition page: *ue, qu, ck, ea.*

Whichever team comes up with the most words in the allotted time wins the game. For extra credit, have students group the words by their pronunciations. For example, *quick* and *quarrel* would be grouped together. *Raquet* would be in another group because the /qu/ sounds different.

# GO!

## DIRECTIONS

Find the misspelled word. If there is none, mark the last answer choice, *(No mistakes)*.

1  A  salad
   (B) kwack
   C  bread
   D  movie
   E  *(No mistakes)*

2  (J) bloo
   K  roof
   L  cream
   M  lemon
   N  *(No mistakes)*

3  A  today
   B  lunch
   (C) lak
   D  shape
   E  *(No mistakes)*

4  J  watch
   K  close
   L  thunder
   (M) rume
   N  *(No mistakes)*

5  A  sack
   B  quiet
   C  barge
   D  flute
   (E) *(No mistakes)*

© McGraw-Hill School Division

## Go over each question on this page as a class.

### Question 1

quack—This is an example of the *qu* rule.

### Question 2

blue

### Question 3

lake

### Question 4

room

Provide some extra questions for students that review letter combinations not tested on this page. For example, *ea*. Words you could use include *team*, *reap*, *steam*, *lead*, and so on.

# SPELLING

## Tricky Words

 **Explain to the class that there are words in the English language that simply do not follow any specific rules. These words have to be memorized.**

In order to help memorize the spellings of these tricky words, students can use the tips provided on the Pupil Edition page.

Have a list of other tricky words prepared to hand out to students to supplement the words found in this section. Some words you might use are:

- *enough*
- *rough*
- *thief*
- *people*
- *phony*
- *school*

Review the "*i* before *e*" rule in detail, with examples and exceptions.

 **Go over the example question as a class.** Tell students that a good way to remember a correct spelling is to ask themselves if a word *looks* correct on the page. If it doesn't *look* right, it might be spelled incorrectly.

---

 ## ON YOUR MARK!
### Spelling: Tricky Words

Some words have spellings that just don't seem to match how the words are pronounced. These words are tricky to spell. For example, the *f* sound in *Fred* can be made by *f*, but also by *ph*, as in *phone*, or *gh* as in *tough*.

> **Here are some tips to help you with tricky spelling words:**
>
> - Make up clues to help you remember the spelling. (*Dessert* is spelled with two *s*'s because you always want seconds!)
>
> - Change the way you say the word to yourself to help with the spelling.
>   (*receive* = re-c-e-ive)
>
> - Think of times you have seen the word in a textbook, or on a sign. Try to remember how it looked. Write the word in different ways. Which one looks correct? (*coff, couf, cough*)

 ## GET SET!

Let's look at some examples.

**Find the spelling error.**

**A** phall
**B** hour
**C** instead
**D** around
**E** *(No mistakes)*

(A) is **correct!** This is because *fall* is misspelled. In this case, *f* is used to make the *f* sound.

---

  ## EXTRA ACTIVITY

Have students think of other ways that they can memorize tricky words. Some ways might be placing similar words together in groups (*cough, laugh*), making up rhymes or sayings (We have *dessert* in the *desert*), or even by simply keeping note cards and writing down all the tricky words they come across when reading.

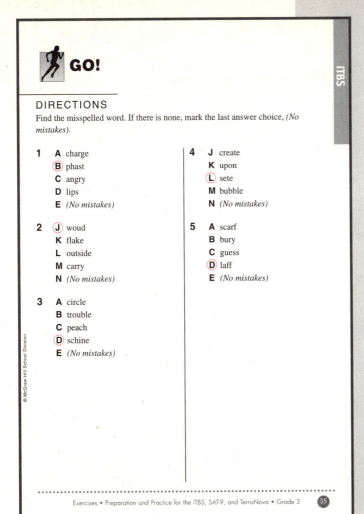

## GO!

### DIRECTIONS

Find the misspelled word. If there is none, mark the last answer choice, *(No mistakes)*.

1. A charge
   - **B phast**
   - C angry
   - D lips
   - E *(No mistakes)*

2. **J woud**
   - K flake
   - L outside
   - M carry
   - N *(No mistakes)*

3. A circle
   - B trouble
   - C peach
   - **D schine**
   - E *(No mistakes)*

4. J create
   - K upon
   - **L sete**
   - M bubble
   - N *(No mistakes)*

5. A scarf
   - B bury
   - C guess
   - **D laff**
   - E *(No mistakes)*

 **Go over each question on this page as a class.**

ITBS

### Question 1

fast

### Question 2

would—Have students pay special attention to this question. Ask them what the correct spelling of the answer should be. Show them how there are two choices for a correct spelling, *would* or *wood*.

### Question 3

shine

### Question 4

seat

### Question 5

laugh

Provide students with an example of a word demonstrating the "*i* before *e*" rule. For example, *receive*.

# Exercise 6

# RULING OUT WRONG ANSWER CHOICES

 **Let students know that it is important to eliminate as many answer choices as they can right away so that there are fewer choices to choose from.**

This improves their odds of choosing the correct answer choices.

Explain that answer choices can be ruled out even when the correct answer isn't known.

In the first example on the Pupil Edition page, the wrong answer choices can be ruled out because they are all places that a person would not live. Now have students look at another version of the same question:

**Where does Mr. Johnson live?**

    **A.** on a flag pole

    **B.** on a ball field

    **C.** on Maple Street*

    **D.** on a bridge

Once again, students can rule out the wrong answer choices even though they do not know Mr. Johnson's address. The other three answer choices are not places a person would live.

 **Go over the example question as a class.** Remind students of the spelling rule that is being demonstrated here.

---

 ## ON YOUR MARK!

### Ruling Out Wrong Answer Choices

Sometimes you can find the right answer to a question, even if you don't know the answer right away! All you have to do is rule out the answer choices you know are wrong. Where does your neighbor Mr. Johnson live?

**A** in a pond

**B** in a library

**(C)** in a house

**D** in a tree

You can answer this question even if you don't know Mr. Johnson. Here's how:

**A:** *Mr. Johnson cannot live in a pond! Rule this out.*

**B:** *Mr. Johnson cannot live in a library! Rule this out.*

**C:** *Mr. Johnson could definitely live in a house. Keep this one, and look at the last answer choice.*

**D:** *Mr. Johnson cannot live in a tree! Rule this out. Answer choice (C) must be correct!*

 ## GET SET!

Let's look at an example. Find the spelling error. Rule out the wrong answer choices first.

**(A)** traceing    You are supposed to drop the *e* before adding *–ing*. This looks wrong, but read choices (B) and (C) to see if they can be ruled out.

**B** strong    This is spelled correctly. Rule it out.

**C** please    This is spelled correctly. Rule it out.

**D** *(No mistakes)*

(A) is **correct!** Every other answer choice has been ruled out.

---

## TEACHING TIP

Let students know that ruling out wrong answer choices will not take the place of practice, but it can help them do better on questions for which they are unsure of the answer. Remind them that they will have a better chance of guessing correctly if they reduce the number of answer choices from which to choose.

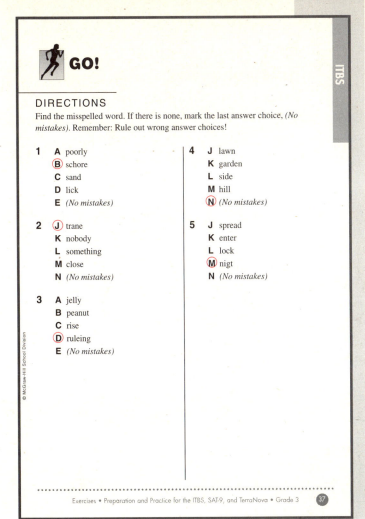

## GO!

### DIRECTIONS

Find the misspelled word. If there is none, mark the last answer choice, *(No mistakes)*. Remember: Rule out wrong answer choices!

**1**
- **A** poorly
- **(B)** schore
- **C** sand
- **D** lick
- **E** *(No mistakes)*

**2**
- **(J)** trane
- **K** nobody
- **L** something
- **M** close
- **N** *(No mistakes)*

**3**
- **A** jelly
- **B** peanut
- **C** rise
- **(D)** ruleing
- **E** *(No mistakes)*

**4**
- **J** lawn
- **K** garden
- **L** side
- **M** hill
- **(N)** *(No mistakes)*

**5**
- **J** spread
- **K** enter
- **L** lock
- **(M)** nigt
- **N** *(No mistakes)*

 **Go over each question on this page as a class.**

Have students eliminate incorrect answer choices for each question. Discuss why certain answer choices can or cannot be eliminated.

## Question 1

shore

## Question 2

train

## Question 3

ruling

## Question 5

night

# Exercise 7

## CAPITALIZATION

## Beginning of a Sentence or Quotation

 **Review with the class the idea that the first word of every sentence should be capitalized.**

Go over some sample sentences on the board. Use both long and short sentences to illustrate that no matter what type of sentence it is, the first word is always capitalized. Some examples you might use are:

- *My dog is named Cooper.*

- *I'm tired.*

- *Stop it!*

- *Once in a while, I like to play board games with my sister.*

Explain to students that even though a quotation often comes in the middle of another sentence, the first word is still capitalized. Write some examples of this on the board. Some examples you might use are:

- *He said, "How are you?"*

- *My friend, Millie, is always saying, "What are you talking about?"*

- *People always ask me, "What time is it?"*

 **Go over the example question as a class.** Ask students to describe why the word *When* is capitalized. (It is the first word in a quotation.)

---

### Exercise 7

## ON YOUR MARK!

### Capitalization: Beginning of a Sentence or Quotation

**The first word of a sentence is always capitalized.**

> *Pools are fun to swim in.*

*Pools* is a common noun and normally would not be capitalized. However, since it is at the beginning of a sentence, it is capitalized.

**The first word in a quotation is also always capitalized.**

> *Roger walked up to the counter and asked, "Can I please buy a movie ticket?"*

In this case, even though the quotation comes in the middle of a sentence, the first word in the quotation, *can*, must be capitalized.

 ## GET SET!

Let's look at an example.

**Find the capitalization error.**

J   On the way home from
K   the circus, Roger Asked "When do
L   clowns take off their make-up?"
M   *(No mistakes)*

(K) is **correct!** The word *asked* does not need to be capitalized. It is not the first word in a quotation or the first word of a sentence.

---

  ## EXTRA ACTIVITY

Have a paragraph prepared to hand out to each student. The paragraph should contain several errors regarding capitalization of first words in sentences and quotations. Instruct students to correct all the errors they can find. Go over the paragraph with the class, sentence by sentence. Answer any questions students have regarding the errors. An example paragraph you might use is:

*when I was seven, I learned to ride my bike. at first, I was scared. my dad said, "you can do it." I decided to try. I got on my bike and my dad held it steady. "don't worry," he said. "I've got you." we practiced and practiced. a few weeks later, I felt ready. "you don't have to hold it this time," I told my dad. i got on the bike and rode it all by myself.*

---

**GO!**

## DIRECTIONS

Find the capitalization error. If there is none, mark the last answer choice, *(No mistakes)*.

1. **A** when we go to the store,
   **B** please remember to hold your
   **C** brother's hand all the time.
   **D** *(No mistakes)*

2. **J** My father said, "it
   **K** is always nice to go on
   **L** a picnic on a beautiful day."
   **M** *(No mistakes)*

3. **J** Mandy and Sharon
   **K** have a new pet. Yesterday
   **L** they got a brand new kitten.
   **M** *(No mistakes)*

4. **A** Last week Margo and Todd
   **B** bought a new car. "It is blue, and
   **C** it has a white roof on it," Margo
      said.
   **D** *(No mistakes)*

5. **J** The house painters are
   **K** coming Today to finish the
   **L** work they started on Friday.
   **M** *(No mistakes)*

6. **A** Clowns are the
   **B** best acts in a circus. Ted said,
   **C** "they make everyone laugh."
   **D** *(No mistakes)*

 **Go over each question on this page as a class.**

## Question 1

The first word of the sentence, *when*, needs to be capitalized.

## Questions 2 and 6

The first word of the quotation should be capitalized.

## Question 5

This question has a capitalized word in the middle of a sentence where it does not belong. *Today* is not a proper noun. Only proper nouns should be capitalized in the middle of a sentence. (Proper nouns are discussed on the next page.)

# CAPITALIZATION

## Nouns, Common Nouns, and Places as Proper Nouns

 **Review the difference between a common noun and a proper noun with the class. Students should be familiar with the following:**

- Nouns are always people, places, or things.

- Common nouns are general words, such as *boy*, *dog*, or *city*.

- Common nouns are never capitalized unless they are the first word of a sentence or quotation, or part of a title.

- Proper nouns are specific people, places, or things, such as *John*, *Rover*, or *Miami*.

- Proper nouns are always capitalized.

- If a proper noun consists of more than one word, for example *King Lear* or *Los Angeles*, both words are capitalized.

 ## TEACHING TIP

Remind students that the word *I* is a proper noun and should always be capitalized.

 **Go over the example question as a class.** Remind students that in this case, both words, *Lake* and *tahoe*, make up the proper noun.

---

 ## ON YOUR MARK!

**Capitalization: Nouns, Common Nouns, and Places as Proper Nouns**

A **noun** is a person, place, or thing. For example, *dog*, *car*, *Katie*, and *Ecuador* are all nouns. There are two basic types of nouns: proper nouns and common nouns.

**Common nouns** always refer to general names for people, places, or things. The words *cat*, *town*, and *pencil* are all common nouns. Common nouns are never capitalized, except at the beginning of a sentence.

**Proper nouns** always refer to a specific person, place, or thing. For example, the words *John*, *Africa*, and *June* are all proper nouns. Proper nouns are *always* capitalized. This exercise focuses on proper nouns that are specific places.

> **TIP:** When a **proper noun** contains more than one word, all the major words must be capitalized. For example, the *United States of America*, and the *Pacific Ocean*.

 ## GET SET!

Now let's look at some examples.

**Find the capitalization error.**

A  The only way we could get to
Ⓑ  Lake tahoe was to take a bus. The bus
C  left early in the morning, so we were tired.
D  *(No mistakes)*

(B) is **correct!** Both *Lake* and *Tahoe* should be capitalized. Together, they form a proper noun, *Lake Tahoe*.

---

  ## EXTRA ACTIVITY

Prepare a set of flash cards with common and proper nouns. Make sure none of them is capitalized. Show each card to the class, and have students tell you whether or not the word should be capitalized. Some words you can use include:

- *boy*        *brian*

- *girl*        *samantha*

- *city*        *new york*

- *ocean*      *pacific ocean*

- *river*       *mississippi river*

- *aunt*        *aunt betty*

## GO!

### DIRECTIONS
Find the capitalization mistake. If there is none, mark the last answer choice, *(No mistakes)*.

1. **A** The kangaroo is a famous
   **B** australian animal. It has big
   **C** feet and can jump far.
   **D** *(No mistakes)*

2. **J** My cousin Larry lives
   **K** on lansdowne Road. He owns
   **L** a car and a truck.
   **M** *(No mistakes)*

3. **A** The city of houston is
   **B** in Texas. During the summer
   **C** it gets very hot there.
   **D** *(No mistakes)*

4. **J** When my family moved
   **K** to the United States, we
   **L** knew we were very lucky.
   **M** *(No mistakes)*

5. **A** New jersey has many
   **B** places to go if you like
   **C** fishing or hiking.
   **D** *(No mistakes)*

6. **J** This year the carnival
   **K** is going to be in the field
   **L** behind fourth Street.
   **M** *(No mistakes)*

7. **A** San diego has a big
   **B** zoo. People come from
   **C** all over to visit it.
   **D** *(No mistakes)*

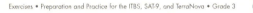

ITBS

## Go over each question on this page as a class.

### Question 1

*Australian* refers to a specific country and should be capitalized.

### Question 2

Both words in a street name need to be capitalized.

### Question 3

*Houston* is the name of a specific city and should be capitalized.

### Question 4

*United States* is a proper noun consisting of two words. There is no mistake.

### Question 5

*New Jersey* is a proper noun consisting of two words, so both words need to be capitalized.

### Question 6

Both words in a street name need to be capitalized.

### Question 7

Both words in a city name need to be capitalized.

# CAPITALIZATION

## People as Proper Nouns

 **This section takes a look at a specific type of proper noun: names of people or living things.**

Remind students that names are always capitalized.

- *Johnny*
- *Sally*
- *Spot*
- *Mittens*
- *Tweetie*

Remind students that when a name is made up of two or more words, all the words are capitalized.

- *Uncle Bob*
- *Aunt Mary Margaret*
- *Grandfather Amos*
- *Billy Joe*
- *Queen Anne*

 **Go over the example question as a class.**

In this example, *grandfather* is not a proper noun, because it is not someone's name.

---

 Exercise 9

## ON YOUR MARK!

### Capitalization: People as Proper Nouns

Proper nouns always refer to a specific person, place, or thing. Proper nouns are *always* capitalized.

This exercise focuses on proper nouns that are a specific person or living thing. For example, the name of a person or pet is a proper noun. So is the word *I*.

My aunt's daughter is named Shelly.

(The words *aunt* and *daughter* are common nouns, while *Shelly* is a proper noun.)

Our Uncle John has a dog named Pickles.

(*Uncle John* and *Pickles* are proper nouns, and *dog* is a common noun.)

**TIP:** When a name has two or more words, all the major words are capitalized. For example, *King Charles*.

 ## GET SET!

Now let's look at an example.

**Find the capitalization error.**

J Sheila and I are going to see a
K movie tomorrow. It is about a boy who
L helps his Grandfather build a car.
M *(No mistakes)*

(L) is **correct!** The word *grandfather* should not be capitalized. In this case, grandfather is a common noun, not a proper noun. It does not name a specific person. If the sentence talked about Grandfather Wilson, *grandfather* would be a proper noun and it would be capitalized.

---

 ### EXTRA ACTIVITY

Have students write down as many names as they can think of in a specific amount of time (e.g., two minutes). See how many different names the class can come up with. Remind them that they can use names of pets or famous animals as well as people. Make sure students are using capital letters where necessary.

### DIRECTIONS

Find the capitalization error. If there is none, mark the last answer choice, *(No mistakes)*.

1  A  He wanted a new book,
   **B**  so i went downstairs and
   C  got one for him to read.
   D  *(No mistakes)*

2  **J**  Everybody thinks miss Bell
   K  is a good teacher, because she
   L  is very patient with us.
   M  *(No mistakes)*

3  A  When you and I get
   B  home today, we will
   C  have to clean our rooms.
   **D**  *(No mistakes)*

4  **J**  Sonja's dog, boomer,
   K  always gets out of the
   L  backyard and runs away.
   M  *(No mistakes)*

5  A  Mr. Brill works in the
   **B**  in the cafeteria. His Aunt
   C  works at the grocery store.
   D  *(No mistakes)*

6  J  Our new librarian,
   **K**  Mr. lee, is very funny.
   L  He tells a joke every day.
   M  *(No mistakes)*

---

 **Go over each question on this page as a class.**

### Question 1

The word *I* is a proper noun and should be capitalized.

### Question 2

Both parts of a person's name must be capitalized.

### Question 4

Names of specific animals are proper nouns.

### Question 5

In this case, *aunt* is not a part of someone's name.

### Question 6

Both parts of a person's name must be capitalized.

## Exercise 10

# CAPITALIZATION

## Dates as Proper Nouns

 **Go over the idea that dates can be considered proper nouns.**

Remind students that proper nouns are always capitalized. Point out to students that all of the following are considered dates:

- *Days of the week*
- *Names of months*
- *Holidays*

As with other proper nouns, all the major words in a date are capitalized.

- *Fourth of July*
- *Labor Day*

Explain to the class that a date always refers to a specific time. Words like *day*, *month*, and *year*, when standing alone, are not capitalized because they do not refer to a specific time.

 **Go over the example question as a class.** Remind students that both words in a proper noun, such as a holiday, are always capitalized.

---

**Exercise 10**

 **ON YOUR MARK!**

### Capitalization: Dates as Proper Nouns

**Proper nouns** always refer to a specific person, place, or thing. Proper nouns are *always* capitalized.

This exercise focuses on proper nouns that are dates. Dates include days of the week, names of months, and holidays. Dates should always be capitalized.

> The last day of school is a Tuesday this year.
>
> (*Tuesday* is a day of the week. It is always capitalized.)
>
> My family always celebrates Flag Day.
>
> (*Flag Day* is a holiday. It is always capitalized.)
>
> Uncle Tommy is going to visit us in October.
>
> (*October* is a month. It is always capitalized.)

> **TIP:** When a holiday has two or more words, all the major words are capitalized, as in *Memorial Day*, *April Fool's Day*, and the *Fourth of July*.

 **GET SET!**

Let's look at an example.

**Find the capitalization error.**

Ⓐ On Arbor day, people plant
B trees to help keep forests growing. My
C brother and I planted one last year.
D *(No mistakes)*

(A) is **correct!** The word *day* is part of a holiday name so it must be capitalized.

44  Exercises • Preparation and Practice for the ITBS, SAT-9, and TerraNova • Grade 3

 **EXTRA ACTIVITY**

Have students write a short paragraph of two or three sentences. The paragraph must include a month, day, and holiday somewhere in it. Go over each student's paragraph, making sure that all dates are correctly capitalized. (Example: *My favorite holiday is Independence Day. It always happens on July 4th. This year it will be on a Tuesday.*)

---

# GO!

ITBS

## DIRECTIONS

Find the capitalization error. If there is none, mark the last answer choice, *(No mistakes)*.

**1**
A Larry's birthday is
B in december. Last year he
C got a new sled from us.
D *(No mistakes)*

**2**
J Yesterday was the first
K day of baseball season. We
L are going to a game on Saturday.
M *(No mistakes)*

**3**
A Every year we do the
B same thing for father's day.
C We take Dad to breakfast.
D *(No mistakes)*

**4**
J My little brother likes
K the month of june, because
L that is when summer camp starts.
M *(No mistakes)*

**5**
A In the United
B States, January 1st is
C New year's Day.
D *(No mistakes)*

**6**
J Election Day is in the
K month of november. This year
L my brother will be able to vote.
M *(No mistakes)*

## Go over each question on this page as a class.

### Questions 1, 4, and 6

Months should always be capitalized.

### Questions 3 and 5

All major words in a holiday should be capitalized.

Prepare additional questions, especially using days of the week and holidays. Give students as much practice as possible with capitalizing dates.

## Exercise 11

# CAPITALIZATION

## Letter Greetings and Closings

 **Go over letter greetings and closings with the class.**

Explain that the first word of a greeting or closing is always capitalized.

 **TEACHING TIP**

Remind students that names and titles in greetings and closings should be capitalized just like always. They are still proper nouns.

Write examples of greetings and closings on the board so students become familiar with them. Some examples you might use are:

- *Sincerely*
- *Regards*
- *Love always*
- *To Whom it May Concern*
- *Dear Sirs*
- *Dear Mrs. Smith*
- *Hello*
- *Your friend*

 **Go over the example question as a class.**

---

### Exercise 11

## ON YOUR MARK!

### Capitalization: Letter Greetings and Closings

A letter always has a greeting and a closing.

The **greeting** is the line that shows who the letter is for. The first word of the greeting is always capitalized.

The **closing** is the ending of the letter. The first word of the closing is always capitalized.

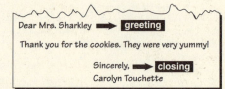

Dear Mrs. Sharkley ➡ greeting

Thank you for the cookies. They were very yummy!

Sincerely, ➡ closing
Carolyn Touchette

 **GET SET!**

Now let's look at an example.

**Find the capitalization error.**

Ⓐ to the Mayville Police,
**B** Thank you for your help at the
**C** parade. You did a fine job all day.
**D** *(No mistakes)*

(A) is **correct!** The word *to* must be capitalized, because it is the first word of the greeting.

46  Exercises • Preparation and Practice for the ITBS, SAT-9, and TerraNova • Grade 3

© McGraw-Hill School Division

---

 **EXTRA ACTIVITY**

Have students write letters as an extra activity to help them understand capitalization. Tell them to choose one person to whom they would like to write a letter. Have them write a short note to the person. They should open the letter with a greeting and end with a closing. Emphasize the importance of using correct capitalization.

© McGraw-Hill School Division

**Go over each question on this page as a class.**

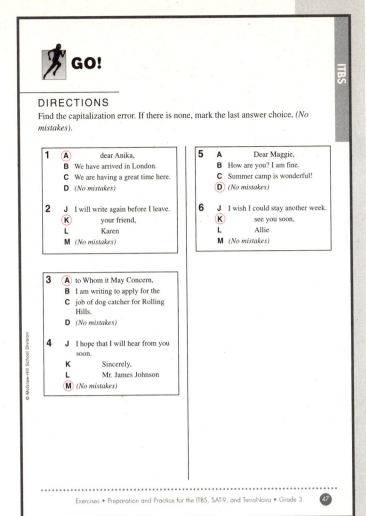

## GO!

### DIRECTIONS

Find the capitalization error. If there is none, mark the last answer choice, *(No mistakes)*.

1  **(A)**      dear Anika,
    **B**    We have arrived in London.
    **C**    We are having a great time here.
    **D**    *(No mistakes)*

2  **J**    I will write again before I leave.
    **(K)**      your friend,
    **L**       Karen
    **M**    *(No mistakes)*

3  **(A)**   to Whom it May Concern,
    **B**    I am writing to apply for the
    **C**    job of dog catcher for Rolling
         Hills.
    **D**    *(No mistakes)*

4  **J**    I hope that I will hear from you
         soon.
    **K**      Sincerely,
    **L**       Mr. James Johnson
    **(M)**   *(No mistakes)*

5  **A**      Dear Maggie,
    **B**    How are you? I am fine.
    **C**    Summer camp is wonderful!
    **(D)**   *(No mistakes)*

6  **J**    I wish I could stay another week.
    **(K)**      see you soon,
    **L**       Allie
    **M**    *(No mistakes)*

### Question 1

The first word in the greeting of a letter needs to be capitalized.

### Question 2

The first word in the closing of a letter needs to be capitalized.

### Question 3

The first word in the greeting of a letter needs to be capitalized.

### Question 6

The first word in the closing of a letter needs to be capitalized.

Remind students that regardless of how many words there are in a greeting or closing, the first word is *always* capitalized.

# PACING YOURSELF

 **Discuss the idea of pacing oneself on an exam with the class.**

Go over each of the three main points on the Pupil Edition page with students, and describe how each one of these tips will help them pace themselves on the ITBS.

Let students know it is important for them to find the pace at which they can answer the most questions correctly within the time allowed for the exam.

The two most important ways for students to increase their pace are:

- **Practice:** The more a student practices on tests that are similar to the ITBS, the more familiar the test will be and the more quickly he will be able to work through the questions.

- **Reading:** Reading improves spelling, punctuation, and just about every other aspect of language arts. If students are comfortable with the skills, they will be able to move through the test more comfortably.

 **Go over the example question as a class.** Tell students to move through the question at a pace that is comfortable for them. In this case, the error is a capitalization error.

---

 ## ON YOUR MARK!
### Pacing Yourself

It is important to take time to answer each ITBS question carefully. But you also don't want to spend so much time on a question that you cannot finish the test. This is why **pacing yourself** is important. Pacing yourself means completing as many questions as you can without rushing or spending too much time on one question. Here are some tips:

- **Do not let yourself get stuck on one question.** If you cannot answer a question, take your best guess and move on.

- **Know the Directions.** When you take the practice tests, pay attention to the directions. That way, you will not have to spend time trying to understand them.

- **Relax.** Don't worry if you don't know an answer. The ITBS is just one way to measure your skills. You'll have plenty of other chances to show what you have learned. The calmer you are, the more likely you are to answer the questions correctly!

 ## GET SET!

Find the capitalization error. Do you know the answer right away? If not, you shouldn't spend too much time trying to figure it out. You should get rid of answer choices you know are wrong, take your best guess, and then move on.

A  Roger needs a new hose for
Ⓑ  his house. the old one has a leak,
C  because the dog chewed on it.
D  *(No mistakes)*

(B) is **correct!** *The* must be capitalized, since it is the first word of a sentence.

---

## TEACHING TIP

Periodically throughout the year, you might want to give students timed quizzes. The quizzes can test spelling, capitalization, punctuation, or usage. Use the Go! exercises as a guide when you set up the quizzes. By timing them, students will be able to keep track of their progress as the year goes on. When it comes time to take the actual exam, students should find that they not only have improved their skills as the year progressed, but also have a good idea of how many questions they can answer in the allotted time.

**GO!**

## DIRECTIONS

Find the capitalization error. If there is none, mark the last answer, (No mistakes).

**1** (A) when it is time for dinner,
  **B** we always wash our hands
  **C** and then help set the table.
  **D** (No mistakes)

**2** **J** Rachel's birthday is
  (K) the same day as columbus day.
  **L** That is how we remember it.
  **M** (No mistakes)

**3** (A)      dear Mr. President,
  **B** I would like to know if
  **C** you could visit my class some day.
  **D** (No mistakes)

**4** **J** I would really like to meet you.
  (K)      best wishes,
  **L**      Thelma Hyatt
  **M** (No mistakes)

**5** **A** It is always nice to
  (B) see my Grandparents. They
  **C** tell lots of interesting stories.
  **D** (No mistakes)

**6** **J** Our principal, Miss White,
  **K** is very nice. She lets us come into
  **L** her office to see her goldfish.
  (M) (No mistakes)

 **Go over each question on this page as a class.**

Questions on this page cover the capitalization skills learned in the exercises on the preceding pages of On Your Mark! Get Set! Go! section. Students should practice ruling out wrong answer choices and not spending too much time on any one question.

## Question 1

The first word in a sentence needs to be capitalized.

## Question 2

The names of holidays need to be capitalized.

## Question 3

The first word in the greeting of a letter needs to be capitalized.

## Question 4

The first word in the closing of a letter needs to be capitalized.

## Question 5

*Grandparents* is not a proper noun and should not be capitalized.

# PUNCTUATION

## Quotations

**Go over what a quotation is with students.**

They should already be familiar with capitalizing the first word of a quotation. Now they will learn other rules that are specific to quotations.

Go over the "Rules for Quotations" box on the Pupil Edition page. Write some quotations on the board without all of the necessary punctuation. Have students come to the board and fix the quotations. Some examples you might use are:

- *Tom said, "I am hungry.*

- *Tom said, "I am hungry, as he walked into the kitchen."*

- *"When are you coming over" asked Theresa.*

- *"I'm not very happy," she said.*

- *"Oh my goodness"!*

- *Sally walked into the room and said "Hello!"*

**Go over the example question as a class.** Ask students which of the above rules has been broken. (Answer: Quotation marks were not placed after a speaker's exact words.)

---

Exercise 13

## ON YOUR MARK!

### Punctuation: Quotations

A **quotation** is a speaker's exact words. **Quotation marks** are used to separate a quotation from the rest of the sentence.

*She said, "Who wants to play a game?"*

**Rules for Quotations**

- Put quotation marks before and after a speaker's exact words.
- Do NOT put quotation marks around words that were not spoken by the speaker.
- Capitalize the first letter of a speaker's words.
- Put commas, periods, question marks, and exclamation marks <u>inside</u> closing quotation marks.
- Use a comma to separate a phrase, such as *she said*, from the quotation.

## GET SET!

Now let's look at some examples.

**Find the punctuation error.**

A  Carlos turned to Esteban and said,

B  "We should do our homework now. Esteban

C  agreed and began to take out his school books.

D  *(No mistakes)*

(B) is **correct!** There must be a quotation mark at the end of the quotation, after *now*.

---

## EXTRA ACTIVITY

Have students write a two- or three-sentence story with at least one quotation. The stories can be about anything they want. Check their stories for correct use of punctuation and capitalization in their quotation.

## GO!

### DIRECTIONS

Find the punctuation error. If there is none, mark the last answer choice, *(No mistakes)*.

**1**
- **A** "What are you doing after
- **B** school?" Jenny asked. We are going
- **C** shopping at the new sneaker store."
- **D** *(No mistakes)*

**2**
- **J** "Excuse me, but can you
- **K** please pass me the gravy" asked
- **L** Ralph. Lenny handed it to him.
- **M** *(No mistakes)*

**3**
- **A** How many plates do we need?
- **B** asked LaShaun. Rachel told her that
- **C** they needed ten plates on the table.
- **D** *(No mistakes)*

**4**
- **J** "What time is it?" asked Jeff.
- **K** Melissa told him that it was almost
- **L** ten, and that he should get ready.
- **M** *(No mistakes)*

**5**
- **A** The teacher asked the class
- **B** who our first president was. "I
- **C** know the answer yelled Shanisse.
- **D** *(No mistakes)*

**6**
- **J** "How do I open this jar"
- **K** asked Melanie." Dad picked it
- **L** up and showed her how to do it.
- **M** *(No mistakes)*

---

 **Go over each question on this page as a class.**

### Question 1

Missing quotation marks at beginning of quotation

### Question 2

Missing comma before end of quotation

### Question 3

Missing quotation marks around exact words spoken

### Question 5

Missing quotation marks and a comma at end of quotation

### Question 6

Missing question mark before end of quotation

# PUNCTUATION

## Endmarks

 **Explain to students that end-marks are the punctuation marks that come at the end of a sentence.**

Emphasize to students that every sentence must have an endmark.

Review the three types of end-marks discussed on the Pupil Edition page. Write some sentences on the board and leave out the end-marks. Have students put the correct endmarks at the end of the sentences. Some examples you might use are:

* *Are you coming over (?)*
* *Stop it (!)*
* *Oh my goodness (!)*
* *Please go away (.)*
* *The dog is on the chair (.)*

 **Go over the example question as a class.** Emphasize to students that they must read carefully in order to find punctuation errors.

---

 **Exercise 14**

## ON YOUR MARK!

### Punctuation: Endmarks

A **punctuation mark** must come at the end of every sentence. Here are the three types of punctuation marks that end a sentence:

A **period** is used to end sentences that are commands or statements.

* A **command** is a sentence that tells or asks someone to do something.

*Please wash the dishes.*

* A **statement** is a sentence that tells something.

*The painting was beautiful.*

A **question mark** is used to end a sentence that asks something.

*What is the answer to question three?*

An **exclamation mark** is used to end a sentence that shows strong feeling.

*"Oh, no!" yelled Omar. "I dropped the pie!"*

 **GET SET!**

Let's look at an example.

**Find the punctuation error.**

Ⓐ Woody and Allen were late By the
**B** time they got to practice, everyone else had
**C** already started throwing the ball around.
**D** *(No mistakes)*

(A) is **correct!** A punctuation mark must be at the end of the sentence after *late*. The punctuation mark should be a period, since this sentence is a statement.

---

  **EXTRA ACTIVITY**

Have students write a paragraph about anything they want. The paragraph must include at least one question and one exclamation. Review their paragraphs for proper use of endmarks.

## GO!

### DIRECTIONS

Find the punctuation error. If there is none, mark the last answer choice, *(No mistakes).*

© McGraw-Hill School Division

1
A Does anyone know where
B the map is Father said it was most
C likely under the front seat of the car.
D *(No mistakes)*

2
J This is where Scarlett's father
K used to work Now he works across
L town in a bigger office building.
M *(No mistakes)*

3
A It is time for school Go
B make sure that your brother is
C dressed and ready to catch the bus.
D *(No mistakes)*

4
J Bryan didn't know where
K the Indian Ocean was? so he
L asked his geography teacher.
M *(No mistakes)*

5
A The man reached
B into his hat and pulled out
C a rabbit. How did he do that
D *(No mistakes)*

6
A Sanjiv and his family
B just moved here from Texas.
C They used to own a ranch.
D *(No mistakes)*

 **Go over each question on this page as a class.**

### Question 1

Missing question mark

### Question 2

Missing period

### Question 3

Missing period

### Question 4

Unnecessary question mark

### Question 5

Missing question mark

# PUNCTUATION

## Possessive Nouns

 **Point out to students that possessive nouns are nouns that show ownership.**

Review singular and plural possessive nouns with the class. Have lists of each type on the board to provide extra examples.

Singular Possessive Nouns

- _Bob's_ cat was hungry.
- _Carol's_ hair was wet.
- The _dog's_ collar is missing.
- _Spot's_ blanket is dirty.
- The _car's_ window is broken.

Plural Possessive Nouns

- The _acrobats'_ wires were high.
- The _ladies'_ hats were funny looking.
- My _parents'_ cars are in the garage.
- Where are the _horses'_ stables?

 **TEACHING TIP**

Have students pay special attention to plural possessives, making sure they put the apostrophe in the correct place.

 **Go over the example question as a class.**

---

## ON YOUR MARK!

### Punctuation: Possessive Nouns

A **possessive noun** is a noun that shows who or what owns or has something.

If a possessive noun is singular, add an apostrophe and then an _s_ to the end of the possessive noun, like this:

_Shari's_ doll has a broken arm.

If the possessive noun is plural, then add apostrophe and an _s_ to the end of the possessive noun, like this:

The _women's_ team is winning!

If the possessive noun is plural and already ends in an _s_, then just an apostrophe is added to the end of the word, like this:

Baseball _players'_ shoes are called cleats.

---

**Singular Possessive Nouns**

My house is two streets away from _Rachel's_ house.
_Woofer's_ collar looks like it is too tight.

**Plural Possessive Nouns**

_Children's_ toys are at the end of the aisle.
The wind blew away my two _brothers'_ hats!

---

 **GET SET!**

Now let's look at an example.

**Find the punctuation error.**

Ⓐ Shannons dog likes to

B sleep under the porch. That is

C why they put a blanket there.

D _(No mistakes)_

(A) is **correct!** The dog belongs to Shannon. _Shannon_ is a singular noun. Therefore, an apostrophe and an _s_ must be added to _Shannon._

---

 ## TEACHING TIP

Make sure students do not confuse possessive nouns with words like _his, hers, theirs, ours,_ and _mine._ These words show possession but are not nouns and do not require an apostrophe.

# GO!

## DIRECTIONS

Find the punctuation error. If there is none, mark the last answer choice, *(No mistakes)*.

1  **A** Wendys first day of school
   **B** is tomorrow. We are having a
   **C** party to celebrate when she gets
      home.
   **D** *(No mistakes)*

2  **J** Mary's mother usually
   **K** drives her to school, but the two
   **L** twin's mother drives on
      Tuesdays.
   **M** *(No mistakes)*

3  **A** Clarissa saw that her
   **B** homework was ruined from
   **C** the boys muddy footprints.
   **D** *(No mistakes)*

4  **J** Cats may have a good
   **K** sense of smell, but nothing
   **L** beats dogs senses of smell.
   **M** *(No mistakes)*

5  **A** Willy's house has
   **B** three bedrooms, while Sams
   **C** house has four of them.
   **D** *(No mistakes)*

6  **J** Our mail carrier got
   **K** all mixed up today. That is
   **L** why we got the Smiths mail.
   **M** *(No mistakes)*

## Go over each question on this page as a class.

### Questions 1 and 5

These sentences need apostrophes added to the singular possessive nouns *Wendys* and *Sams*. The apostrophe should come between the last letter of the name and the *s*.

### Question 2

The word "twins" is plural, so the apostrophe should come after the letter *s*.

### Questions 3, 4, and 6

These sentences need apostrophes added to the plural possessive nouns *boys*, *dogs*, and *Smiths*. The apostrophe should come after the *s* at the end of the word.

# PUNCTUATION

## Contractions

**A contraction is two words that have been combined. The apostrophe shows where the missing letters are.**

Go over the contractions listed on the Pupil Edition page. Make sure that students are familiar with where the apostrophe is placed when combining two words into a contraction. There are general rules but several exceptions, so students should be prepared to memorize as many contractions as they can.

**Go over the example question as a class.**

**Exercise 16**

## ON YOUR MARK!

### Punctuation: Contractions

A contraction is a shortened form of two words. An apostrophe shows where one or more letters have been left out. Here are examples of contractions with the word *not*:

| | | | |
|---|---|---|---|
| has not——▶ *hasn't* | | can not——▶ *can't* | |
| have not——▶ *haven't* | | do not——▶ *don't* | |
| had not——▶ *hadn't* | | does not——▶ *doesn't* | |

Here are some other examples of contractions:

| | | | |
|---|---|---|---|
| I am——▶ *I'm* | | I will——▶ *I'll* | |
| we had/would——▶ *we'd* | | we are——▶ *we're* | |
| he has/is——▶ *he's* | | they have——▶ *they've* | |

> **TIP:** The word *won't* is a special contraction. The spelling of the words *will* and *not* change to *won't*.

 **GET SET!**

Let's look at an example.

A  Where is the paint brush?
B  Brad said it was on the bench,
**C**  but I cant see it anyplace.
D  *(No mistakes)*

(C) is **correct!** *Can't* is a contraction of *can not*. It needs an apostrophe between the *n* and the *t*.

---

 ## EXTRA ACTIVITY

Distribute a short paragraph to the class. Have students list all of the contractions in the paragraph, along with the two words each contraction represents. An example paragraph you can use is:

*Jamie can't wait to go to the park. He hasn't been there in a long time. He'd go there every day if he could, but he can't unless it is nice outside. The park isn't a very nice place to be in the rain.*

**GO!**

 **Go over each question on this page as a class.**

## DIRECTIONS

Find the punctuation error. If there is none, mark the last answer choice, *(No mistakes)*.

**1** Ⓐ Weve got to get to
  **B** the bus stop, or we will
  **C** be late for school today.
  **D** *(No mistakes)*

**2** Ⓙ Mr. Chi isnt the
  **K** most famous man I know.
  **L** I also know an actor.
  **M** *(No mistakes)*

**3** **A** My father tells
  **B** us that at the end of a long day,
  Ⓒ its good to be back home.
  **D** *(No mistakes)*

**4** **J** Madeline has been
  Ⓚ studying all week. Shell
  **L** probably pass the test.
  **M** *(No mistakes)*

**5** **A** When you go camping,
  Ⓑ you dont know if it will rain.
  **C** That's why you bring a tent.
  **D** *(No mistakes)*

**6** **J** Marge has a little dog
  **K** named Fluffy. It's white
  **L** and has a little black nose.
  Ⓜ *(No mistakes)*

**Question 1**

We've

**Question 2**

isn't

**Question 3**

it's

**Question 4**

She'll

**Question 5**

don't

**ITBS**

# PUNCTUATION

## Abbreviations

 **Remind students that abbreviations are shortened forms of words.**

They begin with a capital letter and end with a period.

 ## EXTRA ACTIVITY

Have students write down as many words, along with their abbreviations, that they can think of. See how many different ones the class can come up with.

 **Go over the example question as a class.** Emphasize to students that they must pay special attention to capitalizing abbreviations and placing a period at the end.

---

**Exercise 17**

## ON YOUR MARK!

### Punctuation: Abbreviations

An abbreviation is a shortened form of a word. It begins with a capital letter and ends with a period. Some common abbreviations are:

Dr. = Doctor
Mr. = Mister
Jr. = Junior
St. = Street
Ave. = Avenue

The days of the week can also be abbreviated:

Sun.  Mon.  Tues.  Wed.  Thurs.  Fri.  Sat.

Some of the months can also be abbreviated:

Jan.  Feb.  Mar.  Apr.  Aug.  Sept.  Oct.  Nov.  Dec.

Look at the following sentences and see how abbreviations are used:

Ronnie lives on Maple St.
Roseanne baby-sits for Mrs. Lewis.
Dr. Sparks always gives me a lollipop.
Sammy Davis, Jr. made people laugh.
The sign on the door says, "Open Mon. and Wed. only."

 ## GET SET!

Now let's look at some examples.

**Find the punctuation error.**

Ⓐ Where is Mr Gonzalez? I
B   thought he was going to drive
C   the school bus today.
D   *(No mistakes)*

(A) is **correct!** because *Mr.* is an abbreviation, so it needs a period at the end.

---

 ## EXTRA ACTIVITY

Prepare a paragraph with words in it such as *doctor, mister, street, avenue,* days of the week, and months. Have students rewrite the paragraph, changing all the possible words into their abbreviations. An example paragraph you can use is:

*Today is Tuesday, and I am going to see Doctor Smith. He is a nice doctor. He always gives me a lollipop before I leave. I go to see him twice a year for a check-up. Usually I go in April and December. Mom drives me to the office and waits for me while I go in. I could probably walk there myself because the office is on Pierce Street, which is only two blocks from my house on Baltimore Avenue. But Mom likes to go with me. I like it when she comes.*

## GO!

### DIRECTIONS

Find the punctuation error. If there is none, mark the last answer choice, *(No mistakes)*.

1  A  Mrs. Leone is a good
   B  cook. Everyone loves going
   C  to her house for dinner.
   D  *(No mistakes)*

2  J  When we need a doctor,
   K  we go to Dr Wilson. We like
      him
   L  because he gives us lollipops.
   M  *(No mistakes)*

3  A  Park Ave is a famous
   B  street. It is located in New
   C  York City, New York.
   D  *(No mistakes)*

4  J  My grandparents used
   K  to live on First St, but then
   L  they moved to Maple Road.
   M  *(No mistakes)*

5  A  My favorite show
   B  is Nature World. It comes on
   C  every Tues. afternoon.
   D  *(No mistakes)*

6  A  The date of my
   B  little sister's birthday
   C  is Apr. 17, 2000.
   D  *(No mistakes)*

## Go over each question on this page as a class.

### Question 2

Dr.

### Question 3

Ave.

### Question 4

St.

# Exercise 18

# PUNCTUATION

## Date, Address, Time, and Letter Greeting and Closing

 Point out that each of following—dates, addresses, times, and letter greetings and closings—has special punctuation rules that must be memorized.

Review each of the rules listed on the Pupil Edition page with the class. Make sure that students are familiar with how commas are used in each case, and how abbreviations for a state differ from regular abbreviations (both letters are capitalized and there are no periods).

Explain what a *colon* is and how it is used when writing the time of day.

 Go over the example question as a class. A comma is always placed between the city and state in an address.

---

### Exercise 18

## ON YOUR MARK!

### Punctuation: Date, Address, Time, and Letter Greeting and Closing

**Dates:** A comma separates the month and day from the year:

*October 14, 1906*

**Addresses:** The town or city of an address is separated from the state by a comma. Also, the state's name is usually abbreviated—but without periods—like this:

*Boston, MA*

**Time:** Use a colon to separate the hour from the minutes.

*5:05*

**Letter Greeting:** Place a comma after a letter greeting.

*Dear Mom,*

**Letter Closing:** Place a comma after a letter closing.

*Your friend,*

 ## GET SET!

Now let's look at an example.

**Find the punctuation error.**

A   1824 Jeopardy Lane
Ⓑ   Chicago IL 99227
C   June 27, 1998
D   *(No mistakes)*

(B) is **correct!** A comma must come after *Chicago*.

---

 ## EXTRA ACTIVITY

Prepare a letter and hand out copies to the class. Make sure that the letter has errors for each of the topics covered on the Pupil Edition page. Tell students that they are the teachers and have to correct the letter before it is sent out. To make it more fun, let them use a red or colored pencil for their corrections. An example letter you can use is:

*May 7 2000*

*Dear Larry*

*It is 5,00 in the afternoon. I just got home from soccer practice. I wanted to tell you that I am going to Orlando Florida soon and might be able to visit you. I hope you will be in town.*

*Your friend*

*Eduardo*

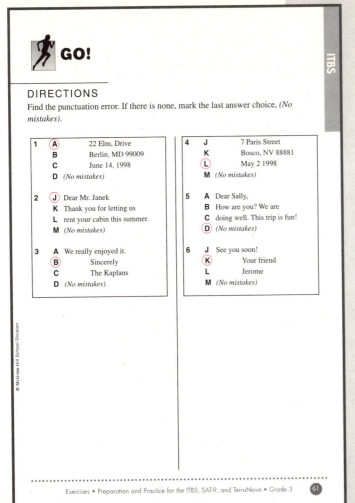

**GO!**

DIRECTIONS

Find the punctuation error. If there is none, mark the last answer choice, *(No mistakes)*.

1  **A**    22 Elm, Drive
   **B**    Berlin, MD 99009
   **C**    June 14, 1998
   **D**    *(No mistakes)*

2  **J**  Dear Mr. Janek
   **K**  Thank you for letting us
   **L**  rent your cabin this summer.
   **M**  *(No mistakes)*

3  **A**  We really enjoyed it.
   **B**         Sincerely
   **C**         The Kaplans
   **D**  *(No mistakes)*

4  **J**    7 Paris Street
   **K**    Bosco, NV 88881
   **L**    May 2 1998
   **M**  *(No mistakes)*

5  **A**  Dear Sally,
   **B**  How are you? We are
   **C**  doing well. This trip is fun!
   **D**  *(No mistakes)*

6  **J**  See you soon!
   **K**      Your friend
   **L**      Jerome
   **M**  *(No mistakes)*

© McGraw-Hill School Division

### Question 1

No comma needed in street name

### Question 2

Comma needed at end of greeting

### Question 3

Comma needed at end of closing

### Question 4

Comma needed before year in date

### Question 6

Comma needed at end of greeting

# FIX THE MISTAKES YOURSELF

 **Make sure students understand that fixing mistakes in their heads as they read will help them succeed on the ITBS.**

It is important that students be able to correct mistakes in paragraphs.

Mistakes that are easy to find in a stand-alone sentence may be more difficult to find when hidden in a larger paragraph. Students must be able to read carefully to find these mistakes.

 ## TEACHING TIP

Students should be given paragraphs to read and correct periodically throughout the school year, emphasizing each language arts topic as it is taught.

 **Go over the example exercise as a class.** The mistakes in the paragraph are:

- *familys*
- *lake!*
- *lake?*
- *Id*

Have students rewrite the paragraph as directed. Review their paragraphs for the correct use of punctuation and capitalization.

---

 **Exercise 19**

## ON YOUR MARK!

### Fix the Mistakes Yourself

When you take the ITBS, try correcting the errors you see as you read them. If you think about how you would write the words as you are reading them, you may be able to find the errors and correct them. This is especially helpful to you on punctuation questions, when errors might be so small they are hard to spot—like a missing period or an incorrectly placed comma.

 ## GET SET!

Let's look at an example.

**Read the paragraph below.**

My familys summer house is on Lake Ontario. On the last day of school in June, my mom always says, "Time to move up to the lake! My favorite thing to do is to catch frogs. I look at their colors and measure their lengths. Then I write that information down in my journal and put the frog back into the lake? Someday, Id like to be a biologist. A biologist studies frogs and other living things.

**Now rewrite the paragraph, correcting all the errors.**

_____
_____
_____
_____
_____
_____
_____
_____

---

 ### EXTRA ACTIVITY

During the year, read through newspapers, magazines, and books, looking for errors in spelling, punctuation, and capitalization. Bring in these examples and have students try to find the mistakes.

## GO!

### DIRECTIONS

Find the punctuation error. If there is none, mark the last answer choice, *(No mistakes)*.

1  A    103 West Palm Drive
   **B**    Oakley FL 23456
   C    January 9, 1992
   D    *(No mistakes)*

2  **J**    Dear Miss LaCroy
   K    Please find with this
   L    letter the signed report card.
   M    *(No mistakes)*

3  A    Thank you for sending it.
   **B**    Sincerely
   C    Mrs. Janet Foo
   D    *(No mistakes)*

4  J    We keep our dog in
   K    the backyard because she is so
   **L**    big. Shes got her own house.
   M    *(No mistakes)*

5  A    "Where is the farm we are
   **B**    going to visit" Carlos asked.
        Mom
   C    told him it was two towns away.
   D    *(No mistakes)*

6  J    Nancy's first art class is
   K    this Saturday. She needs to
        bring
   L    a pen, a pencil, and a notebook.
   **M**    *(No mistakes)*

ITBS

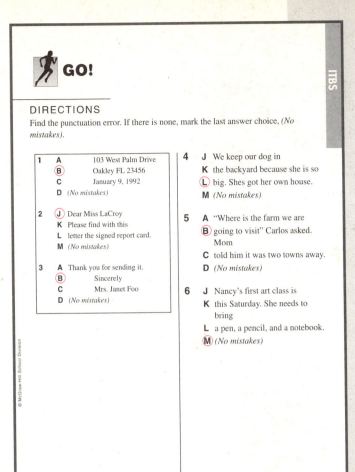

## Go over each question on this page as a class.

Remind students to fix the mistakes in their heads as they answer the questions on this page.

### Questions 1

Comma missing between city and state

### Question 2

Comma missing at end of greeting

### Question 3

Comma missing at end of closing

### Question 4

She's

### Question 5

Missing question mark at end of quotation

# EXPRESSION

## Verb Tense Agreement

 **Explain to students that verb tense is very important. It tells *when* an action takes place: past, present, or future.**

Go over the examples of each tense listed on the Pupil Edition page. Make sure students are aware of the difference between past, present, and future.

Write some sentences on the board to demonstrate how the surrounding words in a sentence give clues to the tense of the verbs.

- *She <u>used</u> to drive a bus <u>when she was younger</u>.* (past)

- *Brady <u>called</u> us <u>last week</u>.* (past)

- *We <u>are driving</u> to the store <u>right now</u>.* (present)

- *<u>Someday</u> I <u>will write</u> a book.* (future)

 **Go over the example question as a class.** After students have answered the question, rewrite it to demonstrate the other tenses.

- *Elisha <u>will borrow</u> my book on Saturday</u>.*

- *Elisha <u>is borrowing</u> my book <u>right now</u>.*

---

 **Exercise 20**

## ON YOUR MARK!

### Expression: Verb Tense Agreement

**Verb tense** tells you when the action happens:

| | |
|---|---|
| Present tense | means it is happening now |
| Past tense | means it happened in the past |
| Future tense | means it will happen in the future |

The words in the sentence usually give you clues that tell you what verb tense to use.

*I **pour** milk in the glass and **drink** the milk*

The two verbs in the present tense tell you the sentence happens now.

*Billy went to the store **yesterday**.*

*Yesterday* tells you the action happened in the past. The verb must be in the past tense.

*Sarah will come to visit us **next month**.*

The words *next month* tell you the action has not happened yet. The verb must be in the future tense.

 ## GET SET!

Let's look at an example.

**Choose the *best* way to write the underlined part of the sentence.**

Elisha <u>borrows</u> my book last Tuesday after school.

Ⓐ borrowed
**B** will borrow
**C** borrowing
**D** *(No mistakes)*

(A) is **correct!** The words *last Tuesday* tell you that the action occurred in the past, and *borrowed* is the past tense of *borrow*.

  ## EXTRA ACTIVITY

Divide the class into three groups. Have the first group write a paragraph in the past tense. Have the second and third groups write paragraphs in the present and future tenses, respectively. The topic can be whatever the students choose. Have students from each group read their paragraphs out loud to demonstrate the differences in verb tense.

# GO!

### DIRECTIONS

Choose the <u>best</u> way to write the underlined part of the sentence.

**1** Marsha <u>sold</u> her doll to Eliza tomorrow for five dollars.

- **A** sells
- **B** has sold
- **C** will sell
- **D** *(No change)*

**2** Margaret <u>brings</u> her book bag to school last week.

- **J** brought
- **K** will bring
- **L** bring
- **M** *(No change)*

**3** Clyde <u>catches</u> the stick when Ben threw it.

- **A** has caught
- **B** caught
- **C** will catch
- **D** *(No change)*

**4** Fred <u>loses</u> his wallet yesterday afternoon.

- **J** lost
- **K** will lose
- **L** has lost
- **M** *(No change)*

**5** They <u>shows</u> us a movie tomorrow in class.

- **A** showing
- **B** have showed
- **C** will show
- **D** *(No change)*

**6** The zoo <u>opened</u> next week for the first time.

- **J** will open
- **K** has opens
- **L** open
- **M** *(No change)*

## Go over each question on this page as a class.

Tell students to look for time indicator words in the sentences. These indicators will provide clues about the correct verb tense.

### Question 1

Future tense

Time indicator: *tomorrow*

### Question 2

Past tense

Time indicator: *last week*

### Question 3

Past tense

Time indicator: *threw*

### Question 4

Past tense

Time indicator: *yesterday*

### Question 5

Future tense

Time indicator: *tomorrow*

### Question 6

Future tense

Time indicator: *next week*

# EXPRESSION

## Sentence Fragments and Run-On Sentences

 **Remind students that a sentence expresses a complete thought.**

If a sentence is incomplete (missing one or more elements), it no longer expresses a complete thought. This is a *sentence fragment* or incomplete sentence. If a sentence is too long (has too many elements), it expresses too many thoughts and is confusing. This is a *run-on sentence*.

Write some examples of complete sentences, fragments, and run-ons on the board. Have students tell you which are complete. Then have them correct the fragments and run-ons. Some examples you might use are:

- *I took a nap*
- *the blue car*
- *the dog was barking the cat was sleeping*
- *I'm a happy girl*
- *bottle of water*
- *today is my birthday it is Monday*

 **Go over the example question as a class.** Ask students to read the answer choices out loud. They should be able to hear how confusing the wrong answer choices sound.

---

**Exercise 21**

 **ON YOUR MARK!**

**Expression: Sentence Fragments and Run-On Sentences**

A **sentence** is a group of words that expresses a complete thought.

*Let's go to the car wash.*

*Grammy's molasses cookies are the best in my neighborhood.*

A **sentence fragment** is a group of words that does not express a complete thought.

*To the car wash*

*Grammy's molasses cookies being the best.*

A **run-on sentence** joins together two or more sentences that should be written separately.

*Let's go to the car wash it will be fun to sit inside the car.*

*Grammy's molasses cookies are the best in my neighborhood she uses a special recipe.*

 **GET SET!**

Let's look at some examples.

**Choose the best way to express the idea.**

A  Byron tossed the softball it went over the fence.
B  Byron, tossing the softball over the fence.
C  Byron tossed the softball, and it went over the fence.
D  Byron tossed the softball. Over the fence.

(A) is **wrong.** This sentence is a run-on. It has two ideas that are not properly joined.

(B) is **wrong.** The sentence does not express a complete thought.

(C) is **correct!** It expresses a complete ideas without being a run-on. Keep this answer choice, but read the last one just in case you missed something.

(D) is **wrong.** The first sentence is correct, but the second is a sentence fragment.

---

★ **EXTRA ACTIVITY**

Play a sentence game with students. Have one student say a word and the next student say another word. For example, one student might say *The* and the next student can say *dog* and each student that follows will continue the story. When a complete sentence has been formed, the next student must say *period* (or another appropriate endmark) or add a word that continues the sentence but doesn't make it a run-on. Then begin a new sentence. For example:

*The – dog – was – sitting – on – the – sofa – period – He – was – wagging – his – tail – period.*

**GO!**

## DIRECTIONS

Choose the <u>best</u> way to express the idea.

**1**
 **A** Living in the water or on land plants needing light.
 **B** Whether they live in water or on land, plants need light.
 **C** Plants need light. In the water or on land.
 **D** Plants in the water or on land they need light.

**2**
 **J** Darryl's dog got out of the yard and ran away.
 **K** Darryl's dog ran away, out of the yard it got.
 **L** Daryl's dog, running away, got out of the yard.
 **M** Out of the yard. Daryl's dog it ran away.

**3**
 **A** Miguel threw the bowling ball it went down the lane.
 **B** Miguel, throwing the bowling ball down the lane.
 **C** Miguel threw the bowling ball, and it went down the lane.
 **D** Miguel threw the bowling ball. Down the lane.

**4**
 **J** For our dinner. Maria served meat and vegetables.
 **K** Maria served meat. And vegetables, for our dinner.
 **L** Maria for our dinner served. Meat and vegetables.
 **M** Maria served meat and vegetables for our dinner.

**5**
 **A** Cars and trucks. In all shapes and sizes they come.
 **B** Cars and trucks come in all shapes and sizes.
 **C** Cars and trucks coming in all shapes and sizes.
 **D** Cars and trucks in all shapes. And sizes come.

**6**
 **J** The pool had to be filled with water before we could swim.
 **K** The pool had to be filled. With water before we could swim.
 **L** Before we could swim. The pool had to be filled with water.
 **M** Before we could swim, the pool had to be filled. With water.

---

 **Go over each question on this page as a class.**

Tell students that on these types of questions, they should read carefully and sound out the sentences in their heads. By sounding out the sentences, students will be able to determine if they are awkward. Point out that if a sentence doesn't sound right, it usually isn't correct.

Remind students to read the instructions carefully. In this case, they are choosing the sentence that is *correct*.

# EXPRESSION

## Sentence Clarity

 **Explain to students that** *clarity* **means how clear something is.**

In this case, sentence clarity refers to how clear, or easy to understand, a sentence is.

Sentences that are not clear are hard to understand and can be confusing to listeners or readers. Students should always try to make their sentences as clear and easy to understand as possible.

Impress upon the students that writing and speaking clearly is something they need to work on all the time, whether they are in school or at home.

 **Go over the example question as a class.** Go over each answer choice carefully, making sure that students understand *why* it is wrong or right.

---

 Exercise 22

## ON YOUR MARK!

### Expression: Sentence Clarity

A sentence that is not clear will be hard for the reader to understand. When you write or speak, make sure that each sentence can be understood easily. Look out for:

- incorrect order of ideas
- misplaced words

**Wrong:** *Flying across the sky, Leon saw an eagle.*

Is Leon flying across the sky? No, because people don't fly. In this case, the ideas in the sentence are out of order.

**Right:** *Leon saw an eagle flying across the sky.*

Now the sentence is easy to understand, because eagles are birds and birds fly.

 ## GET SET!

Let's look at an example.

**Choose the <u>best</u> way to express the idea.**

A  Our cats fish and like to look in at the tank.
B  At the fish in the tank our cats like to look.
C  Our cats like to fish and look in the tank.
D  Our cats like to look at the fish in the tank.

(A) is **wrong.** Do fish look in at the tank? No, they're inside the tank. This is wrong.

(B) is **wrong.** The ideas are all mixed up. Cats is the subject, but it's way at the end of the sentence. It should be at the beginning.

(C) is **wrong.** If cats could fish, then this sentence would be correct.

(D) is **correct!** This sentence makes sense.

---

 ## TEACHING TIP

In order to improve the students' ability to produce clear sentences, have them write paragraphs about topics of their choice on a regular basis throughout the school year.

## GO!

### DIRECTIONS

Choose the best way to express the idea.

**1**
A. Maude pushed the boxes down the stairs.
B. The boxes pushed Maude down the stairs.
C. Down the stairs, Maude the boxes pushed.
D. The boxes Maude pushed down the stairs.

**2**
J. And set it free, the mouse we caught.
K. The mouse, we caught, and set it free.
L. We caught the mouse and set it free.
M. And free we set it, the caught mouse.

**3**
A. The pie we brought and Chantelle brought the flowers.
B. Chantelle brought the flowers and we brought the pie.
C. Chantelle the flowers she brought, and us had the pie.
D. Flowers and pie, Chantelle brought and we brought.

**4**
J. Our dog flies and likes to chase bugs.
K. Flies and bugs like to dog our chase.
L. Our dog likes flies, and to chase bugs.
M. Our dog likes to chase flies and bugs.

**5**
A. Over that hill is where we catch the train.
B. That train is where we catch over the hill.
C. Over the train is where we catch that hill.
D. That hill, over is where we catch the train.

**6**
J. Although he made a great catch, never played before had Steve.
K. Although he had never played before, Steve made a great catch.
L. Steve had a great catch made, although never before did he play.
M. Never playing before, Steve made a great catch although.

## Go over each question on this page as a class.

Remind students to read each answer choice carefully before choosing an answer. For each sentence, they should ask themselves: *Are the ideas in the correct order? Are any words misplaced?* Go over the answer choices in question 1 individually.

### Question 1

Choice *A*: Correct

Choice *B*: Misplaced words—The boxes didn't push Maude. Maude pushed the boxes.

Choice *C*: Incorrect order

Choice *D*: Misplaced words and incorrect order

# EXPRESSION

## Paragraphs

 **Explain to students that all of the sentences in a paragraph should be about a central topic.**

Go over the three ideas listed on the page with the class.

- The **main idea** tells what the paragraph or story is about. For example, the main idea of a fairy tale might be, "A brave knight goes out and has exciting adventures."

- A **topic sentence** introduces the main idea. It is usually the first sentence of a paragraph or story. In our fairy tale example, the topic sentence might be "Once upon a time, there lived a brave knight." This lets us know that the story is going to be about the knight.

- **Time-order** words tell when things in a story or paragraph happen and the order in which they happen. These words help the reader understand the sequence of events in a story.

 **TEACHING TIP**

Go over the idea of concluding sentences as well. Make sure the students understand that a concluding sentence either summarizes a paragraph or provides an understandable conclusion.

 **Go over the example question as a class.**

---

## ON YOUR MARK!

### Expression: Paragraphs

In a **paragraph**, all sentences should work together to tell about, or develop, a main idea.

The **main idea** is what a story or paragraph is all about.

The **topic sentence** usually states the main idea. It is usually the first sentence of the paragraph.

**Time-order words** connect ideas within a sentence. They tell when things happen and in what order. For example:

*first, next, then, later, last, after, before, while, this morning, yesterday, now, as soon as, tomorrow, last year, long ago*

 | Topic Sentence |

*They asked their mother if they could go fly their new kite. Their mother told them they could go after they finished their chores. **First,** Brian and Marta cleaned their rooms. **Then** Brian did the dusting and put the dishes away **while** Marta mopped the floors. When they were done, their mother told them they could go. Brian and Marta spent the rest of the day at the park.*

| Time-Order Words |

 **GET SET!**

Let's look at an example. Read the paragraph about Brian and Marta.

**Choose the best first sentence to add to this paragraph.**

A   All their friends were already there.
B   Brian and Marta wanted to spend the day at the park.
C   Brian and Marta do not like their new kite.
D   The kite flew through the air like a bird.

(B) is **correct!** It tells you the main idea of the paragraph. Brian and Marta wanted to spend the day at the park. The sentences that follow give you the details of that main idea.

---

 ★ **EXTRA ACTIVITY**

Bring in the first paragraph or two from a variety of fairy tales and children's stories. Read them out loud, and have the class pick out the topic sentences and time-order words. See if they can figure out the main idea of the stories from the material provided.

**GO!**

## DIRECTIONS

Use these paragraphs to answer the questions that come after them.

We saw all sorts of animals. I really liked the alligators the best. My sister Sara liked the elephants. While we were there, my dad had our picture taken with a monkey. We look so funny! I have it hanging on my bedroom wall.

**1  Choose the best first sentence to add to this paragraph.**

   A  The zoo is not a fun place to spend an afternoon.

   B  Last year my stepmom took us to the zoo.

   C  Zoos are places where you can see animals.

   D  Zookeepers take care of the animals in a zoo.

**2  Choose the best last sentence to add to this paragraph.**

   J  Next year I am going to buy a monkey.

   K  My stepmom liked the lions the best.

   L  Dad thinks I should clean my room more.

   M  My friends all laugh when they see it.

My family went to visit my grandmother. We thought taking a bus would be more fun than driving oursleves. The ride was long, but I didn't get bored. I watched the farms and towns go by. Once, I saw a bunch of horses in a field. Whenever the bus stopped, I would take a picture of the station for my scrapbook.

**3  Choose the best first sentence to add to this paragraph.**

   A  Last summer I took a long trip on a bus.

   B  My grandmother called us and asked us to ride a bus.

   C  The bus was crowded.

   D  My grandmother likes to bake.

**4  Choose the best last sentence to add to this paragraph.**

   J  I brought my camera with me to my grandmother's.

   K  The horses were running across the field.

   L  When school started, I showed my scrapbook to the class.

   M  My grandmother owns horses and cows.

 **Go over each question on this page as a class.**

## Question 1

Only choice *B* tells who *we* is in the first sentence of the paragraph.

## Question 2

Only choice *M* refers to the picture of a monkey.

## Question 3

Only choice *A* discusses the narrator's ride on a bus.

## Question 4

Only choice *L* refers to the narrator's scrapbook.

# EXPRESSION

## Understanding Main Idea and Sentence Order

 **Explain to students that in between the topic sentence and concluding sentence of a paragraph are the sentences that provide information about the main idea.**

These are called the *detail sentences*.

Among other things, detail sentences provide information that supports the main idea. To do that they must be in the proper order, otherwise the paragraph will be difficult to understand.

Besides being in the proper order, detail sentences must relate directly to the main idea. For example, in a paragraph about baseball equipment, information about other sports equipment would not support the main idea.

 **Go over the example question as a class.** In this example, students are asked to find the detail sentence that does *not* belong in the paragraph.

---

Exercise 24

## ON YOUR MARK!

### Expression: Understanding Main Idea and Sentence Order

As you have already learned, the **main idea** of a paragraph or story is usually stated in the topic sentence. The sentences that come after the topic sentence are detail sentences. **Detail sentences** support the main idea. They explain the main idea in more detail. Detail sentences must be in a logical order. If a sentence is in the wrong place, or does not belong, the paragraph will be hard to understand.

 ## GET SET!

Let's look at an example.

**Use this paragraph to answer the question that comes after it.**

**1** Roger and Corinne played in the yard with their puppy. **2** Their father worked at the bank. **3** The puppy liked it when they threw the ball. **4** The puppy chased the ball all over the yard. **5** Then the puppy got tired and laid down to sleep.

**Which sentence should be left out of this paragraph?**

A   Sentence 1
Ⓑ   Sentence 2
C   Sentence 3
D   Sentence 4

(B) is **correct!** The main idea is Roger and Corinne playing with their puppy. Sentence 2 is about their father working in a bank. It does not support the main idea, so it does not belong.

---

 ## EXTRA ACTIVITY

Ask the students to come up with sentences that could be used in place of sentence 2 in the example. How many can they come up with? Make sure they support the main idea of the paragraph.

## GO!

### DIRECTIONS

Read this paragraph. Then answer the questions that come after it.

© McGraw-Hill School Division

> [1] Anita rode her bike down to the store. [2] It was a blue bike. [3] Her mother had given her a list of things to buy. [4] The first item was jelly. [5] Anita went to the checkout lane and paid for the groceries. [6] Then she placed bread, eggs, and milk in her cart. [7] Afterwards, she had fifty cents left over. [8] Her mother had told her she could spend the change on candy. [9] She was able to buy a whole bag! [10] Anita decided to buy lemon drops.

**1** Which sentence should be left out of this paragraph?

- A Sentence 1
- **B** Sentence 2
- C Sentence 3
- D Sentence 4

**2** Where is the best place for sentence 5 ?

- J Where it is now
- K After sentence 8
- **L** After sentence 6
- M After sentence 2

**3** Where is the best place for sentence 9?

- A Where it is now
- B After sentence 6
- C After sentence 7
- **D** After sentence 10

**4** Choose the best first sentence to add to this paragraph?

- **J** Anita's mother asked Anita to go to the store after school.
- K Anita's favorite way to get around town is on her bicycle.
- L Anita's friends like to borrow her bicycle.
- M Anita hates to do her chores.

---

## Go over each question on this page as a class.

### Question 1

The paragraph is about Anita's trip to the store, not her bike.

### Question 2

Sentence 5 talks about Anita going to the checkout lane and paying for the food. This can't happen before she even places the food in her cart (sentence 6) or after she already has her change (sentences 7 and 8). The only logical place for this sentence is after sentence 6.

### Question 3

Sentence 9 must go after sentence 10 because sentence 9 tells that Anita was able to buy a whole bag of lemon drops. Lemon drops are not introduced until sentence 10.

### Question 4

Only choice *J* refers to Anita's trip to the store.

© McGraw-Hill School Division

# Exercise 25

## SHARE YOUR WRITING WITH OTHERS

 **It is important for students to improve their skills in *spelling, grammar, capitalization*, and *punctuation*. The best way to do this is practice, practice, practice!**

Let students know that the more they read and write, the more they will improve these skills.

Assign writing assignments in class throughout the year. The students should be encouraged to write about anything that interests them. Book reports and movie reviews or stories about favorite athletes or movie stars are all good writing topics. Have students pair with a partner at least once a month to exchange one of their paragraphs. The partner should mark any errors in capitalization, spelling, grammar, and punctuation. Also, the partner can suggest improvements in topic sentences, concluding sentences, and detail sentences.

 **Go over the example question as a class.**

---

### Exercise 25

## ON YOUR MARK!
### Share Your Writing with Others

Memorizing all the spelling, grammar, capitalization, and punctuation rules isn't enough. You also need to practice them. That means writing.

Just as reading helps you notice the relationships between words, writing helps you create those relationships. Show off what you know by sharing your writing with others. Ask your classmate to read your writing and look for:

- Run-on Sentences
- Sentence Fragments
- Punctuation Errors
- Capitalization Errors
- Spelling Errors

If your editor catches these types of mistakes, your writing will be clearer. Plus, you will learn how to be a whiz at ITBS questions!

Learn from your mistakes by noticing what types of errors you make most often. Those are the rules you need to focus on.

 ## GET SET!

Let's look at some examples. Pretend your classmate wrote the question, and you must find the error.

Ⓐ Lana shaked the box
B and listened closely. She wanted
C to guess what was inside it.
D *(No mistakes)*

(A) is **correct!** The past tense of *shake* is *shook*, not *shaked*.

---

 ## EXTRA ACTIVITY

Set up a game in class called "Newspaper." Each week, half of the class will pretend to be writers and write paragraphs about anything they want. They should include several errors in punctuation, capitalization, and expression. The other half of the class will be the editors and correct the articles. Each week the editors and writers should switch.

**GO!**

### DIRECTIONS
Choose the best way to write the underlined part of the sentence.

**1** Daniela <u>eats</u> lunch with Randy yesterday at school.

   **A** has eaten

   **B** will eat

   **C** ate

   **D** *(No change)*

### DIRECTIONS
Choose the best way to express the idea.

**2**  **J** Around boats, dolphins playing and jumping.

   **K** Dolphins play and jump. Like around boats.

   **L** Boats like dolphins to play and jump around.

   **M** Dolphins like to play and jump around boats.

### DIRECTIONS
Use this paragraph to answer the question that comes after it.

> **1** My parents always take my sisters and I on the first night. **2** It is so exciting. **3** The foods all smell so good. **4** I always get popcorn and a soda. **5** My friend Angela likes roller coasters. **6** Before we leave we all buy cotton candy. **7** The noises from the rides and games are so loud you have to shout to be heard. **8** We always play on the bumper cars, and then go on the Ferris wheel. **9** Last year I even won a big prize!

**3** Choose the best first sentence to add to this paragraph.

   **A** Carnivals are like state fairs, but smaller.

   **B** Carnivals always set up in a big field or parking lot.

   **C** The best part of summer is when the carnival comes to town.

   **D** Last year my prize was a giant panda bear.

---

 **Go over each question on this page as a class.**

You might want to have students swap Go! pages and correct each other's work for this exercise to emphasize the importance of sharing writing.

### Question 1

Verb tense—sentence requires the past tense of *eat*. Time indicator: *yesterday*

### Question 2

Only choice *M* presents the words and ideas in a correct and logical order.

### Question 3

Only choice *C* refers to the specific carnival discussed throughout the rest of the paragraph.

# USAGE

**Explain to students that using words and sentences properly is how people make themselves understood.**

Go over the ideas about double negatives and the word *ain't* with the class. (Students should already be familiar with the importance of verb tense agreement.)

- **Double negatives**: *can't not, never not,* and *won't not* are all examples of double negatives. Two negative words should never be used in the same sentence. *Don't* is the contraction for *do not.* Therefore *don't not* means *do not not.* The *not* is repeated and doesn't make sense.

- **Ain't**: Although it is frequently used, *ain't* is not a word. Stress to students that *ain't* should never be used in speaking or writing.

**Go over the example question as a class.** Make sure students understand that *won't not* is a double negative and literally means *will not not.* Explain that this doesn't make sense.

---

**Exercise 26**

# ON YOUR MARK!

## Usage

Using the English language properly helps make sure that people can understand you. Always follow the basic rules of grammar and spelling, whether you are writing a book report for class or a letter to a friend. Here are some common mistakes people make:

**The Double Negative:** This is when two negative words are placed in the same sentence, as in *can't not,* or *not nothing.* Never use two negative words in the same sentence. These negative words cancel each other out.

**Verb Tense Agreement:** The verb tense must agree with the words that surround it. For example:

*She went to the store tomorrow.*

*Went* is past tense of *to go. Tomorrow* tells you that the action takes place in the future. The sentence would be correct if the verb was in the future tense.

*She **will** go to the store **tomorrow**.*

**Ain't:** *Ain't* is not a proper word. Do not use the word *ain't.*

# GET SET!

Let's look at some examples.

**Find the mistake.**

Ⓐ Martin won't not listen to

**B** his teacher. That is why he is always

**C** getting in trouble in the classroom.

**D** (No mistakes)

(A) is **correct!** *Won't not listen* is a double negative. Either *won't listen* or *will not listen* would make this sentence correct.

---

## TEACHING TIP

Constantly remind students to listen to how they and the people around them speak. Have them pay attention to grammatical errors in their speech and practice eliminating them. A good way to do this would be to assign a short two- or three-sentence speech that the students must give to the rest of the class. As each student speaks, keep a list of the grammatical errors the student makes and speak with him or her individually about making improvements.

## GO!

### DIRECTIONS

Find the mistake. If there is none, mark the last answer choice, *(No mistakes)*.

1　**(A)** Amy can't never seem
　　**B** to learn from her mistakes. She
　　**C** always seems to get in trouble.
　　**D** *(No mistakes)*

2　**J** No matter how much
　　**(K)** glue we use, it ain't going to
　　**L** be enough to fix this plate.
　　**M** *(No mistakes)*

3　**A** Jamie has a lemonade
　　**(B)** stand. Last week she earned her
　　**C** enough money for a new doll.
　　**D** *(No mistakes)*

4　**(J)** Our dog Buffy won't not
　　**K** sit down when you want her to.
　　　　She
　　**L** only does it when you give her
　　　　a treat.
　　**M** *(No mistakes)*

5　**A** Brandon is really smart.
　　**B** Last night he told us how his
　　　　boss
　　**(C)** teach him to fix old radios.
　　**D** *(No mistakes)*

6　**J** That isn't how the song
　　**K** is played. It should be played
　　**L** faster, so you can dance to it.
　　**(M)** *(No mistakes)*

© McGraw-Hill School Division

 **Go over each question on this page as a class.**

### Question 1

Double negative

### Question 2

*Ain't* should never be used.

### Question 3

A pronoun should never come directly after a verb. This rule is not discussed on Pupil Edition page 76. Make sure students understand this rule.

### Question 4

Double negative

### Question 5

Verb tense agreement—past tense, *taught*, is needed. Time Indicator: *Last night.*

# USAGE

## Pronouns

**Explain that pronouns are special words that take the place of nouns in a sentence.**

Go over the two types of pronouns, object and subject, thoroughly with your class. Write sentences on the board and have students tell you which pronouns are object pronouns and which are subject pronouns. Some examples you might use are:

- *He likes to eat cake.* (subject)

- *I took her to the store.* (object)

- *They are nice people.* (subject)

- *Sally is fond of him.* (object)

- *Where are you taking us?* (object)

## TEACHING TIP

Make sure students understand the difference between singular and plural pronouns. Also, emphasize the tip box on the Pupil Edition page.

**Go over the example question as a class.** After going over this example, let students know that the reason *He* is the proper pronoun is because it is taking the place of a noun in the subject of the sentence. It is a subject pronoun.

---

Exercise 27

## ON YOUR MARK!

### Usage: Pronouns

A **pronoun** is a word that takes the place of a noun.

**Subject pronouns** replace nouns in the subject of the sentence.

> *Philip* met her there. ⟶ *He* met her there.

**Object pronouns** replace nouns that come after an action verb or the word *for, at, of, with,* or *to.*

> Philip met **Claire** there. ⟶ Philip met **her** there.

A singular noun replaces a singular pronoun.

> *Genna* left the bag at school. ⟶ *She* left the bag at school.

A plural noun replaces a plural pronoun.

> Mark gave **the Clark's** a book. ⟶ Mark gave **them** a book.

| Subject Pronouns | Object Pronouns |
|---|---|
| Singular: *I, you, he, she, it* | Singular: *me, you, him, her, it* |
| Plural: *you, we, they* | Plural: *you, us, them* |

> **TIP:** If there is more than one subject, *I* comes last. *She and I walked home.* If there is more than one object, *me* comes last. *Kyle teases Jenny and* **me.**

## GET SET!

Let's look at an example.

**Find the mistake.**

**A** Willie fell down the
**(B)** hill. Him scraped his knee,
**C** and had a big hole in his pants.
**D** *(No mistakes)*

(B) is **correct!** The subject, *Willie,* should be replaced by the subject pronoun *he,* not by the object pronoun *him.*

© McGraw-Hill School Division

---

## EXTRA ACTIVITY

Prepare a list of sentences for the class, using the following format:

*John and Ralph are twins. (They, Them) are eight years old.*

Students must circle the pronoun that correctly fits into the sentence. Prepare at least two sentences for each possible pronoun. For extra credit, have students label the correct pronouns as subject or object pronouns.

© McGraw-Hill School Division

**GO!**

## DIRECTIONS

Find the mistake. If there is none, mark the answer choice, *(No mistakes)*.

1  A  It was Saturday, and
   B  there was no school. That's
   **C**  why I and Michelle slept late.
   D  *(No mistakes)*

2  J  Bill and Tess are coming
   K  too. Bill's bike broke. That's why
   **L**  them are going to be late.
   M  *(No mistakes)*

3  A  When Liza tasted the
   **B**  pudding, her made a funny
   C  face. Maybe she didn't like it.
   D  *(No mistakes)*

4  J  This is the closest I've
   K  ever been to a live monkey.
   L  It has a really long tail.
   **M**  *(No mistakes)*

5  A  Where is your new
   **B**  puppy? Me heard he had a
   C  big spot on his nose.
   D  *(No mistakes)*

6  J  Charlotte had a bad
   **K**  toothache. That's why her
   L  had to go to the dentist.
   M  *(No mistakes)*

---

 **Go over each question on this page as a class.**

### Question 1

*Michelle and I*

### Question 2

Needs the subject pronoun *they*

### Question 3

Needs the subject pronoun *she*

### Question 5

*Me* should be *I.*

### Question 6

Needs the subject pronoun *she*

# USAGE

## Subject-Verb Agreement

 **Emphasize to students that the subject and verb of a sentence must *always* agree with each other.**

Plural subjects require plural verbs, and singular subjects require singular verbs. Make sure students understand that they should always look at the subject of the sentence to determine whether the verb should be plural or singular.

 ## TEACHING TIP

Explain to the class that *I* is an exception. Verbs used with *I* use the plural form even though it is a singular pronoun:

- *I sing*
- *I walk*
- *I talk*
- *I push*

 **Go over the example question as a class.**

---

 **Exercise 28**

## ON YOUR MARK!

### Usage: Subject-Verb Agreement

In every sentence, the subject and verb must agree with each other. If the subject is plural, the verb must be plural. If the subject is singular, the verb must be singular.

**Wrong:** Jose and Sharon <u>walks</u> to the store. *The subject is plural, but the verb is singular.*

**Correct:** Jose and Sharon <u>walk</u> to the store. *The subject and verb match.*

**Wrong:** She <u>like</u> to play with her dolls. *The subject is singular, but the verb is plural.*

**Correct:** She <u>likes</u> to play with her dolls. *The subject and verb match.*

 ## GET SET!

Let's look at some examples.

**Find the mistake.**

A  When Kyle and Stan
Ⓑ  plays catch, they like to use
C  a ball that is not too hard.
D  *(No mistakes)*

(B) is **correct!** *Plays* is a singular verb, but the subject of the sentence, *Kyle and Stan*, is plural. It should be written *Kyle and Stan* **play** *catch*.

Ⓙ  Mickey want to go
K  to the movie with us, but he
L  is still too young to see it.
M  *(No mistakes)*

(A) is **correct!** The subject, *Mickey*, is singular, but the verb, *want*, is plural. It should be *Mickey* **wants** to go to the movie.

---

  ## EXTRA ACTIVITY

Prepare a list of common verbs in both singular and plural form. Pass these out to students. Have them choose five verbs each and write two sentences for each verb. One sentence should use the singular form of the verb and the other the plural form. Check students' sentences for correct agreement.

## GO!

### DIRECTIONS
Find the mistake. If there is none, mark the last answer choice, *(No mistakes)*.

1  A  Why is the baby crying?
   B  He always cries when he is hungry.
   C  Maybe he want to eat again.
   D  *(No mistakes)*

2  J  Tammi buys her lunch at
   K  school, but I brings mine because
   L  I'd rather eat my Mom's cooking.
   M  *(No mistakes)*

3  A  Brad and I went to
   B  the park yesterday and
   C  flew our kites for an hour.
   D  *(No mistakes)*

4  J  Francine like to paint
   K  pictures. When she grows up
   L  she wants to be an artist.
   M  *(No mistakes)*

5  A  Tanya bakes cookies at
   B  her house, and then she bring
   C  them to school for everyone.
   D  *(No mistakes)*

6  J  Our dog likes going for
   K  long walks. On Saturdays we
   L  walks her all over our town.
   M  *(No mistakes)*

7  A  The water in the stream
   B  are brown. That means we cannot
   C  drink it or swim in it.
   D  *(No mistakes)*

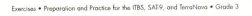

 **Go over each question on this page as a class.**

**Question 1**

*Want* should be *wants*.

**Question 2**

*Brings* should be *bring*.

**Question 4**

*Like* should be *likes*.

**Question 5**

*Bring* should be *brings*.

**Question 6**

*We* is plural and requires the plural verb *walk*.

**Question 7**

*Water* is singular and requires the singular verb *is*.

# USAGE

## Irregular Verbs

### Review the concept of irregular verbs with the class.

Explain that irregular verbs have special spellings for their past-tense forms.

Point out that irregular verbs do not have -ed added to the end to indicate the past tense. Instead, they require a special spelling. These spellings must be memorized.

Discuss the list of irregular verbs on the Pupil Edition page.

### Go over the example questions as a class.

---

## ON YOUR MARK!
### Usage: Irregular Verbs

Irregular verbs are verbs that have special spellings for the past tense. They are different from most verbs. You cannot just add –ed to the end of an irregular verb in order to make it past tense.

**Some Irregular Verbs**

| | | | | | |
|---|---|---|---|---|---|
| come → came | break → | broke | know → | knew |
| have → had | teach → | taught | become → | became |
| buy → bought | give → | gave | bee → | was |
| do → did | say → | said | blow → | blew |
| go → went | run → | ran | fall → | fell |
| see → saw | draw → | drew | feel → | felt |
| hold → held | keep → | kept | begin → | began |

## GET SET!

Now let's look at some examples.

**Find the mistake.**

(A) Chuck taked a trip
B with his family. They went
C to see the Grand Canyon.
D *(No mistakes)*

(A) is **correct!** The past tense of *take* is *took*, not *taked*.

J Last year I went hiking
(K) with my family. We seen a big
L turtle swimming across a lake.
M *(No mistakes)*

(K) is **correct!** The past tense of *see* is *saw*, not *seen*.

---

## TEACHING TIP

You may want to make up note cards for the class. Put the present tense form of the verb on one side of a card and the past tense on the other. Each day, spend five minutes reviewing the cards by showing students the present-tense spelling and having them guess the past-tense spelling.

**GO!**

## DIRECTIONS

Find the mistake. If there is none, mark the last answer choice, *(No mistakes)*.

ITBS

**1**
A The man at the candy
B store is very nice. One time
C he lended me a quarter.
D *(No mistakes)*

**2**
J Barney keeped the bird
K in a large cage. The cage was
L in his room, on a pole.
M *(No mistakes)*

**3**
A Ronnie took off his coat
B and hung it up. Then he put
C his hat and gloves on the shelf.
D *(No mistakes)*

**4**
J Mom gave each of us a
K dollar. I bought a candy bar, and
L my brother buyed a new toy.
M *(No mistakes)*

**5**
A My uncle didn't want
B his car anymore, so he selled
C it to one of his friends.
D *(No mistakes)*

**6**
J Once, on a hot day,
K Andi freezed some juice and
L made her own ice pops.
M *(No mistakes)*

 **Go over each question on this page as a class.**

**Question 1**

lent

**Question 2**

kept

**Question 4**

bought

**Question 5**

sold

**Question 6**

froze

None of the verbs used on this page is found on the chart from the previous page. Let students know that the list provided on Pupil Edition page 82 is not a complete list of all irregular verbs.

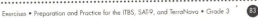

## Exercise 30

# PREPARING FOR THE ITBS

 **Make sure students understand that test preparation is very important to succeeding on a standardized test.**

Go over the preparation list on the Pupil Edition page with the class.

As a teacher, you can help students prepare for the ITBS by making sure they are familiar with all of the language arts skills on which they will be tested. During the school year, constantly review the skills and topics discussed in the Pupil Edition. Answer questions that students have and help to relieve their test-taking anxiety. The more practice the students get, the more familiar with the exam they will be. They will be more relaxed and confident as the day of the exam approaches.

 **Go over the example question as a class.**

---

### Exercise 30

## ON YOUR MARK!
### Preparing for the ITBS

Preparing for the ITBS or any other test requires more than studying. Here are some things other than studying that help you prepare:

**A good night's sleep.** Being well rested is always important, but it is even more important the night before a test.

**A good breakfast.** Eat a good breakfast. Your brain needs energy to think just like your muscles need energy to exercise!

**Avoiding distractions.** Sit away from windows or friends if you can. Make sure that all your attention is focused on your test.

**Relax.** Remember that the test is important, but it is not the most important thing in your life. If you are nervous or scared, it might be harder to pay attention to what you are doing.

 ## GET SET!

The tips above will help you feel at ease when answering questions on the day of the test. Look at this example.

**Choose the best way to write the underlined part of the sentence.**

**Randy did his chores tomorrow.**

A  has done
B  doing
C  will do
D  *(No change)*

(C) is **correct!** The word *tomorrow* tells you that the action will occur in the future, so the verb must be in the future tense. The future tense of *do* is *will do.*

---

## TEACHING TIP

During the school year, try to format as many of your tests, homework assignments, and quizzes as possible in the same manner as the ITBS. That way, students will get practice in the ITBS style of testing and be more comfortable with it when it is time for the test.

# GO!

## DIRECTIONS

Find the mistake. If there is none, mark the last answer choice, *(No mistakes)*.

1  **A** Rayleen earned her a dollar
   **B** just by helping Mrs. Hassett bring
   **C** her groceries into the house.
   **D** *(No mistakes)*

2  **J** The movie starts in one
   **K** hour, and I don't want to miss it.
   **L** You won't not be late, will you?
   **M** *(No mistakes)*

3  **A** If you want to know how
   **B** to fix it, watch me. You ain't
   **C** going to learn by yourself.
   **D** *(No mistakes)*

4  **J** Mom wanted to buy a
   **K** soda, so she went into the store.
   **L** I and Sylvia waited by the car.
   **M** *(No mistakes)*

5  **A** Todd wanted to talk to
   **B** Steffie, but her had to get home
   **C** and let out her dog Scruffy.
   **D** *(No mistakes)*

6  **J** Samuel and Jon sells
   **K** lemonade during the summer.
   **L** They use the money for movies.
   **M** *(No mistakes)*

---

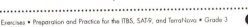 **Go over each question on this page as a class.**

Remind students that, in addition to the preparation steps discussed on Pupil Edition page 84, completing the exercises in this book has been helping them prepare for the ITBS. Congratulate them for having completed the On Your Mark! Get Set! Go! exercise section.

## Question 1

The pronoun *her* is not needed.

## Question 2

Double negative

## Question 3

*Ain't* should never be used.

## Question 4

*I* always comes second when there are two subjects.

## Question 5

The subject pronoun *she* is needed.

## Question 6

Plural subject requires the plural verb *sell*.

# Practice
# Test

## SPELLING

# DIRECTIONS

This test will show how well you can spell.

- Many of the questions contain mistakes in spelling. Some questions do not have any mistakes at all.

- You should look for the mistakes in spelling.

- When you find a mistake, fill in the answer space on your answer sheet that has the same letter as the **line** containing the mistake.

- If there is no mistake, choose the last answer choice.

The samples on this page show you what the questions are like and how to mark your answers.

## SAMPLES

S1 **A** nete
    **B** jump
    **C** call
    **D** neck
    **E** *(No mistakes)*

S2 **J** ball
    **K** nice
    **L** king
    **M** frog
    **N** *(No mistakes)*

Remind students always to read the directions carefully before answering the questions in every section.

## ANSWERS

S1 ●

S2     ●

GO ON ➡

## SPELLING

**1**
**A** kone
**B** cool
**C** wear
**D** play
**E** *(No mistakes)*
cone

**2**
**J** show
**K** lone
**L** sturdie
**M** crate
**N** *(No mistakes)*
sturdy

**3**
**A** treat
**B** face
**C** hollow
**D** mild
**E** *(No mistakes)*

**4**
**J** promise
**K** reply
**L** accept
**M** mooved
**N** *(No mistakes)*
moved

**5**
**A** rent
**B** nise
**C** door
**D** come
**E** *(No mistakes)*
nice

**6**
**J** lace
**K** bow
**L** schoe
**M** mole
**N** *(No mistakes)*
shoe

**7**
**A** pak
**B** sink
**C** pay
**D** call
**E** *(No mistakes)*
pack

**8**
**J** below
**K** writeing
**L** holler
**M** smooth
**N** *(No mistakes)*

For question 8, the
e in *writing* must be
dropped when *-ing*
is added.

**9**
**A** liv
**B** dry
**C** plow
**D** clap
**E** *(No mistakes)*
live

**10**
**J** pool
**K** palm
**L** crib
**M** chace
**N** *(No mistakes)*
chase

© McGraw-Hill School Division

# SPELLING

**11**
- **A** simple
- **B** double
- **(C)** frezing
- **D** accuse
- **E** *(No mistakes)*

freezing

**12**
- **(J)** shoor
- **K** plane
- **L** junk
- **M** tails
- **N** *(No mistakes)*

sure

**13**
- **A** paint
- **(B)** historey
- **C** child
- **D** fruit
- **E** *(No mistakes)*

history

**14**
- **J** splash
- **K** calm
- **L** nose
- **M** place
- **(N)** *(No mistakes)*

**15**
- **(A)** ruond
- **B** smooth
- **C** clown
- **D** moose
- **E** *(No mistakes)*

round

**16**
- **J** parts
- **K** driver
- **(L)** skunck
- **M** banana
- **N** *(No mistakes)*

skunk

**17**
- **A** chain
- **B** goose
- **C** make
- **(D)** fougt
- **E** *(No mistakes)*

Silent letter /h/ is missing.

**18**
- **J** drinking
- **(K)** oranje
- **L** pillow
- **M** turtle
- **N** *(No mistakes)*

orange

**19**
- **(A)** kween
- **B** clean
- **C** steal
- **D** meet
- **E** *(No mistakes)*

*Qu* is pronounced like /kw/ but spelled *qu.*

**20**
- **J** wink
- **K** silly
- **L** enter
- **(M)** phish
- **N** *(No mistakes)*

fish

**GO ON** ➡

**21**  A  please
 B  strap
 C  hello
 D  cannon
 (E)  *(No mistakes)*

**22**  J  crate
 (K)  crowe
 L  ending
 M  truth
 N  *(No mistakes)*
 crow

**23**  A  crane
 B  mouse
 (C)  cought
 D  clay
 E  *(No mistakes)*
 caught

**24**  (J)  bating
 K  throw
 L  wild
 M  clue
 N  *(No mistakes)*
 batting

**25**  A  crush
 (B)  whete
 C  trail
 D  flower
 E  *(No mistakes)*
 wheat

**26**  (J)  cameel
 K  crowd
 L  nice
 M  bench
 N  *(No mistakes)*
 camel

**27**  A  trade
 B  polish
 C  toast
 D  beetle
 (E)  *(No mistakes)*

Remind students that the two best ways to improve their spelling are to memorize the odd words that do not follow rules and to read, read, read!

# DIRECTIONS

This is a test on capitalization. It will show you how well you can use capital letters in sentences.

- You should look for mistakes in capitalization in the sentences on this test.

- When you find a mistake, fill in the answer space that has the same letter as the **line** containing the mistake.

- Some sentences do not have any mistakes at all. If there is no mistake, fill in the last answer space.

The samples on this page show what the questions are like and how to mark your answers.

## SAMPLES

**S1**  **A**  My friend's dog is called
     **(B)**  butch. He has his own
     **C**  house in the backyard.
     **D**  *(No mistakes)*

**S2**  **(J)**  You need to buy a Present
     **K**  for your grandmother. Why
     **L**  not get her a new purse?
     **M**  *(No mistakes)*

**S3**  **A**  In the summer, the beach
     **B**  is my favorite place
     **C**  to go for a vacation.
     **(D)**  *(No mistakes)*

> Remind students that proper nouns are always capitalized, and common nouns are never capitalized unless they are found at the beginning of a sentence or in a title.

## ANSWERS

S1  Ⓐ  ●  Ⓒ  Ⓓ

S2  ●  Ⓚ  Ⓛ  Ⓜ

S3  Ⓐ  Ⓑ  Ⓒ  ●

**GO ON** ➡

# CAPITALIZATION

**1**
  **A** Whenever we visit our
  **B** Uncle Sal, we always bring a lemon
  **C** cake because that is his favorite.
  **(D)** *(No mistakes)*

**2**
  **(J)** Our neighbor, mr. Ramirez,
  **K** is a pilot. He flies big jet
  **L** planes all over the world.
  **M** *(No mistakes)*

**3**
  **(A)** Kim's dog, lucky, is really
  **B** smart. She can sit, play dead,
  **C** and even fetch a stick.
  **D** *(No mistakes)*

**4**
  **J** My house is blue
  **K** and white. It is on the
  **L** north side of the street.
  **(M)** *(No mistakes)*

**5**
  **(A)** people often keep pictures
  **B** in their wallets. My father
  **C** has a picture of me in his.
  **D** *(No mistakes)*

> People's names, pets' names, specific places, holidays, and months are always capitalized.

**6**
  **J** Tracy bought her skates
  **K** in that new hobby store
  **(L)** that is on eighth street.
  **M** *(No mistakes)*

**7**
  **A** Rick and Nancy both have
  **B** the same birthday. They were
  **(C)** both born on july 2nd.
  **D** *(No mistakes)*

**8**
  **J** History is my favorite
  **(K)** subject because i like
  **L** learning about the past.
  **M** *(No mistakes)*

> The word *I* is a proper noun and is always capitalized.

**9**
  **A** Every year our town has
  **(B)** a big thanksgiving day parade.
  **C** We also have a picnic.
  **D** *(No mistakes)*

**10**
J    422 North First Street
(K)   Olean, ny 14766
L    May 7, 1992
M    (No mistakes)

State names and abbreviations are capitalized.

**11**
(A)   Dear miss Carlson,
B    You are my favorite singer.
C    I have all your albums.
D    (No mistakes)

**12**
J    I even joined your fan club.
K    Your biggest fan,
L    Marissa
(M)   (No mistakes)

**13**
A    Willie and Sarah went to
(B)   buy Apples at the local
C    grocery store this morning.
D    (No mistakes)

**14**
J    My cousin has a cat
(K)   named Fuzzy. she is
L    black with white spots.
M    (No mistakes)

The first word of a sentence is always capitalized.

**15**
A    Our cousin, Nigel, lives
B    in England. He owns the
(C)   biggest bakery in london.
D    (No mistakes)

**16**
J    It is very easy to
K    remember Tara's birthday.
(L)   It is on april 1st.
M    (No mistakes)

Months are always capitalized.

**17**
A    Randy went out to
B    dinner last night with
C    his parents. He had steak.
(D)   (No mistakes)

**18**
(J)   only three boys came
K    to the meeting last night,
L    because the weather was bad.
M    (No mistakes)

**19**
A    When he comes over to
B    our house for dinner, Mr.
C    Perez always brings dessert.
(D)   (No mistakes)

**20**
(J)   When i go to the park
K    I like to feed the squirrels.
L    They are fun to watch.
M    (No mistakes)

The word I is always capitalized.

**GO ON** ➡

**21** **(A)** In miami, many people
**B** own boats. Some people
**C** even live on them all year.
**D** *(No mistakes)*

**22** **J** I have to go to the
**K** dentist soon. Maybe I
**(L)** will go on thursday.
**M** *(No mistakes)*

**23** **A** Every summer Mark and
**B** Mindy spend all of
**(C)** august at a summer camp.
**D** *(No mistakes)*

Days of the week and months are always capitalized.

**24** **J** Maria's family is from
**(K)** italy. She even lived
**L** there for three years.
**M** *(No mistakes)*

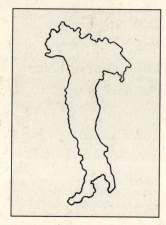

Names of cities and countries are always capitalized.

## DIRECTIONS

This is a test on punctuation. It will show how well you can use periods, question marks, commas, and other kinds of punctuation.

■ You should look for mistakes in punctuation in the sentences on this test.

■ When you find a mistake, fill in the answer space on your answer sheet that has the same letter as the **line** containing the mistake.

■ Some sentences do not have any mistakes at all. If there is no mistake, fill in the last answer space.

The following samples show what the questions on this test are like, and how the answers should be marked.

## SAMPLES

**S1**  A  Where did you find
B  the jacket your mother
Ⓒ  gave you for your birthday
D  *(No mistakes)*

**S2**  J  Dad drove his car
Ⓚ  to the center of, town
L  during the rain storm.
M  *(No mistakes)*

**S3**  A  The amount of daylight
B  grows shorter as the
C  winter months get nearer.
Ⓓ  *(No mistakes)*

## ANSWERS

S1  Ⓐ  Ⓑ  ●  Ⓓ

S2  Ⓙ  ●  Ⓛ  Ⓜ

S3  Ⓐ Ⓑ  Ⓒ  ●

**GO ON** ➡

**1**
**A** Last night I asked?
**B** my father if I could
**C** stay up an hour later.
**D** *(No mistakes)*

**2**
**J** Mr Williams is a friend
**K** of my parents. He also
**L** owns the grocery store.
**M** *(No mistakes)*

**3**
**A** The bus stop is on
**B** Maple Street The bus
**C** stops there every morning.
**D** *(No mistakes)*

Every sentence should have a proper endmark.

**4**
**J** We have to hurry.
**K** Weve only got five
**L** minutes to get home.
**M** *(No mistakes)*

Apostrophe needed in contraction

**5**
**A** The Franklin family
**B** used to live there.
**C** Did you know them.
**D** *(No mistakes)*

**6**
**J** June 17 1995 is
**K** when my big brother
**L** moved to Florida.
**M** *(No mistakes)*

Comma between day and year

**7**
**A** I have to go. Find me
**B** tomorrow. I will be in the room. But
**C** not before noon. Will you?
**D** *(No mistakes)*

**8**
**J** George Washington was
**K** our first President His
**L** picture is on the dollar bill.
**M** *(No mistakes)*

**9**
**A** Where did you go after
**B** school today I wanted
**C** to play baseball.
**D** *(No mistakes)*

Question mark needed after *today*.

**10**
**J** Last year Stacie broke
**K** her arm. She had to
**L** have Dr Smythe fix it.
**M** *(No mistakes)*

**11**
**A** Every day at 600 P.M.
**B** the train goes past my
**C** friend Mike's house.
**D** *(No mistakes)*

There is always a colon in between the hours and minutes of the time in this format.

**12**
J  16 Emory Lane
K  Billings, VT 00235
(L)  November 7 1993
M  *(No mistakes)*

Comma between day and year

**13**
A  Dear Uncle Julio,
B  Thank you for the hat.
C  I wear it every day.
(D)  *(No mistakes)*

**14**
(J)  I will see you in April
K  Love,
L  Shawna
M  *(No mistakes)*

Period after *April*

**15**
(A)  At three oclock, my
B  babysitter picks me up.
C  Then we go home.
D  *(No mistakes)*

When telling time, the word *o'clock* always requires an apostrophe.

**16**
J  There are no wild
(K)  tigers in the US, but
L  you can see them in zoos.
M  *(No mistakes)*

**17**
A  Those cards are for
(B)  Uncle Keito Aunt Jade,
C  and Shijin.
D  *(No mistakes)*

Comman needed in series

**18**
J  The car will not
(K)  start Now what are
L  we going to do?
M  *(No mistakes)*

Period after *start*

**19**
(A)  "Where is your coat"
B  asked Ben. It was a cold
C  spring day in March.
D  *(No mistakes)*

**20**
(J)  When Carla asked? What
K  was the matter, Freddy
L  said he was feeling sick.
M  *(No mistakes)*

**21**
A  In the Midwest, farmers
(B)  grow a lot of corn Much of
C  it is used to feed cattle.
D  *(No mistakes)*

period after *corn*

**GO ON ➡**

**22** J  Do you like
  K  fresh apple pie or
  L  homemade fudge brownies?
  (M) *(No mistakes)*

**23** A  I like playing baseball.
  B  I also enjoy playing
  C  soccer at the park.
  (D) *(No mistakes)*

**24** J  In small towns, the
  K  firefighters are often volunteers.
  (L) That means they don't get paid
  M  *(No mistakes)*

Remind students that a sentence must always begin with a capital letter and end with an endmark—either a period, a question mark, or an exclamation mark.

# PART 1 DIRECTIONS

This is a test on the use of words. It will show how well you can use words according to the standards of correctly written English.

- You should look for mistakes in the sentences on this test.

- When you find a mistake, fill in the answer space on the answer sheet that has the same letter as the **line** containing the mistake.

- Some sentences do not have any mistakes at all. If there is no mistake, fill in the last answer space, *(No mistakes)*.

The samples show on this page show you what the questions are like, and how to mark your answers.

## SAMPLES

**S1** **A** Sally didn't not go to no
**B** movie yesterday. She went
**C** to the theater with us.
**D** *(No mistakes)*

**S2** **J** Ballet and gymnastics
**K** are Genna's favorite activities.
**L** She's good at both of them.
**M** *(No mistakes)*

Remind students that proper usage is vital for sentence clarity. When words are used incorrectly, sentences become hard to understand.

## ANSWERS

**S1** ●

**S2**    ●

**GO ON** ➡

**1**
  **A** In the afternoons, I like
  **(B)** to taking naps. I always
  **C** feel better when I wake up.
  **D** *(No mistakes)*

**2**
  **(J)** Roger try hard to
  **K** get a perfect score on each test.
  **L** He studies every single night.
  **M** *(No mistakes)*

**3**
  **A** Sharon is the busiest
  **B** person I know. Even at night
  **(C)** her is always doing something.
  **D** *(No mistakes)*

> Subject pronoun *she* needed

**4**
  **(J)** Connie telled me how to
  **K** bake bread. Now I try to
  **L** make some once a week.
  **M** *(No mistakes)*

> Subject-verb agreement is incorrect for question 2.

> For question 4, *telled* is the incorrect past tense form for the irregular verb *tell*. *Told* is correct.

**5**
  **A** Jenny told me how much
  **B** she enjoyed J.D. Salinger, so
  **(C)** yesterday I gave her these book.
  **D** *(No mistakes)*

**6**
  **J** Willie hates to
  **K** drive and parks when
  **L** it is dark outside.
  **(M)** *(No mistakes)*

**7**
  **A** Larry walked home with
  **B** us yesterday. He told us
  **C** a lot of funny jokes.
  **(D)** *(No mistakes)*

**8**
  **J** Each child got to
  **(K)** choosed one toy to take
  **L** home from the toy store.
  **M** *(No mistakes)*

**9**
  **A** It is funny to watch
  **(B)** the way kittens plays
  **C** with a ball of yarn.
  **D** *(No mistakes)*

**10**
  **(J)** Andy ain't got time
  **K** to play with us. He has
  **L** too much homework.
  **M** *(No mistakes)*

> *Ain't* is not a proper word and should never be used.

**11** A There is a new movie at
B the theater. Do you want
Ⓒ to go with I and Frank?
D *(No mistakes)*

Frank and I

**12** J It is hard for me to
K find a quiet place to
L study in our house.
Ⓜ *(No mistakes)*

**13** A Last week Mrs. Gomez
Ⓑ teached us about addition,
C subtraction, and multiplication.
D *(No mistakes)*

*Teached* is an incorrect past tense form.

**14** Ⓙ Sam has geeses named
K Oliver and Lulie. They are
L not allowed inside the house.
M *(No mistakes)*

geese

**15** A Carolyn liked to
Ⓑ laid down on her bed when
C she listened to her tapes.
D *(No mistakes)*

**16** J My whole family
K got the flu, but I had the
Ⓛ worstest case of them all.
M *(No mistakes)*

worst

**17** A It is hard to believe that
B one day this caterpillar
C will be a butterfly.
Ⓓ *(No mistakes)*

**GO ON** ➡

# PART 2 DIRECTIONS

This is part 2 of the test about the use of words. It will show how well you can express ideas correctly and effectively. There are several sections to this part of the test. Read the directions for each section carefully. Then mark your answers on your answer sheet.

Important! Inform students that the questions on this page are NOT practice samples! They will be scored.

## DIRECTIONS

For questions 18–21, choose the <u>best</u> way to write the underlined part of the sentence.

**18** Carolyn <u>and</u> Margaret both enjoy going to the movies.

  **J** but
  **K** or
  **L** not
  **(M)** *(No change)*

**19** The captain <u>is making</u> the soldiers march yesterday.

  **A** make
  **B** will make
  **(C)** made      Clue: *yesterday*
  **D** *(No change)*

**20** Can you tell us <u>when</u> you are from?

  **(J)** where
  **K** if
  **L** such
  **M** *(No change)*

**21** Diego <u>picks</u> up a nickel and put it in his pocket.

  **A** has picked
  **(B)** picked      All verbs in a sentence must agree.
  **C** will pick
  **D** *(No change)*

## DIRECTIONS

Sentences must always be complete and have the subject and verb in the correct order.

In questions 22–27, choose the <u>best</u> way to express the idea.

**22** J Movies are better when you watch them on a big TV. Cartoons are too.

K Movies and cartoons are better when you watch them on a big TV.

L Movies are better and cartoons are too when you watch them on a big TV.

M On a big TV, movies and cartoons too are better when you watch them.

**23** A Karen is staying home because she has a bad cold.

B Karen staying home. Because she has a bad cold.

C A bad cold. Karen staying home because of it.

D Karen staying home. Has a bad cold.

**24** J In the lake swimming was a pretty swan yesterday.

K Swimming, there was a pretty swan yesterday in the lake.

L Swimming in the lake, there was a pretty swan, yesterday.

M There was a pretty swan swimming in the lake yesterday.

**25** A Shawn held the heavy rock in one hand.

B In one hand, a heavy rock Shawn held.

C A heavy rock held Shawn in one hand.

D A heavy rock Shawn held in one hand.

**26** J Tina enjoys and likes playing sports.

K Tina enjoys playing sports that she enjoys.

L Tina enjoys playing sports.

M Tina enjoys playing sports and soccer.

**27** A Although the collie was a furry dog, Rachel made it.

B Rachel made it for the collie although it was a furry dog.

C Rachel made it for the collie, which was furry.

D Although the collie was a furry dog, Rachel made a sweater for it.

**GO ON** ➡

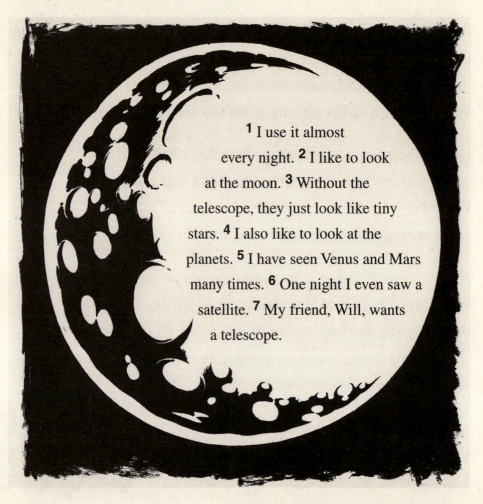
## DIRECTIONS

Use this paragraph to answer questions 28–31.

<sup>1</sup> I use it almost every night. <sup>2</sup> I like to look at the moon. <sup>3</sup> Without the telescope, they just look like tiny stars. <sup>4</sup> I also like to look at the planets. <sup>5</sup> I have seen Venus and Mars many times. <sup>6</sup> One night I even saw a satellite. <sup>7</sup> My friend, Will, wants a telescope.

**28** **Where is the best place for sentence 3?**

(**J**) Between sentences 5 and 6

**K** Between sentences 1 and 2

**L** After sentence 7

**M** Where it is now

Sentences in a paragraph must be in a logical order.

**29** **Choose the best first sentence to add to this paragraph.**

**A** Telescopes make everything look larger.

**B** Telescopes are good for looking at the moon.

(**C**) Last year my parents bought me a telescope.

**D** It is not easy to use a telescope.

This is a topic sentence question.

**30** Which sentence should be left out of this paragraph?

**J** Sentence 1

**K** Sentence 4

**L** Sentence 6

**(M)** Sentence 7

All of the sentences in a paragraph must support the main idea.

**31** Choose the best last sentence to add to this paragraph.

**A** My parents bought it in a science store.

**(B)** My telescope is much more fun than television.

**C** Astronauts landed on the moon several times.

**D** I keep my telescope in my bedroom, on a table.

A concluding sentence should wrap up the paragraph and provide a good, logical ending.

STOP

# On Your Mark, Get Set, Go! Review

## Spelling: Words With Silent Letters

The words below have silent letters in them. The underlined letters don't make a sound when you say the word.

**lamb** \'lam\          **store** \'stȯr\

**knot** \'nät\          **ghost** \'gōst\

> **TIP:** When you spell tricky words, try changing the way you normally say them to yourself. Sound out *every* letter in your head—even the silent ones. For example, say /**kuh not**/ to remind yourself that *knot* is spelled with a *k*.

## Spelling: Letter Combination Sounds

Certain letters sound different when they are next to each other than when they are apart. For example, the *ch* sound in *choice* sounds different than the *c* sound in *cape* or the *h* sound in *Henry*.

**Consonant Sounds**

ro*ck*          *sh*ame          *wh*en          bad*l*y          *th*ere

**Vowel Sounds**

c*ou*ch t*ou*r          b*oo*k          sp*oo*l          d*oe*s

> **TIP:** Think of a word you know, such as a rhyming word, that has the same spelling pattern as the word you want to spell. (*heat, meat, treat*)

## Spelling: Rules for Sounds

- When *c* sounds like an *s*, it is always followed by *e*, *i*, or *y*.
  ra*ce*          fan*cy*          ex*ci*te
- When *g* sounds like a *j*, it is always followed by *e*, *i*, or *y*.
  *ge*rbil          fra*gi*le          *gy*psy
- When *s* sounds like a *z*, it is usually followed by an *e*.
  pha*se*          wi*se*          no*se*

# REVIEW

## Spelling

The spelling skills on this page were originally covered in the On Your Mark! Get Set! Go! section. Refer to the following exercises as necessary:

- Exercise 2      p. 28
- Exercise 3      p. 30
- Exercise 4      p. 32

## EXTRA ACTIVITY

By now, students have probably realized that there are certain words they always seem to spell incorrectly. Have each student make a list of the "Top Five Suspects." Collect each student's list, and read the difficult words on each of their lists. After you have read the word, have the students write it down on a sheet of paper. When you have read all the words, write each word on the board, spelled correctly, and find the number of students who spelled it incorrectly. Write that number next to the word. At the end, the words that were misspelled by the most students are the "Main Suspects." For especially tricky words, try to come up with a good trick for remembering how to spell them.

# REVIEW

## Spelling and Capitalization

The spelling and capitalization skills on this page were originally covered in the On Your Mark! Get Set! Go! section. Refer to the following exercises as necessary:

### SPELLING

### CAPTITALIZATON

### Spelling: Tricky Words

- Make up clues to help you remember the spelling. (*Dessert* is spelled with two *s*'s because you always want seconds!)
- Change the way you say the word to yourself to help with the spelling. (*receive* = re-c-e-ive)
- Think of times you have seen the word. Try to remember how it looked. Write the word in different ways. Which one looks correct? (*coff, couf, cough*)

### Spelling: Adding Suffixes

- When words end in a silent *e*, drop the *e* when adding an ending that begins with a vowel. Example: *prove* becomes *proving*.
- When a one-syllable word ends in one vowel followed by one consonant, double the consonant before adding an ending that begins with a vowel. Example: *sit* becomes *sitting*
- When adding an ending that begins with a consonant, keep the silent *e*. Example: *love* becomes *lovely*
- When a base word ends with a consonant followed by *y*, change the *y* to *i* when adding any ending except endings that begin with *i*. Example: *fly* becomes *flies* or *flying*

### Capitalization: Always Capitalize

- The first word in a sentence. *Exercise is good for you.*
- Proper nouns such as names of people. *James Brown*
- Proper nouns that are names of places. *Bryant Street*
- The first letter of a quotation within a sentence. *Valerie asked, "May I be excused?"*
- Titles that come before a person's name. *Queen Anne*
- The pronoun *I*. *Susan and I went home.*
- The first word of a letter greeting or closing. *Dear Sirs,* and *Yours truly,*
- Holidays, days of the week, and months. *Flag Day, Tuesday,* and *October*

## EXTRA ACTIVITY

For further review on adding suffixes, make a list of ten words and hand it out to students. Have them make as many new words for each word as possible by adding suffixes. The student who makes the most new words by correctly adding suffixes wins a gold star.

### Capitalization: Nouns

A **noun** is a person, place, or thing. For example, *dog*, *car*, *Katie*, and *Ecuador* are all nouns. There are two basic types of nouns: proper nouns, and common nouns.

**Common nouns** always refer to general names for people, places, or things. The words *cat*, *town*, and *pencil* are all common nouns. Common nouns are *never* capitalized, except when they start a sentence.

**Proper nouns** always refer to a specific person, place, or thing. For example, the words *John*, *Africa*, and *June* are all proper nouns. Proper nouns are *always* capitalized.

### Punctuation: Endmarks

 **Period**

Use periods to end a statement.
   *Mustapha plays the trumpet.*

Use periods at the end of an abbreviation.
   *I live next to Mrs. Matthews.*

 **Question Mark**

Use a **question marks** to end a question.
   *Do you like cheese?*

 **Exclamation Mark**

Use **exclamation marks** to end a statement of excitement.

   *Look out for that car!*

# REVIEW

## Capitalization and Punctuation

The capitalization and punctuation skills on this page were originally covered in the On Your Mark! Get Set! Go! section. Refer to the following exercises as necessary:

### CAPITALIZATION

- Exercise 8     p. 40
- Exercise 9     p. 42

### PUNCTUATION

- Exercise 14     p. 52

 **EXTRA ACTIVITY**

For extra practice with capitalization, write a long paragraph, perhaps in the form of a letter, with 25–30 capitalization mistakes. Make a copy for each student, and write the paragraph up on the board. Give the students time to find all the mistakes, and mark them on their copies. Then, go around the room in a circle, asking each student to pick out the very next mistake and explain why it is wrong. Count the number of mistakes that are corrected before one is missed, then either start from the beginning, or continue from the next mistake, and praise the students for having gotten that far.

# REVIEW

## Punctuation

The punctuation skills on this page were originally covered in the On Your Mark! Get Set! Go! section. Refer to the following exercises as necessary:

- Exercise 13    p. 50
- Exercise 18    p. 60

---

### Punctuation: Address, Date, Time, and Letter Greetings and Closings

**Dates:** A comma always separates the month and day from the year:

*October 14, 1906*

**Addresses:** The town or city in an address is always separated from the state by a comma. Also, the initials of the state are usually used instead of the full name, like this:

*Boston, MA (or Massachusetts)*

**Time:** Use a colon to separate the hour from the minutes.

*5:05*

**Letter Greetings and Closings:** Use a comma after a letter greeting and after a letter closing.

*Dear Mom,*
*Yours truly,*

### Punctuation: Quotations

**Quotation marks** show that someone is speaking. They come before and after a person's exact words.

*"These cookies are great!" shouted Claire.*

**Remember these important rules about writing quotations:**

- Quotation marks come at the beginning and end of a person's exact words.
- The first letter inside a quotation is *always* capitalized.
- In most cases, commas, periods, question marks, and exclamation marks go *inside* closing quotation marks.
- Use a comma to separate a phrase, such as *she said*, from the quotation.

---

## EXTRA ACTIVITY

For extra practice with punctuation, have students write an invitation to a party. The party can be whatever they wish, but they must write the invitation in the form of a letter. The letter must include the following:

- *a greeting*
- *a closing*
- *the date of the party*
- *the time of the party*
- *the address of the party*

Check the students' invitations for proper use of punctuation.

## Punctuation: Contractions

A **contraction** is a shortened form of two words:

did not ⟶ didn't

An **apostrophe (')** in a contraction shows where one or more letters has been left out.

is not ⟶ isn't       have not ⟶ haven't

## Punctuation: Abbreviations

An **abbreviation** is a shortened form of a word. It begins with a capital letter and ends with a period. Some common abbreviations are:

Dr. = Doctor
Mr. = Mister
Jr. = Junior
St. = Street
Ave. = Avenue

The days of the week can also be abbreviated:

Sun. Mon. Tues. Wed. Thurs. Fri. Sat.

The months can also be abbreviated:

Jan. Feb. Mar. Apr. Aug. Sept. Oct. Dec.

## Punctuation: Possessive Nouns

A possessive noun is a word that shows who or what owns something.

Change a singular noun to a possessive noun by adding an apostrophe *s*.

**Kelly's** book report is upstairs.

Change a plural noun that ends in *s* to a possessive noun by adding an apostrophe to the end of the word.

The **dogs'** toys are lost.

Change a plural noun that does not end in *s* to a possessive noun by adding an apostrophe *s* to the end of the word.

The **children's** party was over.

ITBS

# REVIEW

## Punctuation

**The punctuation skills on this page were originally covered in the On Your Mark! Get Set! Go! section. Refer to the following exercises as necessary:**

- Exercise 15     p. 54
- Exercise 16     p. 56
- Exercise 17     p. 58

## EXTRA ACTIVITY

Write some sentences on the board that include at least one contraction, one abbreviation, and one possessive noun. Leave out the punctuation. Have students come to the board and insert the missing punctuation. Some examples you might use are:

- *Mr Smith didnt like Jennifers story.*

- *Isnt Peters baseball game on Tues?*

- *The boys friends havent come over since they moved from Charles St*

# REVIEW

## Usage

The usage skills on this page were originally covered in the On Your Mark! Get Set! Go! section. Refer to the following exercises as necessary:

- Exercise 26    p. 76
- Exercise 27    p. 78
- Exercise 28    p. 80

---

### Usage: Pronouns

A **pronoun** is a word that takes the place of one or more nouns. It must match the noun or nouns that it replaces.

A **singular pronoun** replaces a singular noun.

> *Carrie is smart.* ⟶ *She is smart.*

A **plural pronoun** replaces a plural noun or more than one noun.

> *The dogs are barking.* ⟶ *They are barking.*

Use the pronouns *I* and *me* to write about yourself. Use *I* in the subject of a sentence. If there is more than one subject, *I* always comes last.

> *She and I walked home.*

Use *me* after an action verb and words such as *in, into, to, with, by,* or *at*. If there is more than one object, me always comes last.

> *Kyle teases Jenny and me.*

| Subject Pronouns | Object Pronouns |
|---|---|
| Singular: *I, he, she, it,* | Singular: *me, him, her,* |
| Plural: *You, we, they* | Plural: *You, us, them* |

### Usage: Bad English

A **double negative** is two negative words are placed in the same sentence, as in *can't not,* or *not nothing.* Never use two negative words in the same sentence. These negative words cancel each other out.

**Ain't:** *Ain't* is not a proper word. Do not use the word *ain't.*

### Usage: Verbs

An **action verb** is a word that shows action.

> *The rocket shoots up to the moon.*

All verbs must agree with their subjects.

> *I jump*    *She jumps*    *They jump*

---

### TEACHING TIP

Make sure students take time to memorize irregular verb forms. Because these verbs do not follow a particular pattern, the only way students will be able to recognize them is by memorization.

## Expression: Verb Tenses

Verb tenses tell when the action takes place in a sentence.

In most cases, all verb tenses within a sentence must agree.

*The girl **jumped** over the puddle so she **stayed** dry.*

**Past tense** already happened.

*The girl **jumped** over the puddle.*

To form the past tense for most **regular action verbs**, just add -*ed* to the end.

*to look*  *looked*

**Irregular action verbs** are action verbs that have a different spelling than most verbs in the past tense.

*to grow* → *grew*

**Present tense** is happening now.

*The girl **jumps** over the puddle.*

## Expression: Sentences

A **sentence** is a group of words that expresses a complete thought.

*Grammy's molasses cookies are the best in my neighborhood.*

A **sentence fragment** is a group of words that does not express a complete thought.

*Grammy's molasses cookies are.*

ITBS

# REVIEW

## Expression

**The expression skills on this page were originally covered in the On Your Mark! Get Set! Go! sections. Refer to the following exercises as necessary:**

- Exercise 20    p. 64
- Exercise 21    p. 66

## EXTRA ACTIVITY

Write a list of sentence fragments on the board. Some should contain only a subject while others contain only a predicate. Instruct students to write out as many complete sentences as they can, using two (or possibly more) sentence fragments. They are allowed to use conjunctions to combine their sentences but may not add additional verbs, adjectives, or nouns. Inform them that they can probably use the same sentence fragment more than once. Have the class judge whether or not the sentences are acceptable and why. In some cases, the sentences may be grammatically correct but do not make sense. For example:

- *The girl ate the bouncing ball.*

# REVIEW

## Expression

The expression skills on this page were originally covered in the On Your Mark! Get Set! Go! section. Refer to the following exercises as necessary:

- Exercise 22    p. 68
- Exercise 23    p. 70
- Exercise 24    p. 72

---

A **run-on sentence** joins together two or more sentences that should be written separately.

*Grammy's molasses cookies are the best in my neighborhood she uses a special recipe.*

### Expression: Sentence Clarity

When the meaning of a sentence is clear, it has **sentence clarity**. A sentence without sentence clarity is hard to understand. Look out for:

- logical order of words and phrases
- misplaced phrases

### Expression: Paragraphs

A **paragraph** is a group of sentences that are all about the same idea.

A **main idea** is what a piece of writing or a paragraph is about. It is usually stated in the **topic sentence**, first sentence of a paragraph.

**Supporting details** are sentences that help explain the main idea. When a sentence in a paragraph does not talk about the paragraph's main idea, that sentence does not belong in the paragraph.

**Time-order** words connect ideas.

*First, I made a list. Then, I went to the store and bought groceries. After I paid for them, I walked home.*

© McGraw-Hill School Division

## EXTRA ACTIVITY

Have students pick a favorite short story or picture book. Once they have chosen a story or book, they should read it and write down the main idea, the topic sentences, a list of supporting details, and the time-order words from the story. Choose a few of the students' books and read them aloud to the class.

© McGraw-Hill School Division

# SAT-9

# TEACHER
# INTRODUCTION

# WHY *PREPARATION AND PRACTICE FOR THE SAT-9* IS THE BEST PREPARATION FOR STUDENTS

Welcome to the Teacher Edition of *Preparation and Practice for the SAT-9* for grade 3!

By completing each section of this book, students will:

- Increase their knowledge and understanding of language arts skills
- Become familiar with the types of questions that will be asked on the test
- Become aware of and experience first-hand the amount of time they will have to complete the test
- Become accustomed to the style of the test
- Become better writers and speakers
- Learn test-taking techniques and tips that are specifically designed to help students do their best on the SAT-9
- Feel comfortable on the day of the exam

# Parts of This Book

There are eight sections of this Teacher Edition:

### Teacher Introduction

The Teacher Introduction familiarizes you with the purpose and format of *Preparation and Practice for the SAT-9.* It also describes the SAT-9 sections and questions on the test that pertain to language arts skills.

### Student and Class Diagnostic Charts

This section consists of two charts. A student and a class diagnostic chart are included for the Warm-Up Test. You may use these charts to gauge student performance and determine the skills with which students will need the most practice as they prepare for the SAT-9.

### Student Introduction

This section contains some tips and explanations for students as they begin their preparation for the SAT-9. Extra annotations are included for teacher's to help you further explain what is expected of students and to encourage them as they begin their preparation.

### Warm-Up Test

This diagnostic test reveals students' strengths and weaknesses so that you may customize your test preparation accordingly. The skill tested in each question of the Warm-Up Test directly correlates to a skill reviewed in one of the 30 On Your Mark! Get Set! Go! practice exercises.

### On Your Mark! Get Set! Go!

This section consists of 30 practice exercises. Each exercise focuses on a specific language arts skill or test-taking strategy. On Your Mark! introduces and explains the skill. Get Set! provides an example question that tests the skill. (You should go over the question as a class. Get Set! is designed to bridge the gap between On Your Mark! and the test-like questions in Go!) Go! contains questions—similar to SAT-9 questions—that test the skills introduced in the exercise. Have students complete these questions on their own.

### Practice Test

The Practice Test is an exact replica of the actual SAT-9 in style and format. The Practice Test contains the exact number of questions that will appear on the actual test so that students are given a realistic test-taking experience. The Practice Test includes questions from both sections: spelling and language.

### On Your Mark! Get Set! Go! Review

This review section is an overview of the skills contained in On Your Mark! Get Set! Go! Similar skills are grouped together and the On Your Mark! Get Set! Go! exercises to which the skills correspond are noted.

### Index

The index is a brief listing of where you can look to find exercises about specific skills.

# How to Use This Book

This book has been designed so that you may customize your SAT-9 test preparation according to your class's needs and time frame. However, we recommend that you begin your test preparation as early in the school year as possible. This book will yield your students' best SAT-9 scores if you diagnose your students' strengths and weaknesses early and work toward helping them acheive their best performance. Please note that preparing students for a test such as the SAT-9 is a process. As much of their preparation as possible should take place in the classroom and be discussed as a class.

## Warm-Up Test

Have students complete the Warm-Up Test in class. It should be administered as early in the school year as possible. By doing so, students will gain familiarity with the types of questions and the specific skills tested on the SAT-9 *before* they begin working through the skill-specific exercises in this book. Use the student and class diagnostic charts to grade the tests. The results of the Warm-Up Test reveal students' strengths and weaknesses and allow you to focus your test preparation accordingly.

## On Your Mark! Get Set! Go!

We recommend that you review an On Your Mark! Get Set! Go! exercise after completing each chapter in your McGraw-Hill language arts textbook. It is best to go through the On Your Mark! Get Set! Go! section throughout the year so that students can digest the material properly. Consider reviewing On Your Mark! and Get Set! as a class. The Go! sections may be assigned as homework or completed by students individually in class. Having students complete Go! individually will provide the most simulated preparation for the SAT-9. After students have completed the Go! exercises, go over the correct answers as a class. The Princeton Review's research and experience shows this in-class work to be an essential element in effective test preparation.

## Practice Test

The Practice Test should be administered in the weeks prior to the actual exam. Testing conditions should be simulated. For example, no two desks should be placed directly next to each other, students should have two pencils at their disposal, the room should be quiet, and so on.

## On Your Mark! Get Set! Go! Review

Use this review in the few days leading up to the actual exam. Its purpose is to solidify the On Your Mark! Get Set! Go! skills students have learned throughout the school year. Answer any questions students might have and go over the specific exercises and skills with which students are the most concerned. You might want students to read over the section as homework and bring in a list of their questions to class the next day. Address as many of the students concerns as possible before the actual exam.  If students need additional review, consult the On Your Mark! Get Set! Go! exercises that correlate to the skills.

# About the Teacher Pages

Each page of the Pupil Edition is reproduced in this Teacher Edition, either reduced or full-size. Each reduced Pupil Edition page has teacher wrap. Teacher wrap consists of a **column** and a **box**.

- The column serves as a guide for you as you present the material on the Pupil Edition page in an interactive way. Guiding prompts and notes are included to ensure that information pivotal to the exercise is covered.

- The box includes teaching tips and extra activities. The extra activities are often fun, game-like activities for your class. These activities give students the opportunity to learn or apply SAT-9-related skills in a variety of ways.

Teacher wrap pages are punctuated with five icon types that help guide you through the Pupil Edition.

 This icon correlates the teacher wrap to the information in the On Your Mark! section of the Pupil Edition page.

 This icon reminds you to go over the example question in the Get Set! section of the Pupil Edition page.

 This icon reminds you to go over each question on the Go! pages of the Pupil Edition.

 This icon provides a point of emphasis for you to make concerning the exercise on the Pupil Edition page.

 This icon identifies an extra activity.

# About the Annotated Pages

Some pages in the Teacher Edition include full-size Pupil Edition pages. These occur in the Student Introduction, the Warm-Up Test section, and the Practice Test section.

All of these full-size reproductions are highlighted with teacher annotations. These annotations, which appear in magenta ink, provide the following:

- **Correct Answers**

The correct answer to each question is circled in magenta ink.

- **Question Analyses**

Sometimes an annotation offers further explanation of a specific question.

- **Extra Tips**

Certain annotations provide you with extra teaching tips specific to the skill tested on the Pupil Edition page.

- **Hints**

Some annotations offer hints that you can give to your students when they are working through the questions in the exercise or test sections.

# Introduction to the SAT-9

SAT-9 stands for Stanford Achievement Test Series, Ninth Edition. The SAT-9 is a standardized test taken every year by students throughout the country. Talk to your school's test administrator to get the exact testing date for this school year.

The SAT-9 is a multiple-choice test that assesses students' skills in reading, mathematics, language arts, science, and social science.

This book covers the language arts section of the SAT-9, which consists of two parts:

- **Spelling**
- **Language**

The specific number of questions for each skill discussed above and the time allotted for it is broken down as follows on the actual SAT-9:

| Skill | Spelling | Language |
|---|---|---|
| **Number of Items** | 30 | 48 |
| **Timing** | 25 minutes | 45 minutes |

# How Language Arts Skills Are Tested

## Spelling

**Students are asked to determine which of the underlined words, if any, are spelled incorrectly.**

EXAMPLE

   **A** Ben can ern ten dollars shoveling snow.

   **B** Whales and dolphins are mammals.

   **C** Each day I practice the piano.

   **D** No mistake

This question tests students' ability to recognize an incorrectly spelled word. Other spelling questions may involve homophones that are spelled correctly but are used in the wrong context.

## Language

**The language part of the test is divided into four sections. The first section asks students to choose which answer choice has an underlined section with incorrect capitalization, punctuation, or word usage.**

EXAMPLE

When the sun set, we will come in for supper.

   **A** sun have set

   **B** sun sets

   **C** sun are setting

   **D** Correct as is

For this question, students must pick out the answer choice that uses the correct verb tense.

**The second section of the language part of the test asks students to identify mistakes in sentence construction.**

EXAMPLE

The dog ate his food quickly, he drank his water.

    **A**  The dog ate his food quickly, and he drank his water.

    **B**  The dog ate his food quickly. And he drank his water.

    **C**  he dog eating his for quickly and drinking his water.

    **D**  Correct as is

For this question, students must recognize that the sentence is a run-on sentence. They must also demonstrate their understanding of complete sentences in order to select the correct answer choice.

**The third section of the language part of the SAT-9 for grade 3 will include short paragraphs.** Students will read the paragraphs and answer questions that require them to recognize extraneous information, combine sentences, and use descriptive language. Often questions are included that ask which sentences would belong at the beginning or the end of the paragraphs. Questions about the main purpose of the paragraph also appear.

**The fourth and final section of the language part of the SAT-9 for grade 3 assesses students' study skills.** Students will be given an excerpt from a reference source or a dictionary. Questions follow that test a variety of study skills with which students at this grade level should be familiar.

# STUDENT AND CLASS DIAGNOSTIC CHARTS

# How to Use the Student Diagnostic Chart

The Student Diagnostic Chart on page T35 should be used to score the Warm-Up Test in this book. The chart is designed to help you and your individual students determine the areas in which they need the most practice as they begin their preparation for the SAT-9. You will need to make enough copies of the chart for each of your students.

There are two ways to use the Student Diagnostic Chart:

- You can collect the finished Warm-Up Tests from each student and fill out one chart for each student as you grade the tests.
- You can give one copy of the Student Diagnostic Chart to each student and have each student grade their own test as you read aloud the correct answer choices.

*Note: Correct answer choices are marked in the Warm-Up Test of this Teacher Edition.*

## How to Fill Out the Student Diagnostic Chart

For each question number, there is a blank column labeled "Right or Wrong." An "R" or a "W" should be placed in that column for each question on the Warm-Up Test. By looking at the chart upon completion, students will understand which questions they answered incorrectly and to which skills these incorrect answers corresponded. The exercise from the On Your Mark! Get Set! Go! section that teaches the skill is also noted. You should encourage students to spend extra time going over the corresponding exercises covering the skills with which they had the most trouble. The charts will also help you determine which students need the most practice and what skills gave the majority of the students trouble. This way, you can plan your students' SAT-9 preparation schedule accordingly.

# How to Use the Class Diagnostic Chart

The Class Diagnostic Chart on page T36 should be used to record your class's performance on the Warm-Up Test in this book. The chart is designed to help you determine what areas your class needs to practice most as you begin the preparation for the SAT-9. The Class Diagnostic Chart is strictly for your own use. You should not share it with students.

## How to Fill Out the Class Diagnostic Chart

Under the "Name" column, you should write the names of each of your students. Then you should use the completed Student Diagnostic Charts to help you fill out the Class Diagnostic Chart. Fill out one row for each student.

For each question on the Warm-Up Test, there is a corresponding row in the Class Diagnostic Chart. The row is labeled with the question number and the exercise number of the correlating On Your Mark! Get Set! Go! exercise. If a student gets a question wrong, you should mark an "X" in the box underneath that question number. After completing a column for one student, add up all of the "Xs" and put a total for that student in the "Total" row on the top of the page. When you have filled out a row for each student, you should total up the "Xs" for each question. Put the totals in the "Total" column on the right-hand side of the page. Assessing both "Total" columns will help you determine two things: 1) which students are having the most trouble individually, and 2) which questions are giving the class as a whole the most trouble.

You should use the information gathered in the Class Diagnostic Chart to determine which skills to spend the most time reviewing and what students need the most individual practice and guidance.

# Student Diagnostic Chart

| Question # | Correct Answer | Right or Wrong | Exercise # | Skill |
|---|---|---|---|---|
| 1 | A | | 1 | Words with Silent Letters |
| 2 | G | | 1 | Words with Silent Letters |
| 3 | B | | 2 | Words with Two-Letter Sounds |
| 4 | F | | 4 | Adding Endings to Words |
| 5 | B | | 5 | Tricky Spellings |
| 6 | J | | 7 | Capitalizing Titles |
| 7 | B | | 8 | Quotations |
| 8 | G | | 9 | Contractions |
| 9 | D | | 10 | Possessive Nouns |
| 10 | G | | 11 | Adjectives that Compare |
| 11 | A | | 12 | Verbs |
| 12 | F | | 13 | Verb Tenses |
| 13 | C | | 14 | Pronouns |
| 14 | J | | 15 | Capital Letters in Names |
| 15 | A | | 16 | Commas |
| 16 | F | | 19 | Fragments |
| 17 | A | | 18 | Conjunctions |
| 1 | A | | 22 | Supporting Details |
| 2 | H | | 23 | Topic Sentences |
| 3 | A | | 20 | Combining Sentences |
| 4 | H | | 24 | Main Purpose and Audience |
| 5 | B | | 25 | Sentences that don't Support |
| 6 | J | | 27 | Using a Dictionary |
| 7 | D | | 28 | Finding Information |
| 8 | F | | 29 | Classifying Information |

# Class Diagnostic Chart

| Name | Q1-Ex. 1 | Q2-Ex. 1 | Q3-Ex. 2 | Q4-Ex. 4 | Q5-Ex. 5 | Q6-Ex. 7 | Q7-Ex. 8 | Q8-Ex. 9 | Q9-Ex. 10 | Q10-Ex. 11 | Q11-Ex. 12 | Q12-Ex. 13 | Q13-Ex. 14 | Q14-Ex. 15 | Q15-Ex. 16 | Q16-Ex. 19 | Q17-Ex. 18 | Q18-Ex. 22 | Q19-Ex. 23 | Q20-Ex. 20 | Q21-Ex. 24 | Q22-Ex. 25 | Q23-Ex. 27 | Q24-Ex. 28 | Q25-Ex. 29 | Total |
|------|------|------|------|------|------|------|------|------|------|------|------|------|------|------|------|------|------|------|------|------|------|------|------|------|------|-------|
| | | | | | | | | | | | | | | | | | | | | | | | | | | |
| | | | | | | | | | | | | | | | | | | | | | | | | | | |
| | | | | | | | | | | | | | | | | | | | | | | | | | | |
| | | | | | | | | | | | | | | | | | | | | | | | | | | |
| | | | | | | | | | | | | | | | | | | | | | | | | | | |
| | | | | | | | | | | | | | | | | | | | | | | | | | | |
| | | | | | | | | | | | | | | | | | | | | | | | | | | |
| | | | | | | | | | | | | | | | | | | | | | | | | | | |
| | | | | | | | | | | | | | | | | | | | | | | | | | | |
| | | | | | | | | | | | | | | | | | | | | | | | | | | |
| Total | | | | | | | | | | | | | | | | | | | | | | | | | | |

# Practice Test Answer Sheet

## SPELLING

| | | | |
|---|---|---|---|
| SA Ⓐ Ⓑ Ⓒ Ⓓ | 7 Ⓐ Ⓑ Ⓒ Ⓓ | 15 Ⓐ Ⓑ Ⓒ Ⓓ | 23 Ⓐ Ⓑ Ⓒ Ⓓ |
| 1 Ⓐ Ⓑ Ⓒ Ⓓ | 8 Ⓕ Ⓖ Ⓗ Ⓙ | 16 Ⓕ Ⓖ Ⓗ Ⓙ | 24 Ⓕ Ⓖ Ⓗ Ⓙ |
| 2 Ⓕ Ⓖ Ⓗ Ⓙ | 9 Ⓐ Ⓑ Ⓒ Ⓓ | 17 Ⓐ Ⓑ Ⓒ Ⓓ | 25 Ⓐ Ⓑ Ⓒ Ⓓ |
| 3 Ⓐ Ⓑ Ⓒ Ⓓ | 10 Ⓕ Ⓖ Ⓗ Ⓙ | 18 Ⓕ Ⓖ Ⓗ Ⓙ | 26 Ⓕ Ⓖ Ⓗ Ⓙ |
| 4 Ⓕ Ⓖ Ⓗ Ⓙ | 11 Ⓐ Ⓑ Ⓒ Ⓓ | 19 Ⓐ Ⓑ Ⓒ Ⓓ | 27 Ⓐ Ⓑ Ⓒ Ⓓ |
| 5 Ⓐ Ⓑ Ⓒ Ⓓ | 12 Ⓕ Ⓖ Ⓗ Ⓙ | 20 Ⓕ Ⓖ Ⓗ Ⓙ | 28 Ⓕ Ⓖ Ⓗ Ⓙ |
| 6 Ⓕ Ⓖ Ⓗ Ⓙ | 13 Ⓐ Ⓑ Ⓒ Ⓓ | 21 Ⓐ Ⓑ Ⓒ Ⓓ | 29 Ⓐ Ⓑ Ⓒ Ⓓ |
| | 14 Ⓕ Ⓖ Ⓗ Ⓙ | 22 Ⓕ Ⓖ Ⓗ Ⓙ | 30 Ⓕ Ⓖ Ⓗ Ⓙ |

## LANGUAGE

| | | | |
|---|---|---|---|
| SA Ⓐ Ⓑ Ⓒ Ⓓ | 4 Ⓕ Ⓖ Ⓗ Ⓙ | 9 Ⓐ Ⓑ Ⓒ Ⓓ | 14 Ⓕ Ⓖ Ⓗ Ⓙ |
| SB Ⓕ Ⓖ Ⓗ Ⓙ | 5 Ⓐ Ⓑ Ⓒ Ⓓ | 10 Ⓕ Ⓖ Ⓗ Ⓙ | 15 Ⓐ Ⓑ Ⓒ Ⓓ |
| 1 Ⓐ Ⓑ Ⓒ Ⓓ | 6 Ⓕ Ⓖ Ⓗ Ⓙ | 11 Ⓐ Ⓑ Ⓒ Ⓓ | 16 Ⓕ Ⓖ Ⓗ Ⓙ |
| 2 Ⓕ Ⓖ Ⓗ Ⓙ | 7 Ⓐ Ⓑ Ⓒ Ⓓ | 12 Ⓕ Ⓖ Ⓗ Ⓙ | 17 Ⓐ Ⓑ Ⓒ Ⓓ |
| 3 Ⓐ Ⓑ Ⓒ Ⓓ | 8 Ⓕ Ⓖ Ⓗ Ⓙ | 13 Ⓐ Ⓑ Ⓒ Ⓓ | 18 Ⓕ Ⓖ Ⓗ Ⓙ |

| | | | |
|---|---|---|---|
| SA Ⓐ Ⓑ Ⓒ Ⓓ | 20 Ⓕ Ⓖ Ⓗ Ⓙ | 23 Ⓐ Ⓑ Ⓒ Ⓓ | 26 Ⓕ Ⓖ Ⓗ Ⓙ |
| SB Ⓕ Ⓖ Ⓗ Ⓙ | 21 Ⓐ Ⓑ Ⓒ Ⓓ | 24 Ⓕ Ⓖ Ⓗ Ⓙ | 27 Ⓐ Ⓑ Ⓒ Ⓓ |
| 19 Ⓐ Ⓑ Ⓒ Ⓓ | 22 Ⓕ Ⓖ Ⓗ Ⓙ | 25 Ⓐ Ⓑ Ⓒ Ⓓ | 28 Ⓕ Ⓖ Ⓗ Ⓙ |

| | | | |
|---|---|---|---|
| SA Ⓐ Ⓑ Ⓒ Ⓓ | 30 Ⓕ Ⓖ Ⓗ Ⓙ | 33 Ⓐ Ⓑ Ⓒ Ⓓ | 36 Ⓕ Ⓖ Ⓗ Ⓙ |
| 29 Ⓐ Ⓑ Ⓒ Ⓓ | 31 Ⓐ Ⓑ Ⓒ Ⓓ | 34 Ⓕ Ⓖ Ⓗ Ⓙ | 37 Ⓐ Ⓑ Ⓒ Ⓓ |
| | 32 Ⓕ Ⓖ Ⓗ Ⓙ | 35 Ⓐ Ⓑ Ⓒ Ⓓ | 38 Ⓕ Ⓖ Ⓗ Ⓙ |

| | | | |
|---|---|---|---|
| SA Ⓐ Ⓑ Ⓒ Ⓓ | 40 Ⓕ Ⓖ Ⓗ Ⓙ | 43 Ⓐ Ⓑ Ⓒ Ⓓ | 46 Ⓕ Ⓖ Ⓗ Ⓙ |
| 39 Ⓐ Ⓑ Ⓒ Ⓓ | 41 Ⓐ Ⓑ Ⓒ Ⓓ | 44 Ⓕ Ⓖ Ⓗ Ⓙ | 47 Ⓐ Ⓑ Ⓒ Ⓓ |
| | 42 Ⓕ Ⓖ Ⓗ Ⓙ | 45 Ⓐ Ⓑ Ⓒ Ⓓ | 48 Ⓕ Ⓖ Ⓗ Ⓙ |

# STUDENT INTRODUCTION

# INTRODUCTION TO THE SAT-9

## What is the SAT-9?

The Stanford Achievement Test, Ninth Edition (SAT-9) is a multiple-choice test that helps you and your teacher find out how much you have learned in school so far. Now's your chance to show off all that you have learned about reading and writing in class!

## Does the SAT-9 measure how smart I am?

No, not at all. The SAT-9 tests only how well you can use the skills you've learned in class.

## How can I prepare for the SAT-9?

You can use this book to review the types of questions you will see on the test. You can also use this book to learn some simple test-taking tips that will help you do your best. Just like riding a bike or playing the piano, studying for the SAT-9 takes practice. The more you practice, the better you will do and the more confident you'll feel on the day of the test!

It's important to tell students that SAT-9 measures the skills that they are learning in school. It's not a test of their intelligence. Therefore, the best way to prepare for the SAT-9 is by using this book to familiarize themselves with the types of questions that will appear on the test, to review skills they have already been practicing in school, and to learn new test-taking strategies.

# There are four parts of this book.

1. **Warm Up Test**—This test is shorter than the real SAT-9, but it will show you what you know—and what skills you still need to practice.

2. **On Your Mark! Get Set! Go!**—Here's where you really get to roll up your sleeves! First, you will learn the skills that you'll need to know for the test. Then you'll practice what you've learned on questions that are just like the ones on the real SAT-9. Trust us, this is the best part of the book!

3. **Practice Test**—This test is just like the real SAT-9.

4. **On Your Mark! Get Set! Go! Review**—This is a list of all the important things that you will learn in this book. Come back to this part when you need to review or study what you've learned.

You may want to write a timeline on the board to show students how much time you will spend using each part of this book while preparing for the test. This will keep students from feeling overwhelmed and help them maintain a positive attitude about the SAT-9.

# USING THIS BOOK

Here's what you can do to help yourself while you use this book:

### Work carefully.

Completing this book is not a race. Now's the time to work slowly and carefully and to really learn what you need to know. We'll teach you how to go faster later in the book, so you'll be all set to take the real SAT-9 in the time your teacher will give you.

### Pay attention to the directions.

Read all of the directions carefully. The directions tell you how to answer the questions. Always make sure you understand the directions before starting a new set of questions. Pretend you are driving a car, and the directions are the road signs that tell you what's ahead.

### Read the questions and answer choices carefully.

Always read the *entire* question and *all* of the answer choices slowly and carefully. Make sure you've read through *all* of the answer choices before you make your choice, even if you think you have already found the correct answer. There might be a better one!

Reinforce to students the importance of reading all test materials carefully. The directions will often provide valuable information about how to approach the questions.

SAT-9

# Get Rid of the Wrong Answer Choices

This book prepares you for the multiple-choice questions on the SAT-9. On a multiple-choice question, you are given four or five answer choices to choose from. Only one of these choices is the best answer. Here's how to make sure you find it:

1. Read each answer choice, one by one.

2. Decide whether you think each answer choice is right or wrong.

3. Get rid of the answer choices you *know* are wrong.

4. Save any answer choices that might be right or that you aren't sure about.

5. Choose the best answer from the choices you think might be right.

6. If you don't know the answer, take your best guess.

> **Getting rid of wrong answer choices, even only one, makes your chances of picking the correct answer choice a lot better!**
>
> **So remember:**
>
> ✔ Get rid of what you can.
>
> ✔ See what you have left over.
>
> ✔ If you don't know the answer, make your best guess and move on.

Process of elimination is one of the most important strategies students can use to increase their success on standardized tests. Illustrate this concept by playing a guessing game with students. For example, write down four things (e.g., types of animals) on index cards. Share the items with students, and then have one student choose one card. Ask the rest of the class to guess the chosen card. Keep track of the number of guesses. Repeat the game with three cards, two cards, and finally, one card. This should illustrate to students how the chances of guessing correctly increase as the number of choices decreases.

# Pace Yourself

The SAT-9 is a timed test. That means that your teacher is only allowed to let you work on it for a certain amount of time. While you take the test, remember to use your time wisely. Here's how:

### Don't spend too much time on one question.

Some questions on the SAT-9 are harder than others. Don't get stuck on any questions you don't know the answer to. Just make your best guess and move on. You want to be sure you have enough time to answer the easier questions that will come later in the test.

### But don't rush, either!

Going too fast is no good—you will only make silly mistakes. If you don't waste time on difficult questions, you will have enough time to finish the test without rushing.

### Find your own steady pace.

Everyone works at a different pace. Don't compare yourself with others. Just try to answer as many of the questions as you can. Work carefully through each of them. Pick the best answer, and then move on to the next question. When the teacher says time is up, put your pencil down and feel good about all the hard work you have done.

Pacing is an important aspect of taking timed tests. Tell students that they need to strike a balance between working carefully and progressing efficiently through the questions. Remind students that by completing the exercises in this book they will find a pace that works for them.

# MARK YOUR ANSWER CHOICES CORRECTLY

When you take the SAT-9, you will be given the test and an answer sheet. The answer sheet is where you mark your answers. Marking your answers is very simple. Here's how you should answer a question:

1. Read the question.

2. Decide which answer choice is correct. Each answer choice has a letter next to it. Remember the letter that is next to your answer choice.

3. Find the question number on your answer sheet that is the same as the number of the question you are answering.

4. Fill in the bubble that has the same letter as your answer choice.

## Always make sure that you fill in the answer bubbles completely.

 Do NOT fill in half of the bubble. This is wrong.

 Do NOT put a checkmark over the bubble. This is wrong.

 Do NOT scribble inside the bubble. This is wrong.

 DO fill in the bubble completely. This is correct!

Then go on to the next question until you are done with the test. It's that easy!

Explain to students that it's important to fill in the bubbles correctly because a machine scores the test. If their bubbles are not filled in completely, students may not get credit for questions that they have answered correctly.

© McGraw-Hill School Division

# Practice, Practice, Practice!

The more you practice, the more prepared you'll be for the actual test. Remember, the SAT-9 tests what you already know. What you should practice is how to use what you know on the test. The more you practice, the more comfortable you will feel taking the test!

To help students understand the value of practice, lead a discussion about how practicing leads to improvements. For example, ask students to name several activities (e.g., sports, music, art) in which they participate. Then, ask them to discuss how they practice for these activities. Has practice helped them improve their skills? How? In what ways can they see their progress?

# GETTING READY FOR THE SAT-9

You can practice for the SAT-9 even when you're *not* using this book! Here's how:

**Read as much as you can.** Read everything and anything you can get your hands on. Of course, in class, you should read everything your teacher tells you to read. But outside of class, you get to choose what to read. Read comic books, magazines, and cereal boxes. Read signs as you pass by them. Read stories aloud. Listen to others read stories aloud to you. All reading is good reading.

**Play the word game.** When you come across a word you don't understand, play a game: Try to figure out what the word could mean. Ask yourself, "If I had to guess, what do I think the definition of the word would be?"

1. Write down your best guess.

2. Look the word up in a dictionary, or if you're not near a dictionary, ask an adult.

3. Write down the word and its correct definition on an index card. This will help you remember it.

4. Later, go back and read your index cards to see how good your memory is.

Remind students how important it is to practice reading. Reading is exercise for the brain, and the more they exercise their brains–by reading all types of materials–the greater improvement they'll see in their overall performance on the SAT-9. Likewise, playing the word game discussed on this page will help them become stronger readers.

**Pay attention in class.** Not only will you learn cool things, you'll also spend less time wrestling with tricky homework after school and more time playing with your friends!

**Ask questions.** Ask your teacher if you don't understand why an answer is wrong. Other students probably have the same question.

**Learn from your mistakes.** Notice the questions you have trouble with. Find out how to answer them correctly. Ask your teacher to review the skills you need to brush up on.

**Pat yourself on the back.** Congratulate yourself on the things you know well, and keep up the good work!

Answering questions incorrectly can be as valuable as answering questions correctly in preparing for a standardized test. Make sure students understand that it is okay to make mistakes. The important thing is that students learn from their mistakes.

As students work through the tests and exercises in this book, provide them with positive feedback and encourage them with congratulations as they improve their skills. Allowing students to celebrate their progress will help them approach the SAT-9 with confidence and a positive attitude.

SAT-9

# Warm-Up Test

# Spelling

## DIRECTIONS

Find the underlined word that is spelled incorrectly. If none of the underlined words is spelled incorrectly, fill in the letter next to the words *No mistake*.

**1**
- Ⓐ Andrea took the fastest <u>cours</u> to the lake.
- Ⓑ Our teacher has a good sense of <u>humor</u>.
- Ⓒ Cheryl got a <u>package</u> in the mail.
- Ⓓ No mistake

Silent /e/

**2**
- Ⓕ <u>Purple</u> is the color of kings.
- Ⓖ No animals are bigger than <u>wales</u>.
- Ⓗ Take off those <u>muddy</u> boots.
- Ⓙ No mistake

Silent /h/

**3**
- Ⓐ Kerry loves the <u>scent</u> of roses.
- Ⓑ I am <u>thru</u> with my chores.
- Ⓒ Our seats are two <u>rows</u> down.
- Ⓓ No mistake

through

**4**
- Ⓕ Water is <u>driping</u> on the floor.
- Ⓖ Zachary and Josh live on this <u>street</u>.
- Ⓗ Penny <u>says</u> you are very strong.
- Ⓙ No mistake

To add *-ing* to *drip*, the consonant *p* is doubled.

**5**
- Ⓐ On Sundays we go <u>fishing</u>.
- Ⓑ The teacher will <u>desmiss</u> the class early.
- Ⓒ Is this milk still <u>fresh</u>?
- Ⓓ No mistake

dismiss

If students are not sure of an answer, encourage them to rule out answer choices they know are incorrect.

SAT-9

GO ON

## DIRECTIONS

Pay careful attention to the underlined words in each sentence. Look for a punctuation, capitalization, or word usage mistake. If there are mistakes, pick the answer choice that corrects them. If there are no mistakes, mark the last answer choice.

**6** **Our teacher reads the <u>book *Charlotte's Web*</u> to us.**

Ⓕ book *charlotte's Web*

Ⓖ book *Charlotte's web*

Ⓗ book *charlotte's web*

Ⓙ Correct as is

Important words in titles are always capitalized.

**7** **When we got home from vacation, my sister <u>said "I can't wait to sleep in my own bed!</u>**

Ⓐ Said I can't wait to sleep in my own bed!

Ⓑ said, "I can't wait to sleep in my own bed!"

Ⓒ "said I can't wait to sleep" in my own bed!

Ⓓ Correct as is

Quotation marks appear at both the beginning and the end of a person's exact words.

**8** **<u>Dont' eat any more cookies</u> before lunch.**

Ⓕ Do'nt eat any more cookies

Ⓖ Don't eat any more cookies

Ⓗ Dont eat any more cookies

Ⓙ Correct as is

Apostrophes replace missing letters in contractions.

**9** **May I borrow <u>your brother's</u> baseball glove?**

Ⓐ your brothers

Ⓑ your brothers's

Ⓒ your brother

Ⓓ Correct as is

**10** **<u>The chocolate cake is sweetier</u> than the vanilla one.**

Ⓕ chocolate cake is sweet

Ⓖ chocolate cake is sweeter

Ⓗ chocolate cake is sweetest

Ⓙ Correct as is

**11** **I <u>writed</u> the best book report I could.**

Ⓐ wrote

Ⓑ have writed

Ⓒ has wrote

Ⓓ Correct as is

*Write* has an irregular past tense form.

**12** Our teacher <u>will tells us</u> the field trip will be in May.

(F) told us

(G) tell us

(H) has telling us

(J) Correct as is

**13** <u>Me and you can see</u> the stars!

(A) You and me can see

(B) I and you can see

(C) You and I can see

(D) Correct as is

**14** What is the best way to write this name?

<u>Mr. Howard N. Schwartz</u>

(F) Mr. Howard n. Schwartz

(G) mr. howard N. Schwartz

(H) mr. Howard N. Schwartz

(J) Correct as is

**15** Michael ate a sandwich made with <u>turkey, lettuce tomato and bacon.</u>

(A) turkey, lettuce, tomato, and bacon.

(B) turkey, lettuce tomato, and bacon.

(C) turkey, lettuce, tomato and, bacon.

(D) Correct as is

Use commas to separate items in a series.

**DIRECTIONS:**

Look at the words in the box. The words may have a mistake in sentence structure. If there is a mistake, find the answer choice that corrects it. If there is no mistake, mark the last answer choice.

**16** Mary dove into the pool. And started swimming.

(F) Mary dove into the pool and started swimming.

(G) Mary diving into the pool and starting swimming.

(H) Mary dove into the pool, she started swimming.

(J) Correct as is

Avoid sentence fragments. Every sentence should have a subject and a verb.

**17** Will shook the apple tree. Some apples falling out.

(A) Will shook the apple tree, and some apples fell out.

(B) Will shook the apple tree, some apples fell out.

(C) Will shook the apple tree some apples fell out.

(D) Correct as is

SAT-9

© McGraw-Hill School Division

**DIRECTIONS**

Read the paragraph. Then answer the questions that follow it.

---

## Paragraph

He invented them in 1853. He was working as a cook in the Moon Lake House Hotel in Saratoga Springs, New York. One day a customer asked for "very thin french fries." Mr. Crum made them extra thin. That was the birth of the potato chip.

---

**1** **Find the sentence that would go best after the last sentence in the paragraph.**

(A) Next time you eat a potato chip, think of Mr. Crum!

(B) Potato chips taste terrible when they are stale.

(C) Potato chips don't have many vitamins.

(D) Idaho is the state that grows the most potatoes.

> Read the paragraph aloud four times to students, each time placing a different answer choice at the end. Which one goes best with the paragraph?

**2** **Find the best topic sentence for the paragraph.**

(F) Who invented potato chips?

(G) Hotels have good restaurants.

(H) Mr. George Crum made the first potato chip.

(J) Potato chip crumbs are messy.

**3** **What is the best way to combine the last two sentences in the paragraph?**

Ⓐ Mr. Crum made them extra thin, and that was the birth of the potato chip.

Ⓑ Mr. Crum made them extra thin that was the birth of the potato chip.

Ⓒ Mr. Crum made them extra thin, that was the birth of the potato chip.

Ⓓ Extra thin Mr. Crum made them that was the birth of the potato chip

> Two short, related sentences can be combined to form a single, compound sentence.

**4** **This paragraph was most likely written for whom?**

Ⓕ people who never eat snacks

Ⓖ people who grow fruit

Ⓗ people who like to learn interesting facts

Ⓙ people who want to be cooks

**5** **Find the sentence that would not belong in the paragraph.**

Ⓐ Potato chips became a regular choice on the Moon Lake House menu.

Ⓑ Corn chips are also very tasty.

Ⓒ The chips were first called Saratoga Chips because they were invented there.

Ⓓ Chef George Crum liked to please his customers.

> Read the paragraph on page 136 aloud, followed by each of the answer choices. Do any of the sentences seem not to belong?

SAT-9

**6** Read the guide words taken from a page in a dictionary.

> kangaroo—key

Find the word that could be found on the page.

Ⓕ knot

Ⓖ kick

Ⓗ kind

Ⓙ keep

**7** Where can you find the score of yesterday's baseball game?

Ⓐ in an almanac

Ⓑ in an atlas

Ⓒ in a sports book

Ⓓ in a newspaper

**8** Which of these is the category that the other three words belong to?

Ⓕ sports

Ⓖ soccer

Ⓗ basketball

Ⓙ swimming

# On Your Mark, Get Set, Go!

# SPELLING

## Words with Silent Letters

 **Go over the words listed with students.**

Have them say each one aloud. Point out that each word contains a silent letter.

Explain that words are not always spelled the way that they sound.

Go over the tip box on the Pupil Edition page. Have students repeat the words listed in the On Your Mark! section of the Pupil Edition page, altering their pronunciation to include the silent letter.

**Go over the example question as a class.**

---

## ON YOUR MARK!

### Spelling Words With Silent Letters

The words below have silent letters in them. The underlined letters don't make a sound when you say the word.

| | |
|---|---|
| lam**b** \'lam\ | s**t**ore \'stōr\ |
| **k**not \'nät\ | **gh**ost \'gōst\ |
| peo**p**le \'pē-pəl\ | cau**gh**t \'kawt\ |
| dum**b** \'dəm\ | mus**c**le \'mə-səl\ |
| sof**t**en \'so-fən\ | **k**nit \'nit\ |

> **TIP:** When you spell tricky words, try changing the way you normally say them to yourself. Sound out *every* letter in your head—even the silent ones. For example, to remember that the word *knot* begins with a *k*, say **/ke-not/** to yourself. It may sound funny, but this trick will help you remember when a silent letter is needed.

  **GET SET!**

Let's look at an example. Find the underlined word that is misspelled.

I will <u>spread</u> jelly on my <u>toast</u> with a butter <u>nife</u>.
      A             B            C

Ⓐ   spread
Ⓑ   toast
Ⓒ   nife
Ⓓ   No mistake

(A) is **wrong.** It is spelled correctly. Don't be fooled by the *ea* combination. Sometimes *ea* makes a short *e* sound.

(B) is **wrong.** The *oa* combination might look funny, but it is correct.

(C) is **correct!** The word *knife* should begin with a silent *k*.

---

⭐ **EXTRA ACTIVITY**

Create a list on the board of words that have silent letters. After you finish the list, have students say each word twice: first without the silent letter, then with the silent letter.

Some examples you might use are:

- *know*
- *wrap*
- *tore*
- *often*
- *dumb*
- *taught*

Hearing the words with the silent letter pronounced will help students understand why it is silent.

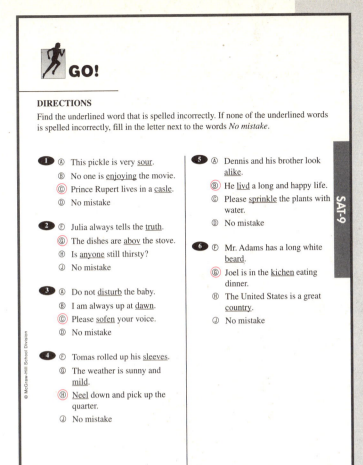

**GO!**

**DIRECTIONS**

Find the underlined word that is spelled incorrectly. If none of the underlined words is spelled incorrectly, fill in the letter next to the words *No mistake*.

**1**
- Ⓐ This pickle is very <u>sour</u>.
- Ⓑ No one is <u>enjoying</u> the movie.
- Ⓒ Prince Rupert lives in a <u>casle</u>.
- Ⓓ No mistake

**2**
- Ⓕ Julia always tells the <u>truth</u>.
- Ⓖ The dishes are <u>abov</u> the stove.
- Ⓗ Is <u>anyone</u> still thirsty?
- Ⓙ No mistake

**3**
- Ⓐ Do not <u>disturb</u> the baby.
- Ⓑ I am always up at <u>dawn</u>.
- Ⓒ Please <u>sofen</u> your voice.
- Ⓓ No mistake

**4**
- Ⓕ Tomas rolled up his <u>sleeves</u>.
- Ⓖ The weather is sunny and <u>mild</u>.
- Ⓗ <u>Neel</u> down and pick up the quarter.
- Ⓙ No mistake

**5**
- Ⓐ Dennis and his brother look <u>alike</u>.
- Ⓑ He <u>livd</u> a long and happy life.
- Ⓒ Please <u>sprinkle</u> the plants with water.
- Ⓓ No mistake

**6**
- Ⓕ Mr. Adams has a long white <u>beard</u>.
- Ⓖ Joel is in the <u>kichen</u> eating dinner.
- Ⓗ The United States is a great <u>country</u>.
- Ⓙ No mistake

SAT-9

 **Go over each question on this page as a class.**

For the questions on this page, extra example words that contain the same silent letter as the misspelled word are included. Share these with students to help them gain familiarity with the sounds and spellings.

### Question 1
Silent /t/: castle—soften, often

### Question 2
Silent /e/: above—store, done

### Question 3
Silent /t/: castle—rustle, whistle

### Question 4
Silent /k/: kneel—knife, knight

### Questions 5 and 6
The incorrectly spelled words in these questions, *lived* and *kitchen*, do not contain silent letters. However, words like these will frequently appear on the SAT-9. Give students some extra words that contain these sounds such as *jumped, roped, pulled, catch, pitcher,* and *stitch*.

Many of the misspelled words on this page are similar to words the students encountered on the previous page. Point out these similarities.

# SPELLING

## Words with Two-Letter Sounds

 **Go over the words listed, having students pay close attention to the underlined letters.**

Explain that when certain letters are next to each other, they make different sounds than when they stand alone.

Using the words listed in the On Your Mark! section of the Pupil Edition page as starting points for ideas, have students come up with other examples of words containing two-letter sounds. Write their ideas on the board.

For consonant sounds, some examples you might use are:

- *rock—sock*
- *shame—should*
- *when—what, why, who, and where*

For vowel sounds:

- *couch—pouch*
- *book—took*
- *foil—oil, boil, and toil*

 **Go over the example question as a class.**

---

## ON YOUR MARK!

### Spelling: Words With Two-Letter Sounds

Certain letters sound different when they are next to each other than they do when they are apart. For example, the *ch* sound in *choice* sounds different than the *c* sound in *cape* or the *h* sound in *Henry*.

**Consonant Sounds**

| | | | | |
|---|---|---|---|---|
| ro<u>ck</u> | <u>sh</u>ame | <u>wh</u>en | ba<u>d</u>ly | wi<u>th</u> |
| <u>ch</u>air | so<u>ng</u> | <u>th</u>ere | <u>ph</u>one | <u>tr</u>eat |

**Vowel Sounds**

| | | | | |
|---|---|---|---|---|
| c<u>ou</u>ch | t<u>ou</u>r | b<u>oo</u>k | sp<u>oo</u>l | d<u>oe</u>s |
| w<u>ea</u>r | h<u>ea</u>t | p<u>ai</u>r | f<u>oi</u>l | bec<u>au</u>se |

> **TIP:** Think of a word you know, such as a rhyming word, that has the same spelling pattern as the word you want to spell. *(heat, meat, treat)*

##  GET SET!

Let's look at an example. Find the underlined word that is misspelled.

The wool <u>jaket</u> feels <u>rough</u> and <u>prickly</u>.
       F        G       H

- Ⓕ jaket
- Ⓖ rough
- Ⓗ prickly
- Ⓙ No mistake

(F) is **correct!** *Jaket* is misspelled. The *k* sound should be spelled with a *ck*. The correct spelling of the word is *jacket*.

(G) is **wrong.** The *gh* might look funny, but sometimes *gh* makes an *f* sound. *Rough* is spelled correctly.

(H) is **wrong.** Sometimes *ck* makes a *k* sound. *Prickly* is spelled correctly.

---

 ## EXTRA ACTIVITY

Distribute a short text or a section of a class reading assignment. Have a student read it aloud, instructing the class to pay close attention to any two-letter sounds. After the student has finished reading, create a list on the board of words from the text that contain two-letter sounds. Write the list horizontally and leave some space below each word. Once you have created a sizable list from the text, expand it using the words listed as starting points for new ideas. For example, *if cheer* appears on the list, write *chair, chick,* and *child* below it.

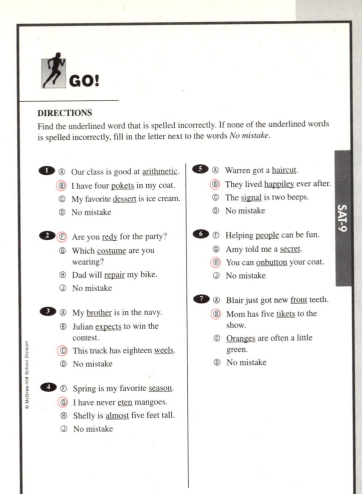

### GO!

**DIRECTIONS**

Find the underlined word that is spelled incorrectly. If none of the underlined words is spelled incorrectly, fill in the letter next to the words *No mistake*.

**1** Ⓐ Our class is good at <u>arithmetic</u>.
　Ⓑ I have four <u>pokets</u> in my coat.
　Ⓒ My favorite <u>dessert</u> is ice cream.
　Ⓓ No mistake

**2** Ⓕ Are you <u>redy</u> for the party?
　Ⓖ Which <u>costume</u> are you wearing?
　Ⓗ Dad will <u>repair</u> my bike.
　Ⓙ No mistake

**3** Ⓐ My <u>brother</u> is in the navy.
　Ⓑ Julian <u>expects</u> to win the contest.
　Ⓒ This truck has eighteen <u>weels</u>.
　Ⓓ No mistake

**4** Ⓕ Spring is my favorite <u>season</u>.
　Ⓖ I have never <u>eten</u> mangoes.
　Ⓗ Shelly is <u>almost</u> five feet tall.
　Ⓙ No mistake

**5** Ⓐ Warren got a <u>haircut</u>.
　Ⓑ They lived <u>happiley</u> ever after.
　Ⓒ The <u>signal</u> is two beeps.
　Ⓓ No mistake

**6** Ⓕ Helping <u>people</u> can be fun.
　Ⓖ Amy told me a <u>secret</u>.
　Ⓗ You can <u>onbutton</u> your coat.
　Ⓙ No mistake

**7** Ⓐ Blair just got new <u>front</u> teeth.
　Ⓑ Mom has five <u>tikets</u> to the show.
　Ⓒ <u>Oranges</u> are often a little green.
　Ⓓ No mistake

**SAT-9**

---

**Go over each question on this page as a class.**

For the questions on this page, extra example words that contain the same two-letter sound as the misspelled word are included. Share these with students to help them gain familiarity with the sounds and spellings.

### Question 1
pockets—jackets, sack

### Question 2
ready—head, instead

### Question 3
wheels—when, white

### Question 4
eaten—heat, beat

### Question 5
happily—badly, shortly

### Question 6
unbutton—unsure, undo

### Question 7
tickets—jackets, socks

Question 6 involves the prefix *un-*. Make sure students are familiar with this two-letter sound in addition to the others listed on Pupil Edition page 142. Some extra words you can provide them as examples include: *unplug*, *untie*, and *unsafe*.

## Exercise 3
# SPELLING

## Words with Confusing Sounds

 **Go over the words in bold in the On Your Mark! section of the Pupil Edition page.**

Explain that some words have groups of letters that may not look like they sound. Students have to memorize these tricky words.

On the board, write some other words that contain the confusing sounds. Some examples you might use are:

- *rough*
- *enough*
- *light*
- *weight*
- *ghoul*

What other words with confusing sounds can students name?

 **Go over the example question as a class.**

---

 **Exercise 3**

## ON YOUR MARK!

### Spelling Words With Confusing Sounds

Some words have groups of letters that may not look like they sound.

*Tough* is pronounced "tuhf."

In the word *tough*, the *gh* makes an *f* sound.

*Eight* is pronounced "ate."

In the word *eight*, the *gh* is silent.

*Ghost* is pronounced "gohst."

In the word *ghost*, the *gh* makes a hard *g* sound.

When you look at answer choices on the SAT-9, always remember that there is often more than one way to spell a sound.

 ## GET SET!

Let's look at an example. Find the underlined word that is misspelled.

I <u>walked</u> into the <u>kitchen</u> and turned on the <u>light</u>.

   A             B             C

Ⓐ   walked
Ⓑ   kitchen
Ⓒ   light
Ⓓ   No mistake

(A) is **wrong.** *Walked* is spelled correctly. It may look funny to you because it is spelled with a silent *l*, but it is correct.

(B) is **wrong.** *Kitchen* is spelled correctly. The *tch* may seem odd, but it is correct.

(C) is **wrong.** *Light* is spelled correctly. The silent *gh* in *light* may look wrong, but it is correct.

(D) is **correct!** All of the choices are spelled correctly.

144   Exercises • Preparation and Practice for the ITBS, SAT-9, and TerraNova • Grade 3

*© McGraw-Hill School Division*

---

 ## EXTRA ACTIVITY

Have students think of ways that they can memorize tricky words. Some ways might be placing similar words together in groups (*cough, laugh*), making up rhymes or sayings (*We <u>ate eight</u> cookies and gained <u>weight</u>*), or even by simply keeping note cards and writing down all the tricky words they come across when reading.

*© McGraw-Hill School Division*

### GO!

**DIRECTIONS:**

Find the underlined word that is spelled wrong. If none of the underlined words is spelled wrong, fill in the letter next to the words *No mistake*.

**1** Ⓐ This bulb is very <u>brigt</u>.
  Ⓑ Gary <u>expects</u> to win the game.
  Ⓒ Put the broom in the <u>corner</u>.
  Ⓓ No mistake

**2** Ⓕ Please <u>compare</u> these two paintings.
  Ⓖ He likes to play <u>rouf</u>.
  Ⓗ A pie is baking in the <u>oven</u>.
  Ⓙ No mistake

**3** Ⓐ Throw the ball with all your <u>migt</u>.
  Ⓑ Do you have a <u>spare</u> pen?
  Ⓒ The mail will arrive <u>soon</u>.
  Ⓓ No mistake

**4** Ⓕ Give your brother a <u>boost</u>.
  Ⓖ This is a <u>touf</u> math problem.
  Ⓗ You can sit on the blue <u>couch</u>.
  Ⓙ No mistake

**5** Ⓐ Put on the <u>gray</u> outfit.
  Ⓑ May I have this <u>dance</u>?
  Ⓒ The two dogs <u>fougt</u> in the yard.
  Ⓓ No mistake

**6** Ⓕ Joaquin ran and <u>caut</u> the ball.
  Ⓖ What is the price on the <u>label</u>?
  Ⓗ How much <u>money</u> does the toy cost?
  Ⓙ No mistake

**7** Ⓐ Look up at the <u>board</u>.
  Ⓑ Turn off the <u>ligt</u> and go to sleep.
  Ⓒ We go <u>barefoot</u> at the beach.
  Ⓓ No mistake

SAT-9

 **Go over each question on this page as a class.**

For the questions on this page, extra example words that contain the same confusing sound as the misspelled word are included. Share these with students to help them gain familiarity with the sounds and spellings.

**Question 1**

bright—light, night

**Question 2**

rough—tough, laugh

**Question 3**

might—light, sight

**Question 4**

tough—cough, rough

**Question 5**

fought—eight, neigh

**Question 6**

caught—taught, right

**Question 7**

light—night, sight

# Exercise 4

## SPELLING

## Rules for Adding Endings to Words

 **Go over the rules for adding endings to words listed on the Pupil Edition page.**

Create three separate columns on the board, one for each ending: *-s*, *-ed*, and *-ing.* Write the rules on the board. Have students copy them on a sheet of paper.

For each example on the Pupil Edition page, have students come up with a similar example. Write their ideas on the board. Some examples you might use are:

- *car/cars—cat/cats*
- *dust/dusted— jump/jumped*
- *hurry/hurried—worry/worried*
- *stomp/stomping— reach/reaching*
- *glide/gliding—taste/tasting*
- *pin/pinning—hit/hitting*

 **Go over the example question as a class.**

---

### Exercise 4

 ## ON YOUR MARK!

### Rules for Adding Endings to Words

**Adding *-s***
- Normally, you just add the *-s.* (car——cars)
- Words ending in *x, z, s, sh,* or *ch* add *-es.* (box——boxes)
- Words ending in *y,* drop the *y* and add *-ies.* (fry——fries)

**Adding *-ed***
- Normally, you just add *-ed.* (dust——dusted)
- Words ending in *y* drop the *y* and add *-ied.* (hurry——hurried)
- Sometimes the consonants are doubled. (skip——skipped)

**Adding *-ing***
- Normally, you just add *-ing.* (stomp——stomping)
- If the word ends in *e,* drop the *e* and add *-ing.* (glide——gliding)
- Sometimes the consonants are doubled. (pin——pinning)

 ## GET SET!

Let's look at an example. Find the underlined word that is misspelled.

I <u>missed</u> my <u>swiming</u> lesson last <u>week</u>.
   F     G         H

- Ⓕ   missed
- Ⓖ   swiming
- Ⓗ   week
- Ⓙ   No mistake

(F) is **wrong.** *Missed* is spelled correctly.

(G) is **correct!** If you add *-ing* to the word *swim,* you must double the *m.*

(H) is **wrong.** *Week* is spelled correctly. Be careful not to confuse *week* with *weak.* They sound the same, but have different meanings.

⁹⁶ McGraw-Hill School Division

146   Exercises • Preparation and Practice for the ITBS, SAT-9, and TerraNova • Grade 3

---

  ## EXTRA ACTIVITY

Erase the examples from the board and break the students into groups of two. Have them quiz each other on the spelling of words with *-s, -ed,* and *-ing* endings. For example, one student might say, "Add an *-ed* to hurry." The other student would then write *hurried.* Encourage students to come up with variations of the examples.

## GO!

**DIRECTIONS**

Find the underlined word that is spelled wrong. If none of the underlined words is spelled wrong, fill in the letter next to the words *No mistake*.

1.
   - Ⓐ My book is <u>buried</u> under this pile somewhere.
   - Ⓑ He <u>filed</u> the cup with water.
   - Ⓒ On Sunday, we will go to the <u>city</u>.
   - Ⓓ No mistake

2.
   - Ⓕ There are <u>many</u> games we can play.
   - Ⓖ We are <u>leaveing</u> next month.
   - Ⓗ My mother never stops <u>loving</u> me.
   - Ⓙ No mistake

3.
   - Ⓐ <u>Cover</u> your mouth when you sneeze.
   - Ⓑ Pete <u>jumpt</u> over the dog.
   - Ⓒ I <u>learned</u> the language easily.
   - Ⓓ No mistake

4.
   - Ⓕ I am <u>sitting</u> in the chair.
   - Ⓖ I <u>found</u> a dollar on the street.
   - Ⓗ My cat is <u>niping</u> my fingers.
   - Ⓙ No mistake

5.
   - Ⓐ If you tease the dog, he will <u>growl</u>.
   - Ⓑ The <u>toys</u> are brand new.
   - Ⓒ He <u>tries</u> very hard at being a good student.
   - Ⓓ No mistake

6.
   - Ⓕ Are you <u>closeing</u> the door?
   - Ⓖ Are you sick or are you <u>faking</u>?
   - Ⓗ My <u>parents</u> are very kind.
   - Ⓙ No mistake

7.
   - Ⓐ The dog <u>marked</u> his territory.
   - Ⓑ Vince likes <u>plane</u> rides.
   - Ⓒ I <u>fixd</u> the radio.
   - Ⓓ No mistake

---

 **Go over each question on this page as a class.**

For the questions on this page, extra example words that contain the same type of ending as the misspelled word are included. Share these with students to help them gain familiarity with the sounds and spellings.

**Question 1**

filled—skipped, pulled

**Question 2**

leaving—gliding, smiling

**Question 3**

jumped—stopped, ripped

**Question 4**

nipping—running, filling

**Question 6**

closing—taking, racing

**Question 7**

fixed—dusted, ruined

## Exercise 5

# SPELLING

## Tricky Spellings

 **Go over the words listed on the Pupil Edition page, pointing out that they have tricky spellings. Emphasize that two vowels or two consonants can sound alike but have different spellings.**

Write some extra words that have tricky spellings on the board. Some examples you might use are:

- ca<u>s</u>e—pla<u>c</u>e
- n<u>e</u>rd—squi<u>r</u>t
- la<u>z</u>y—lo<u>s</u>er
- <u>t</u>on—un<u>d</u>o
- jump—<u>g</u>erm

Make sure students understand the rules for tricky spellings discussed on the Pupil Edition page.

 **Go over the example question as a class.**

---

 **Exercise 5**

# ON YOUR MARK!

## Tricky Spellings

It is easy to confuse some letters with others if they both make the same sound.

| | | |
|---|---|---|
| era<u>s</u>e → ri<u>c</u>e | | <u>t</u>erm → <u>d</u>irt |
| la<u>s</u>er → ra<u>z</u>or | | <u>j</u>et → <u>g</u>em |
| wo<u>n</u> → u<u>n</u>der | | spo<u>ng</u>e → ri<u>dg</u>e |

Did you notice how two vowels or two consonants can sound alike? These rules can help you remember some tricky spellings:

- When the *s* sound is spelled with *c*, it is always followed by *e*, *i*, or *y*.

  ra<u>c</u>e          fan<u>c</u>y          ex<u>c</u>ite

- When the *j* sound is spelled with *g*, it is always followed by *e*, *i*, or *y*.

  <u>g</u>erbil          fra<u>g</u>ile          <u>g</u>ypsy

- Long vowels are always followed by *ge*. Short vowels are always followed by *dge*.

  pa<u>ge</u>          ju<u>dge</u>

 **GET SET!**

Let's look at an example. Find the underlined word that is misspelled.

I <u>terned</u> the music <u>pages</u> while my <u>teacher</u> played the song.
    A              B            C

Ⓐ    terned
Ⓑ    pages
Ⓒ    teacher
Ⓓ    No mistake

(A) is **correct!** An *e* is confused with *u*, *turned*.

(B) is **wrong.** *Pages* is spelled correctly. Adding *s* to *page* is correct.

(C) is **wrong.** *Teacher* is spelled correctly. The *ea* and *ch* combinations are used correctly here.

(D) is **wrong.** Since *turned* is misspelled, this answer choice is incorrect.

148   Exercises • Preparation and Practice for the ITBS, SAT-9, and TerraNova • Grade 3

*© McGraw-Hill School Division*

---

## TEACHING TIP

To emphasize the rules listed on the Pupil Edition page, you might want to make a worksheet listing the rules. Under each rule, you can list several example words including *pace, juicy, city, germs, gym, cage, rage, smidgeon, ridge,* and so on. Photocopy the worksheet and hand it out to students for their reference.

*© McGraw-Hill School Division*

# GO!

**DIRECTIONS**

Find the underlined word that is spelled wrong. If none of the underlined words is spelled wrong, fill in the letter next to the words *No mistake*.

**1**
- Ⓐ Ned <u>thought</u> the show was too long.
- **Ⓑ** Some day I will <u>exploare</u> outer space.
- Ⓒ There is a <u>reward</u> for finding my cat.
- Ⓓ No mistake

**2**
- Ⓕ Drinking <u>milk</u> makes bones stong.
- Ⓖ There are two fillings in my <u>mouth</u>.
- **Ⓗ** Julia likes the <u>uther</u> dress.
- Ⓙ No mistake

**3**
- Ⓐ The <u>only</u> pet I have is a goldfish.
- **Ⓑ** The best <u>tretes</u> are ice cream and cake.
- Ⓒ Do you have an extra <u>pair</u> of socks?
- Ⓓ No mistake

**4**
- **Ⓕ** Please open the <u>curtins</u>.
- Ⓖ We are proud of our <u>school</u>.
- Ⓗ Jack has <u>proof</u> that he is right.
- Ⓙ No mistake

**5**
- Ⓐ Listen to the lion <u>roar</u>!
- Ⓑ This tree has large <u>roots</u>.
- **Ⓒ** She walks at a fast <u>pase</u>.
- Ⓓ No mistake

**6**
- Ⓕ Jerry is mending the <u>roof</u>.
- **Ⓖ** Can we <u>pauze</u> for a rest?
- Ⓗ I need a <u>scrap</u> of paper.
- Ⓙ No mistake

**7**
- Ⓐ <u>Smack</u> that bug before it bites you.
- Ⓑ Her dad has a <u>cabin</u> in the country.
- **Ⓒ** I have four <u>basketes</u> of apples.
- Ⓓ No mistake

**SAT-9**

---

 **Go over each question on this page as a class.**

Questions 1, 3, 4, and 7 require students to understand some tricky spellings not covered on Pupil Edition page 148. Make sure students are familiar with words that include oa, ea, ai, and et. Some examples are toad, road, head, lead, raise, pain, jacket, and socket.

**Question 1**

explore

**Question 2**

other

**Question 3**

treats

**Question 4**

curtains

**Question 5**

pace

**Question 6**

pause

**Question 7**

baskets

## Exercise 6

# RULING OUT WRONG ANSWER CHOICES

**Explain to students that ruling out wrong answer choices is a valuable test-taking strategy.**

Go over the example question in the On Your Mark! section of the Pupil Edition page. Point out to students that they always have a one in four chance of answering a multiple-choice question correctly, even when they have no idea what the answer is.

If they can rule out just one answer choice, their chances of answering correctly go up to one in three. Ruling out two answer choices leaves them with a fifty-fifty chance of answering the question correctly.

For difficult questions, students should always rely on this test-taking strategy. Encourage them to cross through answer choice letters that they can rule out on the test pages. If they can't write on the test, they can use scratch paper to record the wrong answer choice letters.

**Go over the example question as a class.**

### Exercise 6

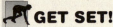

## ON YOUR MARK!

### Ruling Out Wrong Answer Choices

Sometimes you can find the right answer to a question, even if you don't know it right away! All you have to do is rule out the answer choices that you know are wrong. Read the question below:

**Where does your teacher, Mr. Johnson, live?**

Ⓐ   in a pond
Ⓑ   in a library
Ⓒ   in a house
Ⓓ   in a tree

You can answer this question even if you don't know Mr. Johnson.

(A) **is wrong.** Mr. Johnson can't live *in a pond!* Rule this out.

(B) **is wrong.** Mr. Johnson can't live *in a library!* Rule this out.

(C) Mr. Johnson could definitely live *in a house.* Keep this one, and look at the last answer choice.

(D) **is wrong.** Mr. Johnson can't live *in a tree!* Rule this out. Then go back to the answer choice you haven't ruled out. (C) must be **correct!**

## GET SET!

Let's look at an example. Find the underlined word that is misspelled. Rule out the answer choices that you know are wrong.

I finished my <u>job</u> quickly so I <u>could</u> play <u>bal</u>.
         F                G       H

(F) Compare *job* to other rhyming words you know how to spell like *bob, snob,* and *mob. Job* must be spelled correctly.

(G) Compare *could* to rhyming words like *would* and *should. Could* is probably spelled correctly.

(H) Compare *bal* to rhyming words like *mall, call,* and *fall. Bal* seems misspelled. Therefore, (H) must be **correct!**

150   Exercises • Preparation and Practice for the ITBS, SAT-9, and TerraNova • Grade 3

© McGraw-Hill School Division

★ **EXTRA ACTIVITY**

Play twenty questions with students. Think of a person they would know, such as your school principal, and have them guess who it is by asking questions. After the game is over, point out to students that they were able to rule out incorrect answers with each question. For example, if one student asked, "Is this person a girl?" and you answered, "yes," they were able to rule out a huge number of people.

## GO!

### DIRECTIONS

Find the underlined word that is spelled wrong. If none of the underlined words is spelled wrong, fill in the letter next to the words *No mistake*.

**1** Ⓐ Lionel has been waiting <u>such</u> a long time.

Ⓑ Can Susan <u>nit</u> some mittens?

Ⓒ There are old pictures in our <u>attic</u>.

Ⓓ No mistake

**2** Ⓕ Are you <u>ready</u> to play baseball?

Ⓖ My belt is made of <u>leather</u>.

Ⓗ Betsy has a <u>loket</u> with a watch inside.

Ⓙ No mistake

**3** Ⓐ Please take your toys off the <u>floor</u>.

Ⓑ These pants are too <u>tigt</u>.

Ⓒ These sleeves are <u>uneven</u>.

Ⓓ No mistake

**4** Ⓕ You have a <u>message</u> from Cary.

Ⓖ Can you <u>hear</u> the clock ticking?

Ⓗ Where there is a <u>wil</u>, there is a way.

Ⓙ No mistake

**5** Ⓐ Sometimes my puppy <u>desobeys</u> me.

Ⓑ This car has an electric <u>motor</u>.

Ⓒ Would you like to live in a <u>palace</u>?

Ⓓ No mistake

**6** Ⓕ Can you draw a <u>straight</u> line?

Ⓖ I finally <u>finished</u> washing the floor.

Ⓗ Put the <u>nife</u> on the right side.

Ⓙ No mistake

**7** Ⓐ My hair is too short to <u>comb</u>.

Ⓑ May I have a <u>stick</u> of gum?

Ⓒ Ben got a new <u>mouse</u> for his computer.

Ⓓ No mistake

**SAT-9**

## Go over each question on this page as a class.

All of the questions on the page involve the spelling skills taught in Exercises 1 through 6.

Remind students to rule out wrong answer choices as they work through the questions on this page.

### Question 1

Silent /k/ is missing.

### Question 2

*Loket* should be *locket.*

### Question 3

Silent /h/ is missing.

### Question 4

Double consonant *ll* is missing

### Question 5

disobeys

### Question 6

Silent /k/ is missing.

## Exercise 7

# CAPITALIZING TITLES

 **Make sure that students understand it is necessary to capitalize all the important words in titles.**

Have students come up with examples of their favorite books, movies, stories, and so on. Then have students write some of their titles on the board. Check their titles for correct use of capitalization.

Go over the tip box on the Pupil Edition page. Provide some examples to students. Some examples you might use are:

- *Green Eggs and Ham*

- *"What a Wonderful World"*

- *"Ring Around the Rosy"*

 **Go over the example question as a class.**

---

### Exercise 7

## ON YOUR MARK!

### Capitalizing Titles

Capitalize the first word, last word, and all important words in the title of a book, poem, song, short story, film, and newspaper.

Here are some examples of different kinds of titles:

**Book:** *A Wrinkle in Time*

**Song:** "The Star Spangled Banner"

**Newspaper:** *The Smithtown Journal*

> **TIP:** Unimportant words like *a, an, and, the, to, for,* and *as* are not capitalized unless they are the first word in a title.

 ## GET SET!

Let's look at an example. Are the underlined words capitalized correctly?

**Our whole class sang "Three Blind Mice."**

Ⓐ    "Three blind Mice"

Ⓑ    "three blind mice"

Ⓒ    "Three blind mice"

Ⓓ    Correct as is

(A) is **wrong.** *Blind* is an important word in the title. It must be capitalized.

(B) is **wrong.** None of the words in this song title is capitalized.

(C) is **wrong.** Both *blind* and *mice* are important words in the title. They must both be capitalized.

(D) is **correct!** All of the important words in this song title are capitalized.

© McGraw-Hill School Division

---

 ## TEACHING TIP

During the next few weeks, when you or students are reading aloud, point out examples of words that are capitalized because they are titles. Ask students to categorize each example as a book, poem, song, short story, film, or newspaper. In looking at the examples, be sure to point out that unimportant words are not capitalized, unless they are the first word in the title.

© McGraw-Hill School Division

# GO!

## DIRECTIONS

Pay careful attention to the underlined words in each sentence. Look for a punctuation, capitalization, or word usage mistake. If there are mistakes, pick the answer choice that corrects them. If there are no mistakes, mark the last answer choice.

**1** Have you read the **Book** *black* **Beauty**?
- Ⓐ book *black beauty*
- Ⓑ Book *Black Beauty*
- Ⓒ book *Black Beauty*
- Ⓓ Correct as is

**2** When Jill was little, her favorite show was ***Sesame Street***.
- Ⓕ *Sesame street*
- Ⓖ *sesame Street*
- Ⓗ *sesame street*
- Ⓙ Correct as is

**3** Can your class sing "**America the beautiful**"?
- Ⓐ America the Beautiful?
- Ⓑ America The Beautiful?
- Ⓒ "America the Beautiful"?
- Ⓓ Correct as is

**4** Tim will read **the Poem "Trees"** at the recital tonight.
- Ⓕ the poem "Trees"
- Ⓖ the Poem "Trees"
- Ⓗ The poem "Trees"
- Ⓙ Correct as is

**5** In class, we read the **book** **treasure island**.
- Ⓐ Book *Treasure Island.*
- Ⓑ book *Treasure Island.*
- Ⓒ book *Treasure island.*
- Ⓓ Correct as is

SAT-9

## Go over each question on this page as a class.

Have students pay careful attention to questions 1 and 4. Point out that some words in these examples that are not part of the title are incorrectly capitalized: In question 1, the word *book* is incorrectly capitalized, and in question 4, the word *poem* is incorrectly capitalized. Remind students that only words in the actual title should be capitalized.

# USING PUNCTUATION AND CAPITAL LETTERS IN QUOTES

 **Go over the examples listed on the Pupil Edition page with students, asking them to pay careful attention to the use of quotation marks, punctuation, and capital letters.**

Explain the two rules for writing quotations that are outlined on the Pupil Edition page. Discuss how these two rules are evidenced in the three examples provided.

 **Go over the example question as a class.**

---

Exercise 8

## ON YOUR MARK!

### Using Punctuation and Capital Letters in Quotes

Use **quotation marks** to show that someone is speaking.

> Linda said, "Let's go to a movie."
>
> "These cookies are great!" shouted Claire.
>
> "Too bad it is raining," Melissa said. "We could have had a picnic."

Remember these important rules about writing quotations:
- Quotation marks come at the beginning and end of a person's exact words.
- The first letter inside a quotation is always capitalized.

 ## GET SET!

Let's look at an example. Find the punctuation, capitalization, or word usage mistake in the underlined words.

**Barry said, "School was fun today!"**

Ⓕ    Barry said, "school

Ⓖ    Barry said, School

Ⓗ    Barry said, school

Ⓙ    Correct as is

(F) is **wrong**. *School* must be capitalized. It is the beginning of the quotation.

(G) is **wrong**. A quotation mark must come before *School*. Quotation marks show where a quotation begins and ends.

(H) is **wrong**. A quotation mark must come before *school*. Also, *school* must be capitalized since it is the beginning of a quotation.

(J) is **correct!** The quotation marks come before Barry's exact words, and *school* is capitalized because it is the beginning of a quotation.

---

## EXTRA ACTIVITY

Ask two students to come to the front of the class and have a conversation. You might ask one student to tell the other what he or she did over the past weekend. Remind them to ask each other questions as well as make comments. Record their conversation on the board, pointing out to the class your use of quotation marks, punctuation, and capitalization. After you have written a few correct sentences, make some errors: forget the quotation marks, misuse punctuation, or forget to capitalize the first letter inside a quotation. Encourage students to point out the mistakes.

# GO!

**DIRECTIONS**

Pay careful attention to the underlined words in each sentence. Look for a punctuation, capitalization, or word usage mistake. If there are mistakes, pick the answer choice that corrects them. If there are no mistakes, mark the last answer choice.

**1** Dad always **"says Do your homework before you watch television."**

Ⓐ says "do

Ⓑ "Says do

Ⓒ says, "Do

Ⓓ Correct as is

**2** When I woke up this morning, Mom **Asked, "What do you want for breakfast?"**

Ⓕ Asked, "what do you want for breakfast?

Ⓖ asked, "what do you want for breakfast?"

Ⓗ asked, "What do you want for breakfast?"

Ⓙ Correct as is

**3** Patrick Henry **said, "Give me liberty or give me death."**

Ⓐ Said, "give

Ⓑ "Said "give

Ⓒ "Said Give

Ⓓ Correct as is

**4** After Alex finished his chores, his dad **said Good job, Alex.**

Ⓕ said, "Good job, Alex."

Ⓖ said, "Good job, Alex.

Ⓗ "Said, Good job, Alex."

Ⓙ Correct as is

**5** Liz **said, "I** want to be a movie star someday."

Ⓐ "said I

Ⓑ said, I

Ⓒ Said I

Ⓓ Correct as is

SAT-9

 **Go over each question on this page as a class.**

## Question 1

Quotation marks only go around a person's exact words—not words like *says* or *asked*.

## Question 2

Only the first letter inside a quotation is capitalized—not the first letter of the word before the quotation.

## Question 4

Quotation marks must come before and after a direct quotation.

# Exercise 9

## WRITING CONTRACTIONS

 **Explain to your class what a contraction is, and show them how an apostrophe is used in a contraction.**

Go over the examples on the Pupil Edition page. Point out that the verbs in a contraction with *not* do not change their spellings (with the exception of *won't*).

Ask students to come up with other examples of contractions. Write their ideas, along with the two words each contraction represents, on the board. Some examples are:

- *weren't*     *were not*
- *couldn't*     *could not*
- *hasn't*     *has not*
- *she'll*     *she will*
- *they'll*     *they will*

 **Go over the example question as a class.**

---

### Exercise 9

 **ON YOUR MARK!**

**Writing Contractions**

A **contraction** is a shortened form of two words:

    did not —→ didn't

An **apostrophe (')** in a contraction shows where one or more letters has been left out.

A verb in a contraction with *not* usually does not change its spelling. Here are some more examples of contractions with *not*:

| | |
|---|---|
| is not —→ isn't | have not —→ haven't |
| does not —→ doesn't | had not —→ hadn't |
| cannot —→ can't | are not —→ aren't |

The word *won't* is a special contraction. The spelling of the verb *will* changes.

    will not —→ won't

 **GET SET!**

Let's look at an example. How should the underlined words be written?

**Mario hasnt' been in school this week.**

Ⓐ    hasn't been

Ⓑ    ha'snt been

Ⓒ    has'nt been

Ⓓ    Correct as is

(A) is **correct!** The contraction of *has not* is *hasn't*.

(B) is **wrong.** The apostrophe divides the verb *has* in two. That's incorrect.

(C) is **wrong.** The apostrophe in a contraction always takes the place of a missing letter.

(D) is **wrong.** In a contraction, the apostrophe never comes at the end of the word.

156   Exercises • Preparation and Practice for the ITBS, SAT-9, and TerraNova • Grade 3

© McGraw-Hill School Division

---

 **EXTRA ACTIVITY**

Distribute a short paragraph to the class. Have students list all of the contractions in the paragraph, along with the two words each contraction represents. An example paragraph you can use is:

*Sara can't go to the party. She hasn't finished her chores. She promises her parents that she'll do her chores after the party. They say they'll only let her go once her chores are finished. Sara says, "Okay, I'll do the chores." She finishes them just in time. She's going to the party.*

© McGraw-Hill School Division

## GO!

**DIRECTIONS**

Pay careful attention to the underlined words in each sentence. Look for a punctuation, capitalization, or word usage mistake. If there are mistakes, pick the answer choice that corrects them. If there are no mistakes, mark the last answer choice.

**1** <u>Do'esnt that cloud</u> look like a whale?

- Ⓐ Doe'snt that cloud
- Ⓑ Does'nt that cloud
- Ⓒ Doesn't that cloud
- Ⓓ Correct as is

**2** <u>Didn't I see you</u> at the movies on Saturday?

- Ⓕ Did'nt I see you
- Ⓖ Didnt' I see you
- Ⓗ Didnt I see you
- Ⓙ Correct as is

**3** <u>Ill be ready</u> in five minutes.

- Ⓐ I'll be ready
- Ⓑ Il'l be ready
- Ⓒ Ill' be ready
- Ⓓ Correct as is

**4** <u>He isn't going</u> to the fair.

- Ⓕ He isnt' going
- Ⓖ He is'nt going
- Ⓗ He isnot going
- Ⓙ Correct as is

**5** <u>Cal could'nt find</u> a better friend than Dave.

- Ⓐ Cal couldnt find
- Ⓑ Cal couldn't find
- Ⓒ Cal couldnt' find
- Ⓓ Correct as is

SAT-9

---

 **Go over each question on this page as a class.**

Have students pay careful attention to questions 1 and 5. Remind them that an apostrophe shows where one or more letters have been left out in a contraction. The apostrophes in these questions are in the wrong place.

### Question 1

Apostrophe in wrong place

### Question 3

Missing apostrophe between *I* and *ll*

### Question 5

Apostrophe in wrong place

# POSSESSIVE NOUNS

**Go over the rules for changing nouns into possessive nouns, using the three examples provided on the Pupil Edition page.**

Create three columns on the board, separated by the following headings: singular nouns, plural nouns that do not end in *s*, and plural nouns that do end in *s*. Have students come up with examples for each column. Write their ideas on the board.

Have students come up with a sentence for at least one word in each column. The noun that they use from the list on the board should be made into a possessive noun. For example, if one of the singular nouns on the board is *cat*, a student might write, *The cat's ball was under the sofa.*

**Go over the example question as a class.**

Exercise 10

## ON YOUR MARK!

### Possessive Nouns

A **possessive noun** is a word that shows who or what owns something. You change a singular noun to a possessive noun by adding an apostrophe and an *s*.

> ***Kelly's*** *book report is upstairs.*

The word *Kelly's* tells you that the book report belongs to Kelly.

When you need to change a plural noun that DOES NOT end in *s* to a possessive noun, an apostrophe and an *s* goes at the end of the word.

> *The* ***children's*** *party was over.*

The word *children's* tells you that the party was for the children.

When you need to change a plural noun that DOES end in *s* to a possessive noun, only an apostrophe goes at the end of the word.

> *The* ***dogs'*** *toys are lost.*

The word *dogs'* tells you the toys belong to the dogs.

## GET SET!

Let's look at an example. How should the underlined word be written?

This is <u>Brians's</u> dirt bike.

- Ⓕ    Brians'
- Ⓖ    Brians
- Ⓗ    Brian's
- Ⓙ    Correct as is

(F) is **wrong.** *Brian* is just one person. The apostrophe and the *s* are in the wrong order.

(G) is **wrong.** The apostrophe is missing! It must come before the *s*.

(H) is **correct!** *Brian* is a singular noun, so an apostrophe and an *s* are added to show possession.

(J) is **wrong.** *Brian* is singular. Adding an *s*, an apostrophe, and an *s* is wrong.

158   Exercises • Preparation and Practice for the ITBS, SAT-9, and TerraNova • Grade 3

## EXTRA ACTIVITY

As a homework assignment, have students write their own sentences containing possessive nouns. Have students share their sentences with the class. Write them on the board.

Ask students to categorize each of the possessive nouns into one of the three groups: singular nouns, plural nouns that do *not* end in *s*, and plural nouns that *do* end in *s*

## GO!

**DIRECTIONS**

Pay careful attention to the underlined words in each sentence. Look for a punctuation, capitalization, or word usage mistake. If there are mistakes, pick the answer choice that corrects them. If there are no mistakes, mark the last answer choice.

**1** <u>Mrs. McElroy's</u> class is at the modern art museum.
- Ⓐ Mrs. McElroy
- Ⓑ Mrs. McElroys'
- Ⓒ Mrs. McElroys
- Ⓓ Correct as is

**2** Do you know that <u>Jimbo's hot dog stand</u> has the best french fries?
- Ⓕ Jimbos hot dog stand
- Ⓖ Jimbos's hot dog stand
- Ⓗ Jimbos' hot dog stand
- Ⓙ Correct as is

**3** Mr. Hankins carried <u>Governor Coreys'</u> suitcase.
- Ⓐ Governor Coreys
- Ⓑ Governor Corey's
- Ⓒ Governor Corey
- Ⓓ Correct as is

**4** Next weekend we will go to my <u>aunt and uncles' house.</u>
- Ⓕ aunt and uncles house.
- Ⓖ aunt and uncle's house.
- Ⓗ aunt and uncle house.
- Ⓙ Correct as is

**5** <u>The turtles heads</u> were all in their shells.
- Ⓐ The turtles' heads
- Ⓑ The turtle's heads
- Ⓒ The turtles heads'
- Ⓓ Correct as is

 **Go over each question on this page as a class.**

### Question 3

*Governor Corey* is singular so the apostrophe comes at the end of the name and before the added *s*.

### Question 4

The possessive noun is two words—*aunt and uncles'*—but only the second word has an apostrophe.

### Question 5

The possessive noun, *turtles*, is plural because it is connected to the word *heads*. One turtle cannot have more than one head!

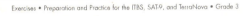

# Exercise 11

## USING ADJECTIVES THAT COMPARE

 **Explain what an adjective is to students.**

Then go over the difference between a comparative adjective and a superlative adjective.

On the board, create two columns: comparative adjectives (compare two nouns) and superlative adjectives (compare more than two nouns). Using the examples on the Pupil Edition page as guides, ask students for additional examples. Write their examples in the appropriate columns.

Explain that some adjectives that are used to compare do *not* follow the usual pattern (-*er, -est*). Go over the examples provided on the Pupil Edition page. Call on students to create sentences with each of the words. Answer any questions students have.

 **Go over the example question as a class.**

---

### Exercise 11

 ## ON YOUR MARK!

### Using Adjectives that Compare

**Adjectives** are words that are used to describe nouns.
> Buddy is **tall**.

A **comparative adjective** compares two nouns. For small words, just add -*er* to the adjective.
> Buddy is **taller** than Christopher.

A **superlative adjective** compares more than two nouns. For small words, just add -*est* to the adjective.
> Buddy is the **tallest** person in his class.

Some adjectives that are used to compare do not follow the usual pattern.

| Adjectives | Comparatives | Superlatives |
| --- | --- | --- |
| bad | worse | worst |
| good | better | best |
| well | better | best |
| many | more | most |

 ## GET SET!

Let's look at an example. How should the underlined word be written?

**Rosa's hair is longest than Clara's hair.**

Ⓐ  longer

Ⓑ  longerest

Ⓒ  long

Ⓓ  Correct as is

(A) is **correct!** *Longer* is a word that compares two people or things. In this case, *longer* compares Rosa's hair to Clara's hair.

(B) is **wrong.** *Longerest* is not a word.

(C) is **wrong.** The word *long* describes, but it does not compare.

(D) is **wrong.** Rosa and Clara are two people. *Longest* should be used to compare *more* than two people or things.

⑯⓪ Exercises • Preparation and Practice for the ITBS, SAT-9, and TerraNova • Grade 3

---

★ ## EXTRA ACTIVITY

Have two students come to the front of the class. Ask the students who are seated to create sentences that compare the two students. You might start with an example, such as, "Gail has shorter hair than Merlene." After students have created a few sentences involving comparative adjectives, have a third student join them. Ask the students who are seated to create sentences that compare the three students. You might offer an example, such as, "Maurice is the tallest of the three students."

Write the students' sentences on the board, circling the comparative and superlative adjectives.

# GO!

## DIRECTIONS

Pay careful attention to the underlined words in each sentence. Look for a punctuation, capitalization, or word usage mistake. If there are mistakes, pick the answer choice that corrects them. If there are no mistakes, mark the last answer choice.

**1** This <u>storm is worser</u> than the one in December.

- Ⓐ storm is worsest
- Ⓑ storm is worst
- Ⓒ storm is worse
- Ⓓ Correct as is

**2** Josie <u>has the redder hair</u> in the class.

- Ⓕ has the reddest hair
- Ⓖ has the more redder hair
- Ⓗ has the reddiest hair
- Ⓙ Correct as is

**3** Kim <u>knows the long song</u> in the world.

- Ⓐ knows the longer song
- Ⓑ knows the longest song
- Ⓒ knows the more long song
- Ⓓ Correct as is

**4** Bobby <u>has a best</u> coin collection.

- Ⓕ has a bestest
- Ⓖ has a more good
- Ⓗ has a good
- Ⓙ Correct as is

**5** This <u>is the best school lunch</u> so far this year.

- Ⓐ is the better school lunch
- Ⓑ is the good school lunch
- Ⓒ is the bestest school lunch
- Ⓓ Correct as is

SAT-9

© McGraw-Hill School Division

Exercises • Preparation and Practice for the ITBS, SAT-9, and TerraNova • Grade 3    161

 **Go over each question on this page as a class.**

## Question 1

Comparative adjective—irregular pattern

## Question 2

Superlative adjective

## Question 3

Superlative adjective

## Question 4

Regular adjective

## Question 5

Superlative adjective—irregular pattern

For question 4, point out to students that Bobby's coin collection is not being compared to anyone else's. The sentence does not include a comparison. Therefore, students simply need to select the correct adjective to describe Bobby's coin collection.

# Exercise 12

## USING VERBS

**Go over what a verb is and explain the difference between the present tense and the past tense.**

On the board, create a list of verbs, taking ideas from the class. Next to each present tense verb, write its past tense form. To help students come up with ideas, have them think about what they do at recess. Their activities at recess are full of action: *run*, *hit*, *jump*, *skip*, *play*, and *yell* are some examples.

Explain that some verbs are irregular. They are spelled in unexpected ways when they are in the past tense. Go over the examples of irregular action verbs provided on the Pupil Edition page. Ask students to come up with additional examples. Add them to the list on the board.

**Go over the example question as a class.**

---

Exercise 12

## ON YOUR MARK!

### Using Verbs

A **verb** is a word that shows action.

*The rocket **shoots** up to the moon.*

A verb in the past tense tells about an action that has already happened. Add *-ed* to most verbs to form the past tense.

| Present Tense | | Past Tense |
|---|---|---|
| look | ⟶ | looked |
| learn | ⟶ | learned |
| lock | ⟶ | locked |

**Irregular action verbs** have a different spelling than most verbs when they are in the past tense. The past tense tells you that the action already happened.

| Present Tense | | Past Tense |
|---|---|---|
| grow | ⟶ | grew |
| get | ⟶ | got |
| give | ⟶ | gave |

 **GET SET!**

Let's look at an example. How should the underlined word be written?

**Yesterday, he <u>holding</u> the baby on his hip.**

- Ⓐ holded
- Ⓑ helded
- Ⓒ held
- Ⓓ Correct as is

(A) is **wrong**. *To hold is an irregular verb. Holded is not correct.*

(B) is **wrong**. *To hold is an irregular verb. Helded is not correct.*

(C) is **correct!** *To hold is an irregular verb. Held is correct!*

(D) is **wrong**. *Holding is in the present tense, but the action in the sentence happened yesterday.*

---

 **TEACHING TIP**

Perform an activity at the front of the class. You might play with two puppets and have them talk to each other. Or you could pretend to get ready in front of an imaginary mirror, donning a coat, combing your hair, and adjusting a hat. Or you might pretend to paint an arrangement of flowers. Try to vary your movements and include as much action as possible. When you are finished, have students write a description of what you did. They should use past tense verbs to describe your actions.

## GO!

**DIRECTIONS**

Pay careful attention to the underlined words in each sentence. Look for a punctuation, capitalization, or word usage mistake. If there are mistakes, pick the answer choice that corrects them. If there are no mistakes, mark the last answer choice.

**1** The plane <u>flied</u> over my house.
Ⓐ fly
Ⓑ flew
Ⓒ have flew
Ⓓ Correct as is

**2** The weather forecaster says snow <u>falled</u> all night.
Ⓕ fell
Ⓖ felled
Ⓗ fall
Ⓙ Correct as is

**3** Last week Ted <u>write</u> a composition about his summer vacation.
Ⓐ wroted
Ⓑ writed
Ⓒ wrote
Ⓓ Correct as is

**4** Grace <u>slided</u> down the water slide.
Ⓕ slid
Ⓖ slide
Ⓗ did slide
Ⓙ Correct as is

**5** When Bill <u>goed</u> to Washington, D.C., he visited the White House.
Ⓐ going
Ⓑ went
Ⓒ have gone
Ⓓ Correct as is

### Go over each question on this page as a class.

Each question on this page tests students' knowledge of irregular past tense action verbs.

For question 3, point out to students that the phrase *Last week* is a clue that the action took place in the past. Therefore, the verb in the sentence must be in the past tense. What are some other phrases that might be clues? Ask students for ideas.

# USING VERB TENSES

 **Go over the difference between the present and the past tense.**

As a class, discuss the examples on the Pupil Edition page.

On the board, write some sentences in the present and past tenses, placing them in two separate columns, one marked present, the other past.

Some examples you might use are:

- *Ms. Cohen <u>bakes</u> chocolate chip cookies.*
- *Ms. Cohen <u>baked</u> chocolate chip cookies.*
- *Adam <u>acts</u> in the school play.*
- *Adam <u>acted</u> in the school play.*

Ask students to come up with additional examples. Write them on the board.

Explain to students that all verb tenses must agree in a sentence, as outlined in the box on the Pupil Edition page. Discuss the examples in the box. Remind students that a verb must also agree with its subject. Answer any questions students have.

 **Go over the example question as a class.**

---

 **Exercise 13**

## ON YOUR MARK!

### Using Verb Tenses

**Verb tenses** tell when the action takes place in a sentence.

**Present tense** is happening now: *The girl **jumps** over the puddle.*

**Past tense** already happened: *The girl **jumped** over the puddle.*

> All verb tenses must agree in a sentence.
>
> *The girl **jumped** over the puddle, so she **stayed** dry.*
>
> In the sentence above, the words *jumped* and *stayed* are both in the past tense. This means that the verb tenses agree.
>
> A verb must also agree with its subject.
>
> *I **jump**.*
>
> *She **jumps**.*
>
> *They **jump**.*

 ## GET SET!

Let's look at an example. How should the underlined word be written?

**Larry <u>drawed</u> a picture last Tuesday.**

Ⓐ draws
Ⓑ drew
Ⓒ is drawing
Ⓓ Correct as is

(A) **is wrong.** *Draws* is in the present tense, and *last Tuesday* is in the past.

(B) **is correct!** *Drew* is the past tense form of the irregular verb *draw*.

(C) **is wrong.** *Is drawing* is in the present tense, and *last Tuesday* is in the past.

(D) **is wrong.** *Drawed* is not a word.

---

  ## EXTRA ACTIVITY

Write several subjects and several verbs on the board. The subjects should be singular and plural. The verbs should be past, present, singular, and plural. Have students match logical subjects and verbs together. Some words you might use are:

- **SUBJECTS:** *Juanita, We, People, Birds, They, He*

- **VERBS:** *like, sits, fly, runs, play*

---

## GO!

**DIRECTIONS**

Pay careful attention to the underlined words in each sentence. Look for a punctuation, capitalization, or word usage mistake. If there are mistakes, pick the answer choice that corrects them. If there are no mistakes, mark the last answer choice.

**1** Yesterday Francis <u>tell me that there</u> will be a spelling test.

  Ⓐ telling me that there will be

  Ⓑ have tell me that there will be

  Ⓒ told me that there will be

  Ⓓ Correct as is

**2** Mom always <u>listening to the radio</u> while she cooks dinner.

  Ⓕ listened to the radio

  Ⓖ listens to the radio

  Ⓗ listen to the radio

  Ⓙ Correct as is

**3** Next week, <u>Grandpa take me</u> to a football game.

  Ⓐ Grandpa taking me

  Ⓑ Grandpa taked me

  Ⓒ Grandpa will take me

  Ⓓ Correct as is

**4** Josie <u>helped me decorate</u> the classroom.

  Ⓕ help me decorate

  Ⓖ helping me decorate

  Ⓗ have helped me decorate

  Ⓙ Correct as is

**5** Keith <u>laugh out loud</u> when he watches a funny television show.

  Ⓐ laughs out loud

  Ⓑ laughed out loud

  Ⓒ laughing out loud

  Ⓓ Correct as is

**SAT-9**

## Go over each question on this page as a class.

### Question 1

Past tense—irregular verb

### Question 2

Present tense

### Question 3

Future tense

### Question 4

Past tense

### Question 5

Present tense

Question 3 is somewhat tricky. It asks students to identify the future tense. The future tense was not covered on the Pupil Edition page 164. Make sure students understand that future tense verbs are preceded by the word *will*. The phrase *Next week* tells students that the action hasn't happened yet, but it *will* happen. It *will* happen in the future.

# PRONOUNS

**Explain that pronouns are special words that take the place of nouns in a sentence.**

Go over the two types of pronouns, object and subject, thoroughly with your class. Write sentences on the board and have students tell you which pronouns are object pronouns and which are subject pronouns. Some examples you might use are:

- _He_ likes to eat cheese. (subject)

- _I took _him_ to the store. (object)

- _We_ are nice people. (subject)

- _Sally is fond of _her_. (object)

- _Where are you taking _them_? (object)

## TEACHING TIP

Make sure students understand that the pronoun _I_ always comes second when paired with another subject. For example, _Carole and I._

**Go over the example question as a class.**

---

**Exercise 14**

## ON YOUR MARK!

### Pronouns

A **pronoun** is a word that takes the place of one or more nouns. It must match the noun or nouns that it replaces.

A **singular pronoun** replaces a singular noun.
_Carrie is smart._ ⟶ **She** is smart.

A **plural pronoun** replaces a plural noun or more than one noun.
_The **dogs** are barking._ ⟶ **They** are barking.

Use the pronouns _I_ and _me_ to write about yourself. Use _I_ in the subject of a sentence. If there is more than one subject, _I_ always comes last.
_She and I walked home._

Use _me_ after an action verb and words such as _in, into, to, with, by,_ or _at._
_Kyle teases Jenny and **me**._

| **Subject Pronouns** | **Object Pronouns** |
|---|---|
| I, you, he, she, it, we, they | me, you, him, her, it, us, them |

## GET SET!

Let's look at an example. How would you write the underlined words?

<u>Ling and me played catch.</u>

Ⓐ .    Ling and I played catch.
Ⓑ    I and Ling played catch.
Ⓒ    Me and Ling played catch.
Ⓓ    Correct as is

(A) is **correct**! Since _I_ is part of the subject, it must come last and it must be _I_, not _me_.

(B) is **wrong.** If there is more than one subject, _I_ always comes last.

(C) is **wrong.** _Me_ is not the correct pronoun to use in a subject.

(D) is **wrong.** Again, _me_ is not the correct pronoun to use in a subject.

166   Exercises • Preparation and Practice for the ITBS, SAT-9, and TerraNova • Grade 3

---

## EXTRA ACTIVITY

Prepare a list of sentences for the class using the following format:

_Sara and Julie are friends. (They, Them) are nine year olds._ Students must circle the pronoun that correctly fits into the sentence. Prepare at least two sentences for each possible pronoun. For extra credit, have students label the correct pronouns as subject or object pronouns.

**GO!**

 **Go over each question on this page as a class.**

## DIRECTIONS

Pay careful attention to the underlined words in each sentence. Look for a punctuation, capitalization, or word usage mistake. If there are mistakes, pick the answer choice that corrects them. If there are no mistakes, mark the last answer choice.

**1** <u>Him and Elsa went</u> to the state fair.

Ⓐ He and Elsa went

Ⓑ Elsa and him went

Ⓒ Her and him went

Ⓓ Correct as is

**2** Fred and his team thought the prize <u>would go to them.</u>

Ⓕ would go to we

Ⓖ would go to they

Ⓗ would go to she

Ⓙ Correct as is

**3** <u>Her and Rebecca had</u> a very exciting day.

Ⓐ Them and Rebecca had

Ⓑ Him and Rebecca had

Ⓒ She and Rebecca had

Ⓓ Correct as is

**4** Jake finally decided <u>to call him.</u>

Ⓕ to call he

Ⓖ to call she

Ⓗ to call we

Ⓙ Correct as is

**5** <u>You and me should</u> do our homework.

Ⓐ You and I should

Ⓑ Me and you should

Ⓒ I and you should

Ⓓ Correct as is

**SAT-9**

### Question 1

*He*: singular—subject

### Question 2

*them*: plural—object

### Question 3

*She*: singular—subject

### Question 4

*him*: singular—object

### Question 5

*You*: singular—subject

*I*: singular—subject

# USING CAPITAL LETTERS

 **Go over the rules for using capital letters with students.**

Write extra examples for each rule on the board. Some examples you might use are:

- *One day I will go on vacation.*
- *Mike Dominic*
- *Lake Michigan*
- *Puritan Street*
- *I asked, "Where are you?"*
- *King James*
- *Mr. Gilmour*
- *Dr. Jeffris*
- *Uncle Tyrone*
- *Lindsey and I*
- *The New York Times*
- *Where the Red Fern Grows*
- *Dear Stella*
- *Sincerely*

 **Go over the example question as a class.**

---

**Exercise 15**

## ON YOUR MARK!

### Using Capital Letters

Always capitalize:

- **The first word in a sentence.**
  *Exercise is good for you.*
- **Proper nouns such as names of people.**
  *Jane Brown*
- **Proper nouns that are names of places.**
  *Bryant Street, Bear Mountain, Mississippi River*
- **The first letter of a quotation within a sentence.**
  *Valerie asked, "May I be excused?"*
- **Titles, when they come before a person's name.**
  *President Lincoln, Queen Anne, Aunt Carol, Mrs. Brown*
- **The pronoun *I*.**
  *Susan and I went home.*
- **The title of a book, song, newspaper, or article.**
  *I am reading the Daily News.*
- **The first word of a letter greeting or closing.**
  *Dear Sirs,*
  *Yours truly,*

 ## GET SET!

Let's look at an example. How should the underlined words be written?

**Mom took me to Eno Lake Park.**

- Ⓐ Mom took me to Eno lake park.
- Ⓑ Mom took me to Eno lake Park.
- Ⓒ Mom took me to Eno Lake park.
- Ⓓ Correct as is

(D) is **correct!** All of the words, *Eno*, *Lake*, and *Park*, should be capitalized.

© McGraw-Hill School Division

---

  ## EXTRA ACTIVITY

Create a brief letter in which there are numerous errors in capitalization. Distribute the letter to students and have them correct the errors. As you discuss the assignment with them, point out which rule from the Pupil Edition page each error is testing. An example letter you can use is:

*dear juan,*

*how are you? it is nice here in florida. my friend, phillip, and i are planning to go swimming in the atlantic ocean this summer. his aunt sally has a house on the water. are you reading any good books? i am reading where the Red fern grows. it is a good book, but it is sad. i hope to hear from you soon.*

*your friend,*

*stanley*

© McGraw-Hill School Division

# GO!

**DIRECTIONS**

Pay careful attention to the underlined words in each sentence. Look for a punctuation, capitalization, or word usage mistake. If there are mistakes, pick the answer choice that corrects them. If there are no mistakes, mark the last answer choice.

**1** Peter visited <u>the grand canyon</u> during his summer vacation.

  Ⓐ the Grand canyon

  Ⓑ the grand Canyon

  Ⓒ the Grand Canyon

  Ⓓ Correct as is

**2** In social studies we learned about <u>president abraham Lincoln.</u>

  Ⓕ president Abraham Lincoln

  Ⓖ President abraham Lincoln

  Ⓗ President Abraham Lincoln

  Ⓙ Correct as is

**3** On <u>Mother's day</u> we like to cook breakfast for Mom.

  Ⓐ Mothers Day

  Ⓑ Mother's Day

  Ⓒ mother's day

  Ⓓ Correct as is

**4** <u>dear mayor Reede,</u>

  Ⓕ dear mayor Reede,

  Ⓖ Dear Mayor Reede,

  Ⓗ Dear Mayor reede,

  Ⓙ Correct as is

**5** Is it colder at the <u>North Pole or the South Pole?</u>

  Ⓐ North Pole or The South Pole?

  Ⓑ north Pole or the south Pole?

  Ⓒ north pole or the south pole?

  Ⓓ Correct as is

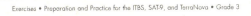

**SAT-9**

## Question 1

*Grand Canyon*—proper noun that is the name of a place

## Question 2

*President*—title before a person's name; *Abraham Lincoln*—proper noun that is the name of a person

## Question 3

*Mother's Day*—holiday

## Question 4

*Dear*—the first word of a letter greeting; *Mayor Reede*—title before a person's name

## Question 5

*North Pole or the South Pole*—proper nouns that are the names of places

Emphasize the importance of capitalizing holidays. This type of proper noun was not covered on Pupil Edition 168.

# Exercise 16
# USING PUNCTUATION

 **Go over the different uses of periods, question marks, exclamation marks, and commas.**

Discuss the examples on the Pupil Edition page. Answer any questions students have. You might want to provide them with some additional examples. Write these examples on the board:

**For periods:**

- *Maria wears lime green pants every Friday.*
- *Mr. Brown likes orange ties.*

**For question marks:**

- *Does Anna own a red hat?*
- *When are you leaving?*

**For exclamation marks:**

- *Janelle hates green!*
- *Stop it!*

**For commas:**

- *Juan prefers purple, blue, and yellow.*
- *He was born on June 12, 1994.*
- *He lives in Tucson, Arizona.*
- *Dear Uncle Ramirez,*
- *Love, Chantal*

Have students come up with their own examples for each of the above.

 **Go over the example question as a class.**

---

 **Exercise 16**

## ON YOUR MARK!

**Using Punctuation**

 **Use periods:**
- **to end a statement.** *Mustapha plays the trumpet.*
- **at the end of an abbreviation.** *I live next to Mrs. Matthews.*

 **Use question marks to end a question.** *Do you like cheese?*

 **Use exclamation marks to end a statement of excitement.** *That's great news!*

 **Use commas:**
- **between items in a series.**
  *I have to clean the bathroom, garage, and my bedroom.*
- **between a day and a year.** *It is March 19th, 1992.*
- **between a city and its state.** *My uncle lives in Miami, Florida.*
- **after the opening or closing of a letter.** *Dear Sara, Sincerely,*

 **GET SET!**

Let's look at an example. How should the underlined words be written?

**I like playing <u>soccer, volleyball, and hockey.</u>**

Ⓐ    soccer volleyball and hockey.
Ⓑ    soccer volleyball, and hockey.
Ⓒ    soccer, volleyball and, hockey.
Ⓓ    Correct as is

(D) is **correct!** Commas must come after every item in a series.

*© McGraw-Hill School Division*

170   Exercises • Preparation and Practice for the ITBS, SAT-9, and TerraNova • Grade 3

---

 **EXTRA ACTIVITY**

As a homework assignment, have students write five sentences for each of the four different punctuation marks: period, question mark, exclamation mark, and comma. Encourage them to be creative and have fun. Discuss the assignment as a class. Have students read some of their sentences aloud. Write these sentences on the board.

*© McGraw-Hill School Division*

## GO!

### DIRECTIONS

Pay careful attention to the underlined words in each sentence. Look for a punctuation, capitalization, or word usage mistake. If there are mistakes, pick the answer choice that corrects them. If there are no mistakes, mark the last answer choice.

**1** Stephanie hit the ball and <u>ran to first base?</u>

  Ⓐ ran to first base.

  Ⓑ ran to first base,

  Ⓒ ran to first base

  Ⓓ Correct as is

**2** Would you rather go <u>to the park or to the zoo.</u>

  Ⓕ to the park or to the zoo!

  Ⓖ to the park or to the zoo?

  Ⓗ to the park or to the zoo,

  Ⓙ Correct as is

**3** Kerry has homework in <u>math spelling and reading.</u>

  Ⓐ math, spelling and reading.

  Ⓑ math, spelling, and reading.

  Ⓒ math, spelling and, reading.

  Ⓓ Correct as is

**4** Mom and I went shopping for <u>pants shirts, and socks.</u>

  Ⓕ pants shirts, and, socks.

  Ⓖ pants, shirts, and socks.

  Ⓗ pants, shirts and socks.

  Ⓙ Correct as is

**5** Rover <u>digs a hole and buried his bone in it.</u>

  Ⓐ dug a hole and buried his bone in it?

  Ⓑ dug a hole and buried his bone in it.

  Ⓒ dig a hole and buried his bone in it

  Ⓓ Correct as is

**SAT-9**

© McGraw-Hill School Division

## Go over each question on this page as a class.

### Question 1

Period—to end a statement

### Question 2

Question mark—to end a question

### Question 3

Commas—between items in a series

### Question 4

Commas—between items in a series

### Question 5

Period—to end a statement

Question 5 also tests students on verb tense agreement, which they learned in a previous exercise. Remind students not to forget what they learned in the previous practice exercises as they move through the exercises in this book.

© McGraw-Hill School Division

## Exercise 17

# FIX THE MISTAKES YOURSELF

 **Encourage students to pay attention to errors as they read.**

This will be particularly helpful in answering punctuation questions on the SAT-9.

 **Go over the example paragraph as a class.** Have students circle the errors. Then students should rewrite the paragraph correctly on the lines provided. The correct paragraph will read as follows:

*My family's summer house is on Lake Ontario. On the last day of school in June, Mom always says, "Time to move up to the lake!" My favorite thing to do is to catch frogs. I look at their colors and measure their lengths. Then I write that information down in my journal and put the frog back into the lake. Someday, I'd like to be a biologist. A biologist studies frogs and other living things.*

### Exercise 17

## ON YOUR MARK!

### Fix the Mistakes Yourself

When you take the SAT-9, try correcting the errors you see as you read them. If you think about how you would write the words as you are reading them, you may be able to find the errors and correct them. This is especially helpful to you on punctuation questions, when errors might be so small that they are hard to spot—like a missing period or an incorrectly placed comma.

 **GET SET!**

Let's look at an example. Read the paragraph below.

> My familys summer house is on Lake Ontario. On the last day of school in June, mom always says, "Time to move up to the lake! My favorite thing to do is to catch frogs. I look at their colors and measure their lengths. Then I write that information down in my journal and put the frog back into the lake? Someday, Id like to be a biologist. A biologist studies frogs and other living things.

Now rewrite the paragraph, correcting all the errors.

_____

_____

_____

_____

_____

_____

© McGraw-Hill School Division

 **TEACHING TIP**

During the year, read through newspapers, magazines, and books, looking for errors in spelling, punctuation, and capitalization. Bring in these examples and have students try to find the mistakes.

© McGraw-Hill School Division

## GO!

**DIRECTIONS**

Pay careful attention to the underlined words in each sentence. Look for a punctuation, capitalization, or word usage mistake. If there are mistakes, pick the answer choice that corrects them. If there are no mistakes, mark the last answer choice.

**1** I think <u>well</u> take a family picture now.

Ⓐ wel'l
Ⓑ we'll
Ⓒ well'
Ⓓ Correct as is

**2** The principal <u>said, "I am proud of the students in my school.</u>

Ⓕ said, I am proud of the students in my school.
Ⓖ Said, "I am proud of the students in my school."
Ⓗ said, "I am proud of the students in my school."
Ⓙ Correct as is

**3** I <u>gone to study</u> hard tonight.

Ⓐ am going to study
Ⓑ goes to study
Ⓒ going to study
Ⓓ Correct as is

**4** Joan says you will find <u>Mr. Winstons</u> coat in the closet.

Ⓕ Mr Winston's
Ⓖ Mr. Winstons'
Ⓗ Mr. Winston's
Ⓙ Correct as is

**5** These gloves are <u>the warm ones I have ever had.</u>

Ⓐ the warmer ones I have ever had
Ⓑ the more warm ones I have ever had
Ⓒ the warmest ones I have ever had
Ⓓ Correct as is

SAT-9

## Go over each question on this page as a class.

Encourage students to fix the mistakes in the example sentences as they read. They can either fix them in their heads, or write the correct sentences on separate sheets of paper. This will help them choose the correct answer.

### Question 1
Mistake in punctuation—contraction

### Question 2
Mistake in punctuation—quotation marks

### Question 3
Mistake in usage—verb tense

### Question 4
Mistake in punctuation—possessive noun

### Question 5
Mistake in usage—superlative adjective

# RUN-ON SENTENCES AND CONJUNCTIONS

**Go over the examples of run-on sentences and conjunctions with students.**

Emphasize that conjunctions—such as *and*, *but*, *because*, *so*, and *if*—can often fix run-on sentences.

On the board, write several run-on sentences and ask students to fix them by inserting conjunctions. Some examples of run-on sentences you might use are:

- *I sing in the shower every morning my brother always complains. (and, but)*

- *Keisha loves spinach her mother made it on her birthday. (so)*

- *Randy dislikes running he plays soccer anyway. (but)*

- *Sarah got a hamster she kept her grades high all year. (because)*

- *I will only go to the park it is sunny outside. (if)*

Discuss with students how they can fix these run-on sentences. Answer any questions students have.

**Go over the example question as a class.**

---

Exercise 18

## ON YOUR MARK!

### Run-On Sentences and Conjunctions

A **run-on sentence** joins together two or more sentences that should be written separately.

*Let's go to the car wash it will be fun to sit inside the car.*

*Grammy's molasses cookies are the best in my neighborhood she uses a special recipe.*

A **conjunction** is a word that joins two ideas together. *And, but, because, so,* and *if* are all conjunctions.

*Conjunctions can fix run-on sentences.*

**Run-on:** *I love Saturdays, I get to stay up late.*

**Complete Sentence:** *I love Saturdays **because** I get to stay up late.*

## GET SET!

Let's look at an example. Can you find the answer choice that is written correctly?

> Angelo washed the dishes he put them away.

Ⓕ Angelo washed the dishes, he also put the dishes away.
Ⓖ Angelo washed the dishes and put them away.
Ⓗ Angelo washed the dishes, he put them away.
Ⓙ Correct as is

(F) is **wrong.** *Also* is not a conjunction. The sentence is still a run-on.

(G) is **correct!** The two ideas are joined together by the word *and.*

(H) is **wrong.** This sentence can't be fixed by just adding a comma.

(J) is **wrong.** This is a run-on sentence, because it has two ideas in it and no conjunction to join them.

---

## TEACHING TIP

Over the next few weeks, be particularly attuned to run-on sentences in students' writing. Circle run-on sentences with a bold-colored pen, such as purple or green, and label them as run-on sentences. Have students rewrite their run-on sentences. Keep a running list of the run-on sentences you find in students' writing. Once a week, discuss them as a class, keeping their authors anonymous. Be sure to offer encouragement, too. You might write, "Good job! No run-on sentences!" or "Great work! Only one run-on!" at the top of students' papers.

**GO!**

 **Go over each question on this page as a class.**

### DIRECTIONS
Pay careful attention to the underlined words in each sentence. Look for a punctuation, capitalization, or word usage mistake. If there are mistakes, pick the answer choice that corrects them. If there are no mistakes, mark the last answer choice.

**1** | Mrs. Bailey went into the bank and deposited his check.

&#9398; Mrs. Bailey went into the bank deposited his check.

&#9399; Mrs. Bailey went into the bank, deposited his check.

&#9400; Mrs. Bailey went into the bank. And depositing his check is what she did.

&#9401; Correct as is

**2** | The crossing guard shivered, it was cold.

&#9401; The crossing guard shivered because it was cold.

&#9403; The crossing guard shivered it was cold.

&#9404; The crossing guard shivered it, was cold.

&#9405; Correct as is

**3** | Ted got into the boat, he started to row.

&#9398; Ted got into the boat. And started to row

&#9399; Ted got into the boat, started to row.

&#9400; Ted got into the boat and started to row.

&#9401; Correct as is

**4** | I flipped the switch the light came on.

&#9403; I flipped the switch, the light came on.

&#9404; I flipped the switch if the light came on.

&#9405; I flipped the switch and the light came on.

&#9406; Correct as is

**SAT-9**

## Question 2
Conjunction *because* fixes run-on

## Question 3
Conjunction *and* fixes run-on

## Question 4
Conjunction *and* fixes run-on

## Exercise 19

# FIXING SENTENCE FRAGMENTS

 **Go over sentences and sentence fragments with students.**

Emphasize that sentences should have both a subject and a verb.

On the board, write several sentence fragments and ask students to fix them. Some examples you might use are:

- *Swim at the pool.*
- *Marion on the diving board.*
- *Did a perfect back flip.*
- *The swimmers along the edge of the pool.*

Ask students to identify what is missing in each sentence fragment. Does it need a subject or a verb?

 **Go over the example question as a class.**

---

 **Exercise 19**

## ON YOUR MARK!

### Fixing Sentence Fragments

A **sentence** is a group of words that expresses a complete thought. It should have a verb that tells you what action is taking place. It should also have a subject, so you know who performs the action.

*Grammy's molasses cookies are the best in my neighborhood.*

A **sentence fragment** is a group of words that does not express a complete thought. A sentence fragment does not have all the important parts that make a complete sentence.

*Ran around the block.* → **Janet** *ran around the block.*

*Micah's favorite shoes.* → *Micah's favorite shoes* **are muddy.**

## GET SET!

Let's look at an example. Is there a mistake in sentence structure?

> I cut the paper. And glued the pieces back together.

Ⓐ   I cut the paper. Glued the pieces back together.

Ⓑ   I cut the paper and glued the pieces back together.

Ⓒ   I cut the paper. To glue the pieces back together.

Ⓓ   Correct as is

(A) is **wrong.** The second sentence has no subject. *Who* glued the pieces back together?

(B) is **correct!** This sentence has a subject, *I*, and verbs, *cut* and *glued.*

(C) is **wrong.** The second sentence has no subject. It is a fragment.

(D) is **wrong.** Never begin a sentence with *and.* It is a conjunction. Conjunctions connect two or more ideas. Conjunctions never come before the first idea.

---

⭐ **EXTRA ACTIVITY**

Play a game with students. Write different fragments on several index cards. Some should include a subject with no verb. Others should include a verb with no subject. Hand out one card to each student. Start a stopwatch and give students one minute to find a partner whose fragment can begin or end their sentence. The first pair to complete a sentence wins a prize.

**GO!**

**DIRECTIONS**

Lok at the words in the box. The words may have a mistake in sentence structure. If there is a mistake, find the answer choice that corrects it. If there is not, mark the last answer choice.

**1** My big sister is going. To college next year.

- Ⓐ My big sister. She is going to college next year.
- Ⓑ My big sister is going to college next year.
- Ⓒ My big sister, going to college next year.
- Ⓓ Correct as is

**2** The cat jumped onto the counter. And started eating the chicken.

- Ⓕ The cat jumped onto the counter and started eating the chicken.
- Ⓖ The cat jumped onto the counter, it started eating the chicken.
- Ⓗ The cat jumping onto the counter and started eating the chicken.
- Ⓙ Correct as is

**3** My father is trying. To get into better shape.

- Ⓐ My father, trying to get into better shape.
- Ⓑ My father. He is trying to get into better shape.
- Ⓒ My father is trying to get into better shape.
- Ⓓ Correct as is

**4** The teacher opened the book. And began reading the story.

- Ⓕ The teacher opening the book and began reading the story.
- Ⓖ The teacher opened the book and began reading the story.
- Ⓗ The teacher opened the book, she began reading the story.
- Ⓙ Correct as is

**SAT-9**

 **Go over each question on this page as a class.**

When discussing the correct answers, have students identify the subjects and verbs.

**Question 1**

Subject—*My big sister*, verb—*is going*

**Question 2**

Subject—*The cat*, verb—*jumped* and *started eating*

**Question 3**

Subject—*My father*, verb—*is trying*

**Question 4**

Subject—*The teacher*, verb—*opened* and *began reading*.

# COMBINING TWO SHORT SENTENCES

 **Go over compound sentences with students.**

Explain that they can combine two short sentences that are related to create a compound sentence. Explain how a compound sentence is made, using a comma and conjunction. Remind students that they already learned about conjunctions.

On the board, write a series of short, related sentences. Ask students to help you combine the two sentences. Some examples you might use are:

- *I love applesauce. It tastes sweet.*

- *Jan cleaned her room. Her missing scarf turned up.*

- *Mario walked to school. His brother rode his bike.*

After you have gone over some examples, read two short sentences aloud to the class, followed by the compound version. Ask students to compare the two. Read a few more examples. What makes the compound version better?

 **Go over the example question as a class.**

---

 ## ON YOUR MARK!

### Combining Two Short Sentences

Two very short sentences can be combined to form one sentence if they have something to do with one another. Sometimes combining two sentences makes the paragraph easier to read.

Two very short sentences that are related sometimes sound choppy.

> *I opened my umbrella. It kept me dry.*

If the sentences are related, they can be combined by a comma and a conjunction such as *and*.

> *I opened my umbrella,* **and** *it kept me dry.*

A **compound sentence** is a sentence that contains two sentences combined into one by a comma and a conjunction such as *and*.

 ## GET SET!

Let's look at an example. Find the <u>best</u> way to combine these sentences.

**Marissa put on her coat. She went outside.**

Ⓐ   Marissa put on her coat, she went outside.

Ⓑ   Marissa put on her coat and, she went outside.

Ⓒ   Marissa put on her coat and went outside.

Ⓓ   Marissa went outside she put on her coat.

(A) is **wrong.** This sentence is a run-on. It is missing a conjunction like *and*.

(B) is **wrong.** The comma is in the wrong place.

(C) is **correct!** The two sentences are combined with *and* correctly.

(D) is **wrong.** This sentence is a run-on. The sentences are combined, but there is no conjunction.

---

  ## EXTRA ACTIVITY

Have one student come up to the board and write a short sentence. Then have another student come up to the board and write another short sentence that relates to the first one. A third student should come to the board and combine the two sentences into a compound sentence, inserting a comma and a conjunction.

## GO!

**DIRECTIONS**

Read each paragraph. Then answer the questions that follow.

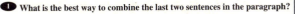

### Paragraph 1

The saguaro cactus is found in Arizona, California, and Mexico. It grows one inch during the first ten years of its life. Eventually, however, it grows to be fifty feet tall. It has pretty flowers. The flowers bloom when it is fifty years old.

**1** **What is the best way to combine the last two sentences in the paragraph?**

Ⓐ It has pretty flowers, they bloom when it is fifty years old.

Ⓑ Pretty flowers it has they bloom when it is fifty years old.

Ⓒ It has pretty flowers or they bloom when it is fifty years old.

Ⓓ It has pretty flowers that bloom when it is fifty years old.

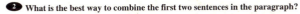

### Paragraph 2

The king penguin is one of the largest penguins in the world. It lives on a very cold island near Antarctica. Like all penguins, it cannot fly. Unlike most other penguins, the king penguin can run with its feet. It doesn't have to hop while it is on land.

**2** **What is the best way to combine the first two sentences in the paragraph?**

Ⓕ The king penguin is one of the largest penguins in the world, it lives on a very cold island near Antarctica.

Ⓖ The king penguin is one of the largest penguins in the world to live on a very cold island near Antarctica.

Ⓗ The king penguin is one of the largest penguins in the world, living on a very cold island near Antarctica.

Ⓙ The king penguin is one of the largest penguins in the world, and lives on a very cold island near Antarctica.

SAT-9

 **Go over each question on this page as a class.**

Remind students that when two adjacent sentences have the same subject, the subject does not need to be repeated in the second sentence. For question 1, the subject is not repeated in the correct answer. Read the correct answer aloud to students. Point out that it does not sound choppy like the other answer choices do.

## Exercise 21

# SHARE YOUR WRITING WITH OTHERS

 **Discuss with students the value of sharing their writing with others.**

Explain that even grown-ups share their writing with others. For example, after an author writes a book, it is reviewed by a number of editors before it is published.

Go over the list of things that students should look for when reading their classmates' writing. When students read classmates' work in class, keep this list on the board.

 **Go over the example question as a class.**

---

 **Exercise 21**

# ON YOUR MARK!

## Share Your Writing with Others

Share your writing with others. Ask your classmate to read over your work and to look for:

- Run-on sentences
- Sentence fragments
- Sentences that do not belong
- Topic sentences that do not state the main idea
- Supporting sentences that are out of order
- Compound sentences that are not joined correctly

Ask your classmate which mistakes you make most often. Then go back and review the skills you still have trouble with.

 **GET SET!**

Let's look at an example. Pretend you are reviewing your classmate's writing. Is there a mistake in sentence structure?

> Pat fell asleep at the movies she was very tired.

Ⓐ  Pat fell asleep at the movies because she was very tired.
Ⓑ  Pat fell asleep at the movies, she was very tired.
Ⓒ  Pat falling asleep at the movies because she was very tired.
Ⓓ  Correct as is

(A) is **correct!** The conjunction *because* connects the two ideas.

(B) is **wrong.** This is a run-on. A comma cannot connect these two ideas.

(C) is **wrong.** The verb *falling* is incomplete. It needs a helping verb.

(D) is **wrong.** This is a run-on. There is nothing that connects the two ideas.

180  Exercises • Preparation and Practice for the ITBS, SAT-9, and TerraNova • Grade 3

© McGraw-Hill School Division

---

  **EXTRA ACTIVITY**

After students have written a brief paragraph about the topic of their choice, break them into groups of two. Have them exchange papers and read each other's work. In class, allow them time to discuss each other's work. You might repeat this assignment throughout the year, assigning students different partners each time.

© McGraw-Hill School Division

## GO!

### DIRECTIONS

Look at the words in the box. The words may have a mistake in sentence structure. If there is a mistake, find the answer choice that corrects it. If there is not, mark the last answer choice.

**1** | Mr. McGill passed out the costumes, and the cast put them on.

- Ⓐ Mr. McGill passed out the costumes the cast put them on.
- Ⓑ Mr. McGill passed out the costumes, the cast put them on.
- Ⓒ Mr. McGill passed out the costumes. And putting them on is what the cast did.
- Ⓓ Correct as is

**2** | Theresa is learning. To play the guitar.

- Ⓕ Theresa, learning to play the guitar.
- Ⓖ Theresa. She is learning to play the guitar.
- Ⓗ Theresa is learning to play the guitar.
- Ⓙ Correct as is

**3** | The people cheered the mayor's speech, they agreed with him.

- Ⓐ The people cheering the mayor's speech because they agreed with him.
- Ⓑ The people cheered the mayor's speech because they agreed with him.
- Ⓒ The people cheered the mayor's speech they agreed with him.
- Ⓓ Correct as is

**4** | I read a book. It was about farming.

- Ⓕ I read a book and about farming.
- Ⓖ I reading a book and it was about farming.
- Ⓗ I read a book about farming.
- Ⓙ Correct as is

SAT-9

 **Go over each question on this page as a class.**

These questions cover material that students learned in previous exercises. Remind them that the mistakes in these questions are the types of errors they should look for when reading a classmate's writing. You might want to have students swap Go! pages and correct each other's work for this exercise to emphasize the importance of sharing writing.

### Question 2
Fixing sentence fragments

### Question 3
Run-on sentences and conjunctions

### Question 4
Combining two short sentences

## Exercise 22

# MAIN IDEAS AND SUPPORTING DETAILS IN WRITING

 **Go over the elements of a paragraph with students.**

Explain the terms in bold on the Pupil Edition page.

On the board, write the following brief paragraph:

*Every night, Jeremy helps set the table for dinner. First, he puts place mats on the table. Then, he puts plates and glasses on the place mats. He makes sure everyone has a plate and a glass. Jeremy feeds his turtle every day. Finally, he puts napkins and silverware on the table. Jeremy enjoys helping out.*

Point out to students that this is a paragraph. Then ask them to help you determine its main idea. Then ask them if any sentences do not belong. They should point to the sentence *Jeremy feeds his turtle every day.* Explain to students that this sentence does not support the main idea. Put a line through this sentence on the board. Finally, ask students to help you label the supporting details and the time-order words.

 **Go over the example question as a class.**

---

### Exercise 22

## ON YOUR MARK!

### Main Ideas and Supporting Details in Writing

A **paragraph** is a group of sentences that is about one idea.

A **main idea** is what a piece of writing or a paragraph is all about.

**Supporting details** are sentences that help explain the main idea.

Use **time-order** words to connect ideas.

*First, I made a list. Then, I went to the store and bought groceries. After I paid for them, I walked home.*

## GET SET!

Let's look at an example. Is there a sentence that does not belong in this paragraph?

> ¹ Maria is writing a report about dolphins. ² She needs to find some books about dolphins so she can write her report. ³ Maria decides to go to the library to learn about dolphins. ⁴ The library was just built last year.

Ⓐ Sentence 1
Ⓑ Sentence 2
Ⓒ Sentence 3
Ⓓ Sentence 4

(A) is **wrong.** Sentence 1 tells you Maria's report on dolphins is the main idea of the paragraph.

(B) is **wrong.** Sentence 2 tells you a detail about the main idea. It explains what she needs to write her report on dolphins.

(C) is **wrong.** Sentence 3 also tells you another detail about the main idea. It explains where Maria will go to learn about dolphins.

(D) is **correct!** Sentence 4 does not belong in this paragraph. It tells you a detail about the library, but that is not the main idea of the paragraph.

---

## TEACHING TIP

Bring in the first paragraph or two from a variety of fairy tales and children's stories. Read them out loud and have the class pick out the topic sentences and time-order words. See if they can figure out the main idea of the stories from the material provided.

**GO!**

**DIRECTIONS**

Read the paragraph. Then answer the question that follows it.

---

**Paragraph 1**

Maybe you know that mammals are animals whose babies drink milk. You probably don't know that the world's smallest mammal is the bumble bee bat. It lives only in an Asian country called Thailand. The adult bat is no bigger than a bumble bee. It is less than one and a half inches long. It would take 228 of them to weigh a pound!

**1** Find the sentence that would go best after the last sentence in the paragraph above.

Ⓐ The river that runs beside the bumble bee bat's home is called the Kwae Noi.

Ⓑ The next time you see a bumble bee, imagine a mammal that size!

Ⓒ The bumble bee bat has more than one name.

Ⓓ The bumble bee bat is not a bee.

---

**Paragraph 2**

Louis Pasteur discovered that germs cause most contagious diseases. This discovery helped to make and keep people healthy in many ways. Hospitals became cleaner so people would not catch diseases there. Medicines were invented that keep us safe from many diseases.

**2** Find the sentence that would go best after the last sentence in the paragraph above.

Ⓕ Paul Ehrlich was another great medical scientist.

Ⓖ We still take those medicines today.

Ⓗ Milk is very important for your health.

Ⓙ Louis Pasteur was a citizen of France.

---

 **Go over each question on this page as a class.**

Ask students to come up with the main idea of each paragraph on this page. Doing so will help them answer the questions.

**Question 1**

Main idea—the bumble bee bat

**Question 2**

Main idea—results of germ discovery

# Exercise 23

# PARAGRAPHS

 **Explain what a topic sentence is in further detail.**

Make sure students understand that a topic sentence is the first sentence of a paragraph and often contains the main idea.

On the board, write the following paragraph:

*My brother Sam loves vegetables. He eats carrots every day after school. When my parents make spinach, he smiles from ear to ear. He even likes to have peas at breakfast. He can't get enough vegetables.*

Using this paragraph, ask students to help you determine the main idea, topic sentence, and supporting details. Ask students to come up with additional supporting details for this paragraph. Make sure their sentences support the main idea. If they do not, discuss this as a class.

**Go over the example question as a class.**

---

## ON YOUR MARK!

### Paragraphs

You just learned that the **main idea** of a paragraph is what the rest of the paragraph is about. The main idea can be found in the first sentence of a paragraph.

A **topic sentence** is the first sentence of a paragraph. It tells you the main idea of the paragraph.

Every sentence in the paragraph must be about the main idea stated in the topic sentence. Those sentences are called **supporting details**.

| | |
|---|---|
| Topic Sentence: | *Andreas is my best friend.* |
| Detail: | *I have known him my whole life.* |
| Detail: | *We do everything together.* |
| Detail: | *Andreas is fun to hang out with because he is so funny.* |

 ## GET SET!

Let's look at an example. Read the paragraph. What is the best topic sentence for the paragraph?

> He puts on his cap and gets out his glove. He hopes he will be the third baseman again. He wants to be a famous player when he grows up.

- Ⓕ He finished his homework.
- Ⓖ Caesar has many friends.
- Ⓗ His dad is the coach.
- Ⓙ Caesar gets ready for his baseball game.

(F) is **wrong.** Is the paragraph about Caesar finishing his homework? No, it's about Caesar playing baseball.

(G) is **wrong.** Is this paragraph about Caesar's friends? No.

(H) is **wrong.** Is this paragraph about Caesar's coach? No.

(J) is **correct!** Is this paragraph about Caesar getting ready for his baseball game? Yes, it is! This topic sentence states the main idea of the paragraph.

---

## EXTRA ACTIVITY

Have students pick a favorite short story or picture book. Once they have chosen a story or book, they should read it and write down the main idea, the topic sentences, and a list of some supporting details. Choose a few of the students' books and read them aloud to the class.

## GO!

**DIRECTIONS**

Read the paragraph. Then answer the question that follows it.

---

### Paragraph 1

Some islands in the Caribbean Sea and the Pacific Ocean are also part of the United States. These islands are American Samoa, Guam, and Puerto Rico. Four million people live on the islands. They are all United States citizens.

---

**1** **Find the best topic sentence for the paragraph.**

Ⓐ The United States is made up of more than just fifty states.

Ⓑ Alaska and Hawaii are also part of the United States.

Ⓒ Lots of people take vacations in the Virgin Islands.

Ⓓ Citizens of the United States have many rights.

---

### Paragraph 2

At top speed, red kangaroos can make sixteen-foot jumps. "Reds" can run up to thirty miles per hour! Even a lazy, slow hop can be as far as six feet! The kangaroo can go fast because it has a long, heavy, and powerful tail that keeps it balanced.

---

**2** **Find the best topic sentence for the paragraph.**

Ⓕ Sometimes red kangaroos hop slowly.

Ⓖ Red kangaroos are amazing animals.

Ⓗ Kangaroos live in Australia.

Ⓙ Kangaroo babies stay in their mothers' pouches.

## Go over each question on this page as a class.

In Exercise 6, students learned about ruling out wrong answer choices. As a class, discuss how this might be helpful in answering these types of questions. Encourage students to cross out sentences that are clearly not the best topic sentence.

## Exercise 24

# KNOWING MAIN PURPOSE AND AUDIENCE

 **Go over the terms** *main purpose* **and** *audience* **with students.**

As a class, discuss why it is important to have a main purpose and an audience in mind when writing.

Tell students to imagine you have given them the following two assignments:

- *Write a paragraph telling your classmates what you did last summer.*

- *Write a paragraph telling your best friend about your summer vacation.*

Ask students how these two assignments differ. Be sure to discuss main purpose and audience. Ask students how they might approach each assignment differently.

 **Go over the example question as a class.**

---

 ## ON YOUR MARK!

### Knowing Main Purpose and Audience

A **main purpose** is the reason you write something. Do you have something exciting to tell your readers? Do you want to make your readers laugh? Do you want to convince your readers to do something? These are all purposes for writing.

An **audience** is the person or group you would like to have read your writing. Are you writing a story for young people? Then young people would be your audience. Are you writing to people who like trains? Then people who know something about trains would be your audience. Think about your audience before you begin. It will help you make your main purpose clear to your audience.

 ## GET SET!

Let's look at an example. Read the paragraph.

> Always make sure to keep your lawn mower blade sharpened. A dull blade will tear the grass instead of cut it. Grass that is torn will dry out and look brown.

This paragraph was <u>most likely</u> written for whom?

Ⓕ someone who just bought his or her first lawn mower
Ⓖ someone who hires people to cut his or her lawn
Ⓗ someone who cuts grass for a living
Ⓙ someone who sells lawn supplies

(F) is **correct!** A person who has never had a lawn mower needs to know this information.

(G) is **wrong.** People who don't cut their own grass don't need to know about caring for a lawn mower.

(H) is **wrong.** A person who cuts grass for a living probably already knows this information.

(J) is **wrong.** A person who sells lawn supplies already knows this information.

---

 ## EXTRA ACTIVITY

Have students write a paragraph with a very specific purpose and audience in mind. Some ideas you might use are:

- *In a paragraph, tell your parents what you do at recess.*

- *In a paragraph, describe a parent to your classmates.*

- *In a paragraph, tell your teacher what your favorite book is.*

After students have written their paragraphs, revisit the concepts of *main purpose* and *audience* with students. How was their writing guided by these concepts?

**GO!**

**DIRECTIONS**

Read the paragraph. Then answer the question that follows it.

### Paragraph 1

The bald eagle was chosen as our national bird in 1782. It was selected because it looks magnificent, and it is a good hunter and protector of its young. The term "bald" doesn't mean that it doesn't have feathers on its head. It's taken from an old word, piebald, that means "marked with white."

1 **This paragraph was most likely written for whom?**

Ⓐ Scientists who study birds

Ⓑ Doctors who take care of birds

Ⓒ Students of American history

Ⓓ People who dislike birds

### Paragraph 2

My grandmother lives in DeWitt, New York. She lives two blocks from my house. I ride my bike to visit her after school. She makes great spaghetti sauce. Sometimes I help her. I stir the sauce while it simmers in the pot.

2 **Find the main reason the author wrote this paragraph.**

Ⓕ To tell about spaghetti sauce

Ⓖ To explain how far away her grandmother lives

Ⓗ To tell about her grandmother

Ⓙ To explain why DeWitt is a nice place

 **Go over each question on this page as a class.**

## Question 1

Audience question

## Question 2

Main purpose question

# Exercise 25

## WHAT BELONGS IN A PARAGRAPH AND WHAT DOES NOT?

**Go over what *does* and *does not* belong in a paragraph with students.**

Remind students that they already learned about main ideas and supporting details in a paragraph. Review these concepts if necessary.

Then explain to students that any sentence that doesn't relate to the main idea of a paragraph does not belong in the paragraph. It should be eliminated. To emphasize this concept, write the following paragraph on the board:

*Rani loves to be outside. Every day after school, she climbs trees with her friends. Every Saturday, she goes for a walk with her mom. Last Sunday, she went to a birthday party. In the summer, she roller skates in the park. Rani is happiest when she is outside.*

Ask students to determine the main idea of the paragraph. Have students pick out the sentence that doesn't belong. Ask them to explain why it doesn't belong. Then, have students come up with an additional supporting detail to put in place of the sentence that doesn't belong. Encourage them to be creative. You might start them off with an example, such as *She always looks for butterflies in her backyard.* Make sure their supporting details refer back to the main idea. If not, discuss why as a class.

**Go over the example question as a class.**

---

Exercise 25

## ON YOUR MARK!

### What Belongs in a Paragraph and What Does Not?

All paragraphs have a main idea. When a sentence in a paragraph does not talk about the paragraph's main idea, that sentence does not belong in the paragraph.

Use these steps to find out whether a sentence belongs in a paragraph.

1. When you read a paragraph, ask yourself, "What is this paragraph mostly about?"
2. Go back and reread the supporting detail sentences. As you read each sentence, ask yourself, "Does this sentence tell me more about the main idea?"
3. When you read a sentence that does not belong, it will usually stand out in the paragraph. Read the paragraph again without that sentence. If the sentence does not belong, the paragraph will be easier to read without it.

## GET SET!

Let's look at an example. Read the paragraph. Then decide which sentence would <u>not</u> belong in the paragraph.

> Scientists say that monkeys are a lot like people. Monkeys can use their hands to hold things like humans do. Young monkeys have playmates like human children do, too.

Ⓐ    Monkeys eat bananas like humans do.
Ⓑ    Monkeys also have hands and feet, and walk on their hind legs.
Ⓒ    Some people keep monkeys as pets.
Ⓓ    Monkeys even seem to get happy, sad, and angry like humans do.

(A) is **wrong**. It belongs. It tells us how monkeys are like people.

(B) is **wrong**. It belongs. It also tells us how monkeys are like people.

(C) is **correct!** It does not belong. It does not relate to the topic sentence.

(D) is **wrong**. It belongs. It compares the feelings of humans and monkeys.

---

## EXTRA ACTIVITY

Create a worksheet that lists a series of main ideas. For each main idea, have students write one sentence that would be an appropriate supporting detail.

## GO!

**DIRECTIONS**

Read the paragraph. Then answer the question that follows.

---

**Paragraph 1**

Do you know that the world's smallest mammal is the bumble bee bat? It lives in an Asian country called Thailand. The adult bat is no bigger than a bumble bee.

---

**1** Find the sentence that would **not** belong in the paragraph.

Ⓐ The bumble bee bat's wings are only six inches wide.

Ⓑ The bumble bee bat is less than one and a half inches long.

Ⓒ Some people are afraid of bats.

Ⓓ It would take 228 of them to weigh a pound!

---

Dear Felicia,

I am sorry that you have the chicken pox. I had it last year and it made me itch like crazy. Soon you will be better and we will get together. I have a new game that I think you'll like. It's about the circus. Feel better soon. Don't scratch too much.

Your friend,

Natalie

---

**2** Find the sentence that would **not** belong in the paragraph.

Ⓕ How long have you been sick?

Ⓖ I want to be a doctor when I grow up.

Ⓗ Sometimes lotion helps the itching go away.

Ⓙ I can't wait to see you again.

SAT-9

 **Go over each question on this page as a class.**

Students should try to come up with the main idea of each paragraph *before* looking at the answer choices. That way, they will have a better idea of what does *not* belong in the paragraph.

## Question 1

Choice *C* does not belong because the fear of bats is irrelevant to the paragraph.

## Question 2

Choice *G* doesn't belong because it is the only sentence that does not directly relate to Felicia and the chicken pox.

## Exercise 26
# PACING YOURSELF

**Go over the tips students can follow for pacing themselves on the SAT-9.**

Ask students if they have any questions. Remind them that they will be well prepared for the SAT-9 after completing the exercises in this book. Encourage them to be confident in what they know.

Explain to students that pacing themselves as they move through the test will increase their chances of succeeding. They should not spend too much time on difficult questions. Instead, they should return to the difficult questions at the end of the test and make their best guess if time allows.

**Go over the example question as a class.**

---

# ON YOUR MARK!

## Pacing Yourself

**Pacing yourself** means using the time you have to complete as many questions as you can without rushing or spending too much time on one question. Here are some tips that will help you work at a careful but steady pace:

- **Do not get stuck on one question.** If you cannot answer a question and you have been trying for a while, take your best guess and move on.
- **Know the directions.** When you take the practice tests, pay attention to the directions so that on the real exam, you will not have to spend time trying to understand them.
- **Relax as best you can.** Don't worry if you don't know an answer. The SAT-9 is just one way to measure your skills. The calmer you are, the more likely you are to answer the questions correctly!

# GET SET!

Practice pacing yourself on this example question. Read the paragraph. Then find the sentence that would be the best topic sentence for the paragraph.

> There is no school, so I don't have to worry about homework. I get to play outside every day. I wish that summer could last all year long.

- Ⓕ    Summer is my favorite time of year.
- Ⓖ    There are four seasons in a year.
- Ⓗ    I like to watch the fireworks on July 4th.
- Ⓙ    Some kids think winter is more fun than summer.

(F) is **correct!** The supporting details talk about summer being the writer's favorite time of year.

(G) is **wrong.** It talks about *all* of the seasons, not just summer.

(H) is **wrong.** It is a supporting detail, not a topic sentence.

(J) is **wrong.** The paragraph is not about how other kids feel about winter.

---

## TEACHING TIP

Encourage students to get in the habit of pacing themselves. Make it a game and practice with everyday activities, such as getting ready to go outside for recess.

Later, place a time limit on some in-class assignments. Start with easy assignments, then move on to more difficult ones. In general, encourage students to feel comfortable with time constraints. Try to teach them to be efficient in their work but not overly conscious of time.

**GO!**

**DIRECTIONS:**

Read the paragraph. Then answer the question that follows.

---

**Paragraph 1**

Some islands in the Caribbean Sea and the Pacific Ocean are a part of the United States. These islands are American Samoa, Guam, and Puerto Rico. Four million people live on the islands.

---

**1** Find the sentence that would **not** belong in the paragraph.

Ⓐ The United States is made up of more than just fifty states.

Ⓑ The island of Puerto Rico is close to Florida.

Ⓒ People on these islands are all United States citizens.

Ⓓ My family vacations wherever the weather is warm.

---

**Paragraph 2**

We bring our fishing rods, bait, and tackle box. We wait for the fish to bite our line. Then we reel them in as gently as we can. After we catch a fish, we always put it back into the lake.

---

**2** Find the best topic sentence for the paragraph above.

Ⓕ In the summer, my brother and I go up to Lake Ontario to fish.

Ⓖ Some fish take a nibble of the bait and swim away!

Ⓗ Sometimes we measure the length of the fish.

Ⓘ We usually catch a small fish called perch.

 **Go over each question on this page as a class.**

These questions test material that students learned in previous exercises. Have students answer these questions in a set amount of time. This will familiarize them with pacing themselves. Make it formal by announcing when students may begin and when they should "put their pencils down." Afterwards, ask them if they paced themselves well. If not, why?

**Question 1**

Identifying correct supporting details

**Question 2**

Determining the topic sentence

## Exercise 27
# USING A DICTIONARY

 **Go over the different parts of a dictionary listed on the Pupil Edition page with students.**

Hand out dictionaries to students. If you don't have enough for each student, have them share. Tell them to open their dictionaries to a particular page. Point out the guide words and entry words on the page, as well as the definitions, pronunciations, and pronunciation keys.

Ask a student to select another page and lead the class in finding these same parts. Repeat this with other students, until they are comfortable with the different parts of a dictionary.

### TEACHING TIP

Review alphabetical order with students. Understanding alphabetical order is an essential part of using a dictionary successfully.

 **Go over the example question as a class.**

---

# ON YOUR MARK!

## Using a Dictionary

A **dictionary** is a book that tells you what words mean. It also shows you how to spell and say the words.

**Guide words** appear at the top of every page. The first guide word is the first word on that page. The second guide word is the last word on that page.

**Entry words** are the words that are listed in the dictionary. They are listed in alphabetical order.

A **definition** is the meaning of a word.

A **pronunciation** \prō-nun-sē-'ā-shən\ shows you how to say an entry word. It breaks the word down syllable by syllable. The pronunciation is listed next to each entry word, as it is in the word *pronunciation*, above.

A **pronunciation key** helps you read the respelled pronunciations. In some dictionaries, the key appears at the bottom of every other page.

 GET SET!

Let's look at an example. Read the guide words taken from a page in a dictionary.

> lab—lag

**Find the word that could be found on the page.**

- (A) lace
- (B) lamp
- (C) laugh
- (D) knot

(A) is **correct!** In alphabetical order, *lace* belongs between *lab* and *lag*.

(B) is **wrong.** *Lamp* belongs on a page after this one.

(C) is **wrong.** *Laugh* belongs on a page after this one.

(D) is **wrong.** *Knot* belongs on a page before this one.

---

### EXTRA ACTIVITY

Create a worksheet that presents several tasks students must complete using a dictionary. Some examples you might use are:

- Find the word *lamp* in the dictionary. What are the guide words on that page?

- Write out the pronunciation for the word *important*.

- What is the definition of *cheerful*?

- Find the word *television* in the dictionary. List three entry words from that page.

Have students complete these tasks in a set amount of time. Remind them to stay calm and pace themselves.

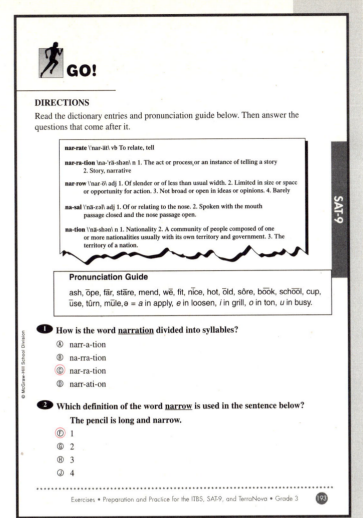

## GO!

**DIRECTIONS**

Read the dictionary entries and pronunciation guide below. Then answer the questions that come after it.

> **nar·rate** \'nar-āt\ vb To relate, tell
>
> **nar·ra·tion** \na-'rā-shən\ n 1. The act or process, or an instance of telling a story 2. Story, narrative
>
> **nar·row** \'nar-ō\ adj 1. Of slender or of less than usual width. 2. Limited in size or space or opportunity for action. 3. Not broad or open in ideas or opinions. 4. Barely
>
> **na·sal** \'nā-zəl\ adj 1. Of or relating to the nose. 2. Spoken with the mouth passage closed and the nose passage open.
>
> **na·tion** \'nā-shən\ n 1. Nationality 2. A community of people composed of one or more nationalities usually with its own territory and government. 3. The territory of a nation.

**Pronunciation Guide**

ash, ōpe, fär, stāre, mend, wē, fit, nīce, hot, ōld, sôre, bŏŏk, schōōl, cup, ūse, tûrn, mūle, ə = a in apply, e in loosen, i in grill, o in ton, u in busy.

**1** How is the word <u>narration</u> divided into syllables?

Ⓐ narr-a-tion

Ⓑ na-rra-tion

Ⓒ nar-ra-tion

Ⓓ narr-ati-on

**2** Which definition of the word <u>narrow</u> is used in the sentence below?

The pencil is long and narrow.

Ⓕ 1

Ⓖ 2

Ⓗ 3

Ⓙ 4

## Go over each question on this page as a class.

To answer these questions, students are presented with information sources: a series of dictionary entries and a pronunciation guide. Before answering these questions, students should only skim the information sources instead of reading them word for word. Once they reach the questions, they can refer back to the information sources as necessary.

After students answer questions 1 and 2, you might point out all the parts of the information sources that they did *not* use to answer the questions on this page. For example, they did not need the pronunciation guide to answer these questions correctly. However, for some questions on the SAT-9, these sections will be important. It is crucial that students understand how to use *all* the different parts of a dictionary.

## Exercise 28

# PLACES TO FIND INFORMATION

 **Go over the different information sources with students.**

If possible, show students real examples of a dictionary, thesaurus, atlas, encyclopedia, almanac, newspaper, and textbook. Pass them around the room. Answer any questions students have.

Ask students in which place they can find the answer to a series of questions. Some examples you might use are:

- Where can you find a map of Texas?

- Where can you find the correct spelling of *broom*?

- Where can you find a word that has a similar meaning to *happy*?

As students name the correct place to find the answer, hold up the source.

 **Go over the example question as a class.**

---

 **Exercise 28**

## ON YOUR MARK!

### Places to Find Information

A **dictionary** gives the meaning, spelling, and pronunciation of words.

A **thesaurus** helps you find words with similar meanings.

An **atlas** is a book of maps.

An **encyclopedia** is a set of books that tells you facts about people, places, and things.

An **almanac** gives general information using facts and numbers.

A **newspaper** tells about daily events.

A **textbook** gives information about subjects studied in school. You can use history books, language books, spelling books, and math books to find information when you need it.

 **GET SET!**

Let's look at an example.

**You can use an atlas to—**

Ⓕ    find out how to say the word *guess*

Ⓖ    find out where the Red Sea is

Ⓗ    learn about a boy who saved someone's life today

Ⓙ    find another word that means the same as *small*

(F) is **wrong.** You would use a dictionary to find this.

(G) is **correct!** An atlas has maps that can show you where the Red Sea is.

(H) is **wrong.** You would find this information in a newspaper.

(J) is **wrong.** You would find this information in a thesaurus.

---

 **EXTRA ACTIVITY**

Create a worksheet that lists the seven sources covered in this exercise: dictionary, thesaurus, atlas, encyclopedia, almanac, newspaper, and textbook. For each source, have students come up with three questions they could answer using that source. Their questions might be similar to the ones you asked in going over the sources.

As an extra assignment, break students into groups of two. Have them answer each other's questions by looking in the information sources.

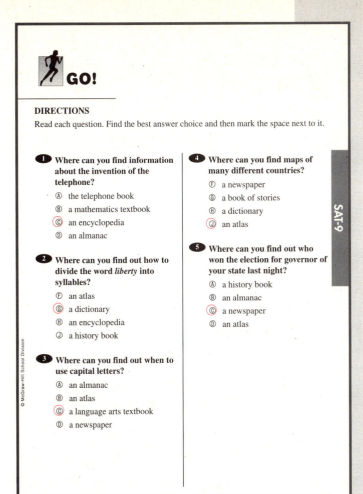

**Go over each question on this page as a class.**

## GO!

### DIRECTIONS

Read each question. Find the best answer choice and then mark the space next to it.

1. **Where can you find information about the invention of the telephone?**
   - Ⓐ the telephone book
   - Ⓑ a mathematics textbook
   - Ⓒ an encyclopedia
   - Ⓓ an almanac

2. **Where can you find out how to divide the word *liberty* into syllables?**
   - Ⓕ an atlas
   - Ⓖ a dictionary
   - Ⓗ an encyclopedia
   - Ⓙ a history book

3. **Where can you find out when to use capital letters?**
   - Ⓐ an almanac
   - Ⓑ an atlas
   - Ⓒ a language arts textbook
   - Ⓓ a newspaper

4. **Where can you find maps of many different countries?**
   - Ⓕ a newspaper
   - Ⓖ a book of stories
   - Ⓗ a dictionary
   - Ⓙ an atlas

5. **Where can you find out who won the election for governor of your state last night?**
   - Ⓐ a history book
   - Ⓑ an almanac
   - Ⓒ a newspaper
   - Ⓓ an atlas

SAT-9

Throughout the year, encourage students to familiarize themselves with different sources of information. You might create a section of the room, or even a table, that contains the different sources.

Bring in a newspaper from time to time. Read some headlines to the class to give them a sense of the kind of information they can find there.

© McGraw-Hill School Division

# HOW TO FIND INFORMATION INSIDE A BOOK

## Go over how to use an index.

Explain that an index appears in alphabetical order and that some subjects are arranged under general headings.

Using one of your class textbooks, show students how to use the index. Have them flip through it. Ask them some questions, such as:

- On what page can we find information about X?

- Does this textbook contain information about Y?

Questions on the SAT-9 will ask students to use their index knowledge to classify terms. Most questions will ask students to determine which word out of four doesn't belong with the other three. Make sure students understand these types of questions.

## Go over the example question as a class.

---

## ON YOUR MARK!

### How to Find Information Inside a Book

You just learned what kind of information is inside an encyclopedia, dictionary, almanac, textbook, newspaper, atlas, and almanac. Those are some big books! How do you know where to find the specific information you are looking for? Books like encyclopedias, almanacs, and textbooks are set up in a way that helps you find information inside them quickly.

An **index** usually appears at the back of a book. It is a list that is in alphabetical order. It tells you where to find all the important things in the book.

The exact words for the things you are looking for will not always be listed in the index. Sometimes they may be listed under a more general name or category. For example, if you are looking for information about Earth, you might find it listed under the topic heading *Planets*.

## GET SET!

Let's look at an example. Which of these is the category that the other words belong to?

- Ⓐ    snow
- Ⓑ    wind
- Ⓒ    rain
- Ⓓ    weather

(D) is **correct!** *Weather* is a general name or category for *snow*, *wind*, and *rain* because snow, wind, and rain are all types of weather.

---

### TEACHING TIP

To help students understand the difference between general and specific topic headings, try this in-class exercise.

Call out a series of *general* topic headings and have students come up with five subjects that fall under each. Some examples you might use are: *animals, flowers, American states, famous television stars,* and *vegetables.* Write their ideas on one side of the board. Then, call out a series of *specific* topic headings and have students come up with a general heading under which each might fall. Some examples you might use are: diamonds, rabbits, gloves, and Pluto. Write their ideas on the other side of the board. Ask students to compare the two lists. How are the topics on each list different?

# GO!

**DIRECTIONS**

Read each question. Select the best answer choice and mark the space next to it.

**1** Which of these is the category that the other three words belong to?

Ⓐ bee
Ⓑ fly
Ⓒ bug
Ⓓ moth

**2** Which of these is the category that the other three words belong to?

Ⓕ necklace
Ⓖ jewelry
Ⓗ ring
Ⓙ bracelet

**3** Which of these is the category that the other three words belong to?

Ⓐ water
Ⓑ drink
Ⓒ soda
Ⓓ juice

**4** Which of these is the category that the other three words belong to?

Ⓕ goat
Ⓖ giraffe
Ⓗ animal
Ⓙ nonkey

**5** Which of these is the category that the other three words belong to?

Ⓐ finger
Ⓑ hand
Ⓒ palm
Ⓓ thumb

 **Go over each question on this page as a class.**

Show students how specific and general topics function in a real index. Using one of your class' textbooks, ask students to look up a specific topic in the index—one you know will *not* be there. Once they discover it is not there, ask them to come up with a more general topic, one that would include the missing topic. Try that and see what happens. Repeat this with other specific topics that you know are missing.

## Exercise 30

# BE SURE TO READ ALL OF THE ANSWER CHOICES

 **Go over the importance of reading all of the answer choices when taking the SAT-9.**

Discuss the tip box on the Pupil Edition page.

Remind students that ruling out wrong answer choices is a valuable test-taking strategy. If they do not know the answer but can rule out two answer choices, they still have a fifty-fifty chance of answering the question correctly.

Ask students if, in answering questions for the previous exercises, they ruled out wrong answer choices. Has that strategy been helpful?

 **Go over the example question as a class.**

---

Exercise 30

## ON YOUR MARK!

### Be Sure to Read All of the Answer Choices

Sometimes when you read a question, you might think the first answer choice you read is correct. It may be correct, but always read all of the answer choices before you decide. If you mark the first answer choice you think is correct, you might miss a better one that comes later.

> **TIP:** Always get rid of the wrong answer choices first. Put a finger over the wrong answer choices as you rule out each one. It will help you remember to read all of the choices before you mark your answer.

 **GET SET!**

The tips above will help you feel at ease when answering questions like this one and those on the next page on the day of the real test. Look at this example. Read the guide words taken from a page in a dictionary.

> dragon—drama

**Find the word that could be found on the page.**

Ⓐ   drastic
Ⓑ   drab
Ⓒ   drain
Ⓓ   drape

(A) is **wrong.** *Drastic* belongs on a page after this one.

(B) is **wrong.** *Drab* belongs on a page before this one.

(C) is **correct!** *Drain* would come between *dragon* and *drama*.

(D) is **wrong.** *Drape* belongs on a page after this one.

---

 ## TEACHING TIP

On the board, write a multiple-choice question to which students will *not* know the answer. In addition to the correct answer, provide three incorrect answer choices that can be easily discounted. Make sure students read every answer choice. Show students how ruling out wrong answer choices can lead to the correct answer—even on extremely difficult questions. Point out that students would not have been able to rule out the wrong choices if they had not read every answer choice.

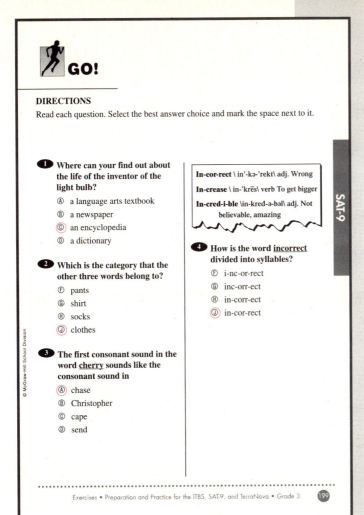

## GO!

**DIRECTIONS**

Read each question. Select the best answer choice and mark the space next to it.

**1** Where can your find out about the life of the inventor of the light bulb?

- Ⓐ a language arts textbook
- Ⓑ a newspaper
- Ⓒ an encyclopedia
- Ⓓ a dictionary

**2** Which is the category that the other three words belong to?

- Ⓕ pants
- Ⓖ shirt
- Ⓗ socks
- Ⓙ clothes

**3** The first consonant sound in the word <u>cherry</u> sounds like the consonant sound in

- Ⓐ chase
- Ⓑ Christopher
- Ⓒ cape
- Ⓓ send

In-cor-rect \ in'-kə-'rekt\ adj. Wrong

In-crease \ in-'krēs\ verb To get bigger

In-cred-i-ble \in-kred-ə-bəl\ adj. Not believable, amazing

**SAT-9**

**4** How is the word <u>incorrect</u> divided into syllables?

- Ⓕ i-nc-or-rect
- Ⓖ inc-orr-ect
- Ⓗ in-corr-ect
- Ⓙ in-cor-rect

© McGraw-Hill School Division

These questions test students on material they learned in previous exercises. Remind them to read *all* of the answer choices before answering the questions and to rule out wrong choices first.

**Question 1**

Places to find information

**Question 2**

Specific *vs.* general topics—indexes

**Question 3**

Tricky spellings

**Question 4**

Using a dictionary

© McGraw-Hill School Division

# Practice Test

## Spelling

**DIRECTIONS**

Look carefully at each group of sentences below. If an underlined word is spelled wrong, fill in the letter next to that sentence. If no underlined word is spelled wrong, fill in the letter next to the words *No Mistake*.

**SAMPLE**

(A) Please finish washing the flor.

(B) Terry won the award.

(C) We cheer for our team.

(D) No mistake

**1** (A) Ben can ern ten dollars shoveling snow.

(B) Whales and dolphins are mammals.

(C) Each day I practice the piano.

(D) No mistake

earn

**2** (F) That movie was too scary.

(G) The clowns in the circus were funny.

(H) The logs burnd in the fireplace.

(J) No mistake

Must add -ed

**3** (A) The robin observed me from its nest.

(B) My muther is very kind.

(C) We were taught to be polite.

(D) No mistake

mother

**4** (F) Mom sketched a picture of our house.

(G) Jan fell asleep very quickley.

(H) Dad likes pancakes for breakfast.

(J) No mistake

quickly

**5** (A) Did you make this sweater?

(B) I like honey on my bread.

(C) Chris has a baby turtle.

(D) No mistake

**6** (F) The cow ate grass in the meadow.

(G) Rosa puts sugar on her oatmeal.

(H) I like to do worsheetes.

(J) No mistake

worksheets

**7** (A) My napsack is all packed.

(B) Spread the sheet over the bed.

(C) There are many families in our building.

(D) No mistake

Silent /k/ is missing.

**8** (F) Thunder is rumbleing in the sky.

(G) Dad had to straighten my tie.

(H) Perhaps it will rain today.

(J) No mistake

To add *-ing* to a word that ends in *e*, drop the *e*.

**9**
(A) There is a full <u>moon</u> tonight.
(B) A dollar is one <u>hundred</u> cents.
(C) Help Beth <u>search</u> for her ring.
(D) No mistake

**10**
(F) <u>Hurry</u>, or we will be late.
(G) Do you <u>stil</u> take piano lessons?
(H) The <u>petals</u> on this rose are opening.
(J) No mistake

still

**11**
(A) Bullies make me <u>angry</u>.
(B) Turkey is her <u>favorite</u> food.
(C) <u>Onbutton</u> your coat and hang it up.
(D) No mistake

Unbutton

**12**
(F) Mr. Nason <u>ledes</u> our band.
(G) Please play that song <u>again</u>.
(H) The one in the <u>middle</u> is Jeff.
(J) No mistake

Words with two-letter sounds: *leads—heat, beat, sea*

**13**
(A) I am <u>proud</u> to be an American.
(B) <u>Cactus</u> plants need very little water.
(C) A <u>mountin</u> is taller than a hill.
(D) No mistake

mountain

**14**
(F) I <u>cought</u> a lot when I was sick.
(G) His belt is made of <u>leather</u>.
(H) Michael Jordan is a <u>famous</u> person.
(J) No mistake

coughed

**15**
(A) The balloon <u>burst</u> with a pop.
(B) <u>Cherries</u> come in different colors.
(C) Jack likes <u>shoping</u> for toys.
(D) No mistake

Double the *p* when adding *-ing*.

**16**
(F) The ring is too small for my <u>thumb</u>.
(G) This painter uses <u>vivid</u> colors.
(H) Cherry <u>blossoms</u> are beautiful.
(J) No mistake

**17**
(A) Do you want to <u>descuss</u> the trip?
(B) Dave <u>bought</u> a new basketball.
(C) I like to <u>wear</u> hats.
(D) No mistake

discuss

**18**
(F) She has six dimes in her <u>purs</u>.
(G) George Washington is my <u>hero</u>.
(H) The cat has black and white <u>paws</u>.
(J) No mistake

Silent /e/ is missing.

**19**
(A) She has never been to this <u>plase</u>.
(B) <u>Salty</u> snacks make me thirsty.
(C) That was a <u>careless</u> mistake.
(D) No mistake

place

**20**
(F) <u>Running</u> makes me <u>thirsty</u>.
(G) Kittens are very <u>playful</u>.
(H) Football can be a <u>rouf</u> game.
(J) No mistake

*Gh* makes the /f/ sound in *rough*.

**21**

Ⓐ Our class went to the art <u>museum</u>.

Ⓑ Orange <u>juice</u> is good for you.

Ⓒ She likes butter <u>cookies</u>.

Ⓓ No mistake

**22**

Ⓕ Josh says <u>fried</u> eggs are the best.

Ⓖ Rebecca was <u>thankful</u> for the gift.

Ⓗ Farmers produce <u>cheeze</u> from milk.

Ⓙ No mistake

cheese

**23**

Ⓐ I helped to <u>paint</u> the house.

Ⓑ The baby crawls on her hands and <u>knees</u>.

Ⓒ We have <u>eight</u> people in our club.

Ⓓ No mistake

**24**

Ⓕ The horse ate the whole <u>apple</u>.

Ⓖ The water in the pool was <u>warm</u>.

Ⓗ I <u>migt</u> try out for the team.

Ⓙ No mistake

Silent /h/ is missing.

**25**

Ⓐ Bread is made from <u>weat</u>.

Ⓑ Take the cake out of the <u>oven</u>.

Ⓒ It is a <u>pleasure</u> to meet you.

Ⓓ No mistake

Silent /h/ is missing.

**26**

Ⓕ Carl <u>studied</u> for the spelling test.

Ⓖ He always eats lunch at <u>noon</u>.

Ⓗ The doctor says I am <u>helthy</u>.

Ⓙ No mistake

healthy

**27**

Ⓐ Be sure to <u>fassen</u> your jacket buttons.

Ⓑ We <u>search</u> for shells on the beach.

Ⓒ Lisa was born in <u>March</u>.

Ⓓ No mistake

Silent /t/ is missing.

**28**

Ⓕ Jack took the telephone <u>message</u>.

Ⓖ Who is the <u>author</u> of *Black Beauty?*

Ⓗ We have <u>choares</u> to do each week.

Ⓙ No mistake

chores

**29**

Ⓐ Peach pie is my <u>favorite</u>.

Ⓑ Fran <u>craked</u> the walnut shell.

Ⓒ You ate a large <u>amount</u> of grapes.

Ⓓ No mistake

cracked

**30**

Ⓕ That <u>word</u> is easy to spell.

Ⓖ Bob is learning to <u>whisle</u>.

Ⓗ A <u>square</u> has four sides.

Ⓙ No mistake

Silent /t/ is missing.

SAT-9

GO ON

**DIRECTIONS**

Pay careful attention to the underlined words in each sentence. They might show a mistake in punctuation, capitalization, or word usage. If there are mistakes, pick the answer choice that corrects them. If you cannot find a mistake, pick the last answer choice.

**SAMPLE A**

My mother was <u>borned in March</u>.

Ⓐ born in March

Ⓑ born on march

Ⓒ borns in march

Ⓓ Correct as is

**SAMPLE B**

My cousin Frank lives in <u>Saint Louis</u>.

Ⓕ Saint louis

Ⓖ saint louis

Ⓗ saint Louis

Ⓙ Correct as is

**1** Ben Franklin <u>said, "a penny saved is a penny earned."</u>

Ⓐ says "a

Ⓑ said, "A

Ⓒ said, A

Ⓓ Correct as is

> The first letter inside a quotation is always capitalized.

**2** The sheriff jumped on his horse and <u>chased after the thief?</u>

Ⓕ chase after the thief?

Ⓖ chases after the thief.

Ⓗ chased after the thief.

Ⓙ Correct as is

> Statement

**3** When the <u>sun set</u>, we will come in for supper.

Ⓐ sun have set

Ⓑ sun sets

Ⓒ sun are setting

Ⓓ Correct as is

> Subject-verb agreement

**4** They <u>said this here</u> pencil is the best.

Ⓕ said this

Ⓖ saying this here

Ⓗ says this

Ⓙ Correct as is

**5** We <u>saw Prime Minister Blair</u> on television last week.

Ⓐ seen prime minister Blair

Ⓑ see Prime Minister Blair

Ⓒ seeing prime minister Blair

Ⓓ Correct as is

> Titles—when they come before a person's name—are always capitalized.

**6** <u>Mr. Johnsons'</u> pets have the best life!

Ⓕ Mr. Johnsons

Ⓖ Mr. Johnson's

Ⓗ Mr. Johnsons's

Ⓙ Correct as is

*Mr. Johnson's is a singular, possessive noun.*

**7** Which is the best way to write the beginning of this letter?

<u>Dear mayor Foster,</u>

Ⓐ dear Mayor Foster,

Ⓑ Dear Mayor Foster,

Ⓒ dear mayor Foster

Ⓓ Correct as is

**8** <u>Have'nt you ever</u> seen a lion?

Ⓕ Havent' you ever

Ⓖ Havent you ever

Ⓗ Haven't you ever

Ⓙ Correct as is

*Apostrophes show where one or more letters are missing.*

**9** Jim <u>runned</u> in the first race.

Ⓐ ran

Ⓑ running

Ⓒ run

Ⓓ Correct as is

**10** I <u>packed my baseball my glove and two books,</u> for the trip.

Ⓕ packing my baseball, my glove and two books

Ⓖ packed my baseball, my glove, and two books

Ⓗ packed my baseball, my glove, and, two book

Ⓙ Correct as is

**11** Taylor <u>is the bestest speller</u> in the class.

Ⓐ is the goodest speller

Ⓑ is the best speller

Ⓒ is the most good

Ⓓ Correct as is

*Best: irregular superlative adjective*

**12** Will has seen the <u>movie *star wars*</u> six times!

Ⓕ Movie *Star Wars*

Ⓖ movie *Star Wars*

Ⓗ Movie *star wars*

Ⓙ Correct as is

*Important words in titles of a film are always capitalized.*

**13** Manuel <u>and me thought we'd</u> do well on the test.

Ⓐ and I thought wed'

Ⓑ and I thought we'd

Ⓒ and me thinks we'd

Ⓓ Correct as is

*If there is more than one subject, I always comes last.*

© McGraw-Hill School Division

SAT-9

**14** When I finished painting the wall, my brother Timmy <u>said, good job!"</u>

   Ⓕ said good job!

   Ⓖ said, "Good job!"

   Ⓗ said", good job!

   Ⓙ Correct as is

> First word in quotation is capitalized.

**15** For <u>breakfast we often have</u> hot or cold cereal.

   Ⓐ breakfast we often could of had

   Ⓑ breakfast we often have has

   Ⓒ breakfast we often has

   Ⓓ Correct as is

**16** I don't really like <u>string beans?</u>

   Ⓕ string beans.

   Ⓖ String beans.

   Ⓗ string Beans!

   Ⓙ Correct as is

> Use a period to end a statement.

**17** Every Saturday, Blair <u>listened to music</u> after she does her chores.

   Ⓐ listen to music

   Ⓑ listens to music

   Ⓒ listening to music

   Ⓓ Correct as is

**18** We visited <u>the Grand Canyon.</u>

   Ⓕ the grand canyon

   Ⓖ The Grand Canyon

   Ⓗ the Grand canyon

   Ⓙ Correct as is

> Always capitalize names of specific places.

## DIRECTIONS

Read the words that are boxed. You may find an error in sentence structure. If you do, pick the answer choice that is clearest and correct. If you find no errors, choose "Correct as is."

### SAMPLE A

**Dad drove the car. To the mall.**

   Ⓐ Dad drove the car he drove it to the mall.

   Ⓑ Dad driving the car to the mall.

   Ⓒ Dad drove the car to the mall.

   Ⓓ Correct as is

### SAMPLE B

**Paul changed his clothes to get cooler.**

   Ⓕ Paul changed his clothes, he got cooler.

   Ⓖ Paul changing his clothes to get cooler.

   Ⓗ Paul changing his clothes he got cooler.

   Ⓙ Correct as is

**19** My cousin Christian is planning. To be a doctor.

   Ⓐ My cousin Christian is planning to be a doctor.

   Ⓑ My cousin Christian, planning to be a doctor.

   Ⓒ My cousin Christian. He is planning to be a doctor.

   Ⓓ Correct as is

> Every sentence should have a subject and a verb.

© McGraw-Hill School Division

**20** **This week my neighbors want to go camping.**

F My neighbors, this week, want to go camping.

G They want to go camping this week, my neighbors.

H Camping this week my neighbors want to go.

J Correct as is

**21** **Max decided to make breakfast for his mom and dad.**

A To make breakfast for his mom and dad is what Max decided to do.

B For his mom and dad Max decided to make breakfast.

C Max, he decided to make breakfast for his mom and dad.

D Correct as is

**22** **The dog ate his food quickly, he drank his water.**

F The dog ate his food quickly, and he drank his water.

G The dog ate his food quickly. And drank his water.

H The dog eating his food quickly and drinking his water.

J Correct as is

For questions 22, 23, and 25, remind students that conjunctions can fix run-on sentences.

**23** **She pitched the ball the batter missed it.**

A She pitched the ball, and the batter missed it.

B She pitched the ball, the batter missed it.

C She pitched the ball. The batter missing it.

D Correct as is

**24** **Ten people in my class. They like to play checkers.**

F Ten people in my class liking to play checkers.

G There are ten people in my class, they like to play checkers.

H Ten people in my class like to play checkers.

J Correct as is

**25** **Victor would not eat the peach, it was not ripe.**

A Victor would not eat the peach it was not ripe.

B Victor not eating the peach because it was not ripe.

C Victor would not eat the peach because it was not ripe.

D Correct as is

SAT-9

**26** **My horse passed all the others. And won the race.**

- Ⓕ My horse passing all the others and won the race.
- Ⓖ My horse passed all the others, it won the race.
- Ⓗ My horse passed all the others and won the race.
- Ⓙ Correct as is

**27** **Jack put on his bathing suit and walked to the beach.**

- Ⓐ Jack put on his bathing suit walked to the beach.
- Ⓑ Jack put on his bathing suit. And walking to the beach is what he did.
- Ⓒ Jack put on his bathing suit, walked to the beach.
- Ⓓ Correct as is

**28** **I fell asleep and dreamed about summer vacation.**

- Ⓕ I falling asleep sleep and dreamed about summer vacation.
- Ⓖ I fell asleep I dreamed about summer vacation.
- Ⓗ I fell asleep and dreamed. About summer vacation.
- Ⓙ Correct as is

Remind students to check each sentence for a subject and a verb. In question 26, there is no subject in *And won the race.* It is a fragment.

# DIRECTIONS

Read each short paragraph. Then read the questions that come after each paragraph.

**SAMPLE**

Last week our class went to the art museum. We saw art from Egypt, Greece, and Rome that was created 3,000 years ago. We saw beautiful paintings that were made 400 years ago in Italy. We also saw strange-looking metal statues that were made just last year. I wonder what kind of art there will be 400 years from now.

**Which sentence would go best after the last sentence in this paragraph?**

- Ⓐ We ate lunch in the museum cafeteria.
- Ⓑ Some of the paintings from Italy were very large.
- Ⓒ I can't even imagine what art will look like then.
- Ⓓ I liked the art from Greece the best.

Students should try using each sentence at the end of the paragraph to decide which is best.

## Paragraph 1

Blue whales are most likely the biggest animals that ever lived. They can grow to be 100 feet long! The adult blue whale's favorite food is krill, which is one of the smallest animals in the world. They eat as much as 4,000 pounds of it a day! Baby blue whales like to drink milk. They don't like to eat krill.

**29** **Which is the best combination of the last two sentences?**

Ⓐ Baby blue whales like drinking milk, and they don't like to eat krill.

Ⓑ Baby blue whales like drinking milk, not eating krill.

Ⓒ Krill drinks milk for the baby blue whales who do not.

Ⓓ Drinking milk is for baby blue whales, not krill.

**30** **Which sentence would not belong in this paragraph?**

Ⓕ Blue whales are even bigger than dinosaurs were.

Ⓖ Just the heart of a blue whale weighs about 1,000 pounds.

Ⓗ Blue whales also eat tiny plants called plankton.

Ⓙ Blue whales can dive for up to one hour.

## Paragraph 2

Camp Sunburst is for boys and girls ages eight through fourteen. Campers play many sports, including baseball, softball, basketball, volleyball, and tennis. Camp Sunburst has many other interesting activities for campers. Some of these are swimming, hiking, arts and crafts, putting on plays, and woodworking. We also offer computer classes. We offer classes in how to use a video camera.

**31** **Which would be the best topic sentence for the paragraph?**

Ⓐ Camp Sunburst is not for adults.

Ⓑ Camp Sunburst is a great summer camp for your children.

Ⓒ We play lots of games at Camp Sunburst.

Ⓓ Camp Sunburst is not far from where you live.

**32** **Which sentence would not belong in this paragraph?**

Ⓕ Camp Sunburst is located in Raymond, Maine.

Ⓖ Campers can attend for two, four, six, or eight weeks.

Ⓗ There are hundreds of summer camps in Maine.

Ⓙ Every summer, older campers take a trip to climb Mount Washington.

GO ON

SAT-9

© McGraw-Hill School Division

**33** **Which answer choice is the best combination of the last two sentences?**

Ⓐ We also offer computer classes, we offer classes in how to use a video camera.

Ⓑ We also offer computer classes and classes in how to use a video camera.

Ⓒ We also offer computer classes, but we offer classes in how to use a video camera.

Ⓓ Computer classes we also offer and classes in how to use a video camera.

When two short sentences have the same subject, the subject does not need to be repeated.

## Paragraph 3

When oil taken from the ground is heated, it separates into different liquids. One of those liquids is the gasoline that makes cars run. Surprisingly, oil is also used to make the roads that cars drive on! And that's not all. Scientists use oil to make plastic, paint, and clothes.

**34** **This paragraph was most likely written for whom?**

Ⓕ Scientists

Ⓖ Students

Ⓗ Experts on oil

Ⓙ People who use after-shave

Ask students how they can determine audience. What clues in the paragraph suggest that it was written for students? What clues rule out the incorrect answer choices?

**35** **Which would be the best topic sentence for the paragraph?**

Ⓐ Peanut oil is often used for cooking

Ⓑ Oil isn't very important for people

Ⓒ Oil has made life better and easier for people.

Ⓓ Oil has made many people rich.

The topic sentence should include the main idea.

© McGraw-Hill School Division

## Paragraph 4

Dear Monica,

We just moved here, but I already miss you and my other friends in Rockland. Everything here is so different. Most people in Elyria have never even seen the ocean! Mom says there are lots of nice things about Elyria. I'm not sure.

Your friend,

Penny

**36** **Which sentence would be best to add after "I'm not sure"?**

Ⓕ Nobody here has ever swum in the ocean.

Ⓖ Right now it's hard to believe.

Ⓗ Remember when we went sailing together?

Ⓙ We just moved to Elyria.

**37** **Why did Penny write this letter?**

Ⓐ To tell her friend that she moved to a new town

Ⓑ To tell how much she misses her old home and friends

Ⓒ To tell how much she likes her new town

Ⓓ To tell Monica that she has moved to Rockland

Ask students how they can determine an author's main purpose. What clues in the paragraph suggest that Penny wrote this letter to tell how much she misses her old home and friends? What clues rule out the incorrect answer choices?

**38** **What is the best way to combine the last two sentences?**

Ⓕ Mom says there are lots of nice things about Elyria I'm not sure.

Ⓖ There are lots of nice things about Elyria mom says and I'm not sure.

Ⓗ Lots of nice things there are about Elyria mom says, I'm not sure.

Ⓙ Mom says there are lots of nice things about Elyria, but I'm not sure.

SAT-9

# DIRECTIONS

Read each question. Select the best answer choice and mark the space next to it.

## SAMPLE

These are guide words from a page in the dictionary.

| walnut—war |
| --- |

Which of these words could be found on that page?

- Ⓐ wave
- Ⓑ water
- Ⓒ want
- Ⓓ wait

**39** The guide words below are from a page in the dictionary.

| bird—bold |
| --- |

Which of these words could be found on that page?

- Ⓐ biggest
- Ⓑ board
- Ⓒ bright
- Ⓓ burn

For questions 39 and 40, remind students that the correct answer choices are *entry words*. Entry words are the words that are listed in the dictionary.

For questions 41 and 42, remind students that distinguishing between specific and general topic headings is important in using an index.

**40** Read the dictionary guide words below.

| rest—robe |
| --- |

Which of these words could be found on that page?

- Ⓕ return
- Ⓖ rattle
- Ⓗ remember
- Ⓙ rotate

**41** Find the word that is the main heading for the other three words.

- Ⓐ pants
- Ⓑ suit
- Ⓒ clothes
- Ⓓ tie

**42** Which word is the category that the other three words belong to?

- Ⓕ rain
- Ⓖ storm
- Ⓗ snow
- Ⓙ weather

© McGraw-Hill School Division

**43** Where can you find out if your favorite golfer won a game yesterday?

Ⓐ a newspaper

Ⓑ an almanac

Ⓒ a history book

Ⓓ an encyclopedia

The word *yesterday* is important.

**44** Where can you find out how to use quotation marks?

Ⓕ an encyclopedia

Ⓖ a language arts textbook

Ⓗ a newspaper

Ⓙ an almanac

**45** Where can you find information about American Indians?

Ⓐ an atlas

Ⓑ a newspaper

Ⓒ an encyclopedia

Ⓓ a dictionary

SAT-9

**false** [fôls] adj. 1. Not real 2. Wrong 3. Not true

**fam-i-ly** [fam-ə-lē] n. 1. A group composed of one or two parents and their children 2. A group of plants or animals that are related to one another

**fa-mous** [fā-məs] adj. 1. Very well-known 2. Deserving to be remembered

**fan** [fan] n. 1. A device that is often in the shape of a section of a circle and is waved back and forth by hand to cool the air 2. A machine with a set of rotating blades driven by a motor which is used to cool the air 3. Something shaped like a hand fan 4. An enthusiastic follower or admirer

**fang** [fəng] n. 1. one of the long sharp teeth used by animals to grab, hold, and tear apart their prey 2. One of the long hollow or grooved teeth of a poisonous snake

**fan-tas-tic** [fan-tas-tik] dj. 1. created by the imagination or like something created by the imagination 2. hardly believable

**Pronunciation Guide**

ash, āpe, fär, stâre, mend, wē, fit, nīce, hot, ōld, sôre, bōok, schōōl, cup, ūse tûrn, müle, ə = *a* in able, *e* in loosen, *i* in grill, *o* in ton, *u* in busy.

---

**46** How is the word <u>fantastic</u> correctly divided into syllables?

- Ⓕ fan-tast-ic
- Ⓖ fa-ntas-tic
- Ⓗ fan-tas-tic  *(circled)*
- Ⓙ fan-ta-stic

**47** Which definition of the word <u>fan</u> is used in the sentence below?

**Marina is a fan of funny movies.**

- Ⓐ 1
- Ⓑ 2
- Ⓒ 3
- Ⓓ 4  *(circled)*

*Students can replace the word fan in the sentence with each of the four definitions. Marina is an enthusiastic follower of funny movies is the only answer that makes sense.*

**48** The first vowel sound in <u>famous</u> sounds most like the vowel sound in—

- Ⓕ about
- Ⓖ ape  *(circled)*
- Ⓗ ash
- Ⓙ far

*Students should use the pronunciation guide to answer this question.*

# On Your Mark, Get Set, Go! Review

## Spelling: Words With Silent Letters

The words below have silent letters in them. The underlined letters don't make a sound when you say the word.

lam**b** \lām\        store \stōr\

**k**not \nôt\        **gh**ost \gōst\

> **TIP:** When you have to spell tricky words, try changing the way you normally say them to yourself. Sound out *every* letter in your head—even the silent ones. For example, say **/kuh not/** to remind yourself that *knot* is spelled with a *k*.

## Spelling: Words With Two-Letter Sounds

Certain letters sound different when they are next to each other than when they are apart. For example, the *ch* sound in *choice* sounds different than the *c* sound in *cape* or the *h* sound in *Henry*.

**Consonant Sounds**

ro**ck**    **sh**ame    **wh**en    bad**ly**    **th**ere

**Vowel Sounds**

c**ou**ch    t**ou**r    b**oo**k    sp**oo**l    d**oe**s

> **TIP:** Think of a word you know, such as a rhyming word, that has the same spelling pattern as the word you want to spell. *(heat, meat, treat)*

## Spelling: Rules for Sounds

- When the *s* sound is spelled with *c*, it is always followed by *e*, *i*, or *y*.

  ra**ce**    fan**cy**    ex**ci**te

- When the *j* sound is spelled with *g*, it is always followed by *e*, *i*, or *y*.

  **ge**rbil    fra**gi**le    **gy**psy

- Long vowels are always followed by *ge*. Short vowels are always followed by *dge*.

  pa**ge**    ju**dge**

SAT-9

© McGraw-Hill School Division

# REVIEW

## Spelling

**The spelling skills on this page were originally covered in the On Your Mark! Get Set! Go! section. Refer to the following exercises as necessary:**

- Exercise 1      p. 140
- Exercise 2      p. 142
- Exercise 3      p. 144
- Exercise 5      p. 148

## EXTRA ACTIVITY

By now, students have probably realized that there are certain words they always seem to spell incorrectly. Have each student make a list of the "Top Five Suspects." Collect each student's list, and read the difficult words on each of their lists. After you have read the word, have the students write it down on a sheet of paper. When you have read all the words, write each word on the board, spelled correctly, and find the number of students who spelled it incorrectly. Write that number next to the word. At the end, the words that were misspelled by the most students are the "Main Suspects." For especially tricky words, try to come up with a good trick for remembering how to spell them.

© McGraw-Hill School Division

# REVIEW

## Spelling and Capitalization

The spelling and capitalization skills on this page were originally covered in the On Your Mark! Get Set! Go! section. Refer to the following exercises as necessary:

### SPELLING

- Exercise 4        p. 146

### CAPITALIZATON

- Exercise 7        p. 152
- Exercise 8        p. 154
- Exercise 15       p. 168

---

### Rules for Adding Endings to Words

**Adding -s**
- Normally, you just add the -s. (car ⟶ cars)
- Words ending in x, z, s, sh, or ch add -es. (box ⟶ boxes)
- Words ending in y drop the y and add -ies. (fry ⟶ fries)

**Adding -ed**
- Normally, you just add -ed. (dust ⟶ dusted)
- Words ending in y drop the y and add -ied. (hurry ⟶ hurried)
- Sometimes you double the consonant at the end. (skip ⟶ skipped)

**Adding -ing**
- Normally, you just add -ing. (stomp ⟶ stomping)
- If the word ends in e drop the e and add -ing. (glide ⟶ gliding)
- Sometimes you double the consonant at the end. (pin ⟶ pinning)

### Capitalization

**Always Capitalize:**
- The first word in a sentence
  *Exercise is good for you.*
- Proper nouns such as names of people
  *James Brown*
- Proper nouns that are names of places
  *Bryant Street, Bear Mountain, Mississippi River*
- The first letter of a quotation within a sentence
  *Valerie asked, "May I be excused?"*
- Titles when they come before a person's name
  *President Lincoln, Queen Anne, Aunt Carol, Mrs. Brown*
- The pronoun *I*
  *Susan and I went home.*
- The title of a book, song, newspaper, or article
  *I am reading* The Daily News.
- The first word of a letter greeting or closing
  *Dear Sirs,        Yours truly,*

---

## TEACHING TIP

For further review on adding suffixes, make a list of ten words and hand it out to students. Have them make as many new words for each word as possible by adding suffixes. The student who makes the most new words by correctly adding suffixes wins a gold star.

## Punctuation

**Use periods to end a statement.**
*Mustapha plays the trumpet.*

**Use periods at the end of an abbreviation.**
*I live next to Mrs. Matthews.*

**Use question marks to end a question.**
*Do you like cheese?*

**Use exclamation marks to end a statement of excitement.**
*Look out for that car!*

**Use commas between items in a series.**
*I have to clean the bathroom, garage, and my bedroom.*

**Use commas between a day and a year.**
*I was born on March 19th, 1992.*

**Use commas between a city and its state.**
*My uncle lives in Miami, Florida.*

**Use commas after the opening or closing of a letter.**
*Dear Sara,      Sincerely,*

## Quotations

**Quotation marks** show that someone is speaking. They come before and after a person's exact words.

*"These cookies are great!" shouted Claire.*

**Remember these important rules about writing quotations:**

- Quotation marks come at the beginning and end of a person's exact words.
- The first letter inside a quotation is *always* capitalized.

SAT-9

# Punctuation and Quotations

The punctuation and quotation skills on this page were originally covered in the On Your Mark! Get Set! Go! section. Refer to the following exercises as necessary:

## PUNCTUATION

- Exercise 16      p. 170

## QUOTATIONS

- Exercise 8      p. 154

## TEACHING TIP

For extra practice with punctuation, give students a short story and leave out all of the punctuation. For extra credit, students should insert the missing punctuation marks. Make sure you include quotations in the story.

# REVIEW

## Contractions and Pronouns

The contraction and pronoun skills on this page were originally covered in the On Your Mark! Get Set! Go! section. Refer to the following exercises as necessary:

### CONTRACTIONS

- Exercise 9     p. 156

### PRONOUNS

- Exercise 14     p. 166

---

### Contractions

A **contraction** is a shortened form of two words:

*did not* ⟶ *didn't*

An **apostrophe (')** in a contraction shows where one or more letters have been left out.

*is not* ⟶ *isn't*     *have not* ⟶ *haven't*

### Pronouns

A **pronoun** is a word that takes the place of one or more nouns. It must match the noun or nouns that it replaces.

A **singular pronoun** replaces a singular noun.

**Carrie** *is smart.* ⟶ **She** *is smart.*

A **plural pronoun** replaces a plural noun or more than one noun.

**The dogs** *are barking.* ⟶ **They** *are barking.*

Use the pronouns *I* and *me* to write about yourself. Use *I* in the subject of a sentence. If there is more than one subject, *I* always comes last.

*She and **I** walked home.*

Use *me* after an action verb and words such as *in, into, to, with, by,* or *at.* If there is more than one object, *me* always comes last.

*Kyle teases Jenny and **me**.*

| Subject Pronouns | Object Pronouns |
|---|---|
| I, you, he, she, it, we, they | me, you, him, her, it, us, them |

---

## EXTRA ACTIVITY

For extra practice with contractions, have students get into groups of three or four. Hand each group a list of ten contractions that do not include the apostrophe. Start a stopwatch and give students a set amount of time to insert the apostrophes in the correct places and write down the two words from which the contraction comes.

## Possessive Nouns

A **possessive noun** is a word that shows who or what owns something.

Change a singular noun to a possessive noun by adding an apostrophe and an *s*.

> **Kelly's** book report is upstairs.

Change a plural noun that ends in *s* to a possessive noun by adding an apostrophe to the end of the word.

> The **dogs'** toys are lost.

Change a plural noun that does not end in *s* to a possessive noun by adding an apostrophe and an *s* at the end of the word.

> The **children's** party was over.

## Adjectives that Compare

**Adjectives** are words that are used to describe nouns. *Buddy is* **tall**.

A **comparative adjective** compares two nouns. For small words, just add *-er* to the adjective. *Buddy is* **taller** *than Christopher.*

A **superlative adjective** compares more than two nouns. For small words, just add *-est* to the adjective. *Buddy is the* **tallest** *person in his class.*

Some adjectives that compare do not follow the usual pattern.

> *bad*  *worse* → *worst*

## Verbs

An **action verb** is a word that shows action.

*The rocket* **shoots** *up to the moon.*

A verb must agree with its subject.

> *I* **jump**     *She* **jumps**     *They* **jump**

SAT-9

# REVIEW

## Possessive Nouns, Comparative Adjectives, and Verbs

The skills on this page were originally covered in the On Your Mark! Get Set! Go! section. Refer to the following exercises as necessary:

### POSSESSIVE NOUNS

- Exercise 10     p. 158

### COMPARATIVE ADJECTIVES

- Exercise 11     p. 160

### VERBS

- Exercise 12     p. 162

## EXTRA ACTIVITY

To practice using comparative adjectives, have students think of two people that they know well. It could be their parents, their siblings, their friends, or their relatives. Have students write a short paragraph comparing the two people. Check their paragraphs for correct use of comparative and superlative adjectives.

# REVIEW

## Verb Tenses, Fragments, Run-Ons, Conjunctions, and Compound Sentences

The skills on this page were originally covered in the On Your Mark! Get Set! Go! section. Refer to the following exercises as necessary:

---

## Verb Tenses

**Verb tenses** tell when the action takes place in a sentence. In most cases, **all verb tenses must match within a sentence.**

> The girl **jumped** over the puddle, so she **stayed** dry.

**Past tense** means something already happened.

> The girl **jumped** over the puddle.

To form the past tense for most **regular action verbs**, just add *-ed* to the end.

> look⟶looked

**Irregular action verbs** are action verbs that have a different spelling than most verbs when they are in the past tense.

> grow⟶grew

**Present tense** means something is happening now.

> The girl **jumps** over the puddle.

## Sentence Fragments

A **sentence** is a group of words that expresses a complete thought.

> *Grammy's molasses cookies are the best in my neighborhood.*

A **sentence fragment** is a group of words that does not express a complete thought.

> *Are the best in my neighborhood.*

## Run-On Sentences

A **run-on sentence** joins together two or more sentences that should be written separately.

> *I love Saturdays I get to stay up late.*

## Conjunctions and Compound Sentences

A **conjunction** is a word that joins two ideas together. *And, but, because, so,* and *if* are all conjunctions.

A **compound sentence** is a sentence that contains two sentences combined into one by a comma and a conjunction.

> *I love Saturdays **because** I get to stay up late.*

---

### TEACHING TIP

Understanding complete sentences is extremely important to success on the SAT-9. Throughout the school year, check students' sentences frequently to make sure they are complete and coherent. Assign short writing assignments on a regular basis so you can track student progress in sentence construction.

## Paragraphs

A **paragraph** is a group of sentences that talks about the same idea.

A **main idea** is what a piece of writing or a paragraph is about. It is usually stated in the **topic sentence**, which is the first sentence of a paragraph.

**Supporting details** are sentences that help explain the main idea. If a sentence in a paragraph does not talk about the paragraph's main idea, that sentence does not belong in the paragraph.

**Time-order** words connect ideas.

*First*, I made a list. *Then*, I went to the store and bought groceries. *After* I paid for them, I walked home.

## Main Purpose and Audience

A **main purpose** is the reason why you write something.

An **audience** is the person or group you would like to have read your writing.

## Using a Dictionary

A **dictionary** is a book that tells you what words mean. It also shows you how to spell and say the words.

**Guide words** appear at the top of every page. The first guide word is the first word on that page. The second guide word is the last word on that page.

**Entry words** are the words that are listed in the dictionary. They are listed in alphabetical order.

A **definition** is the meaning of a word.

A **pronunciation** \pro-nun-sē-'ā-shən\ shows you how to say an entry word. It breaks the word down syllable by syllable. The pronunciation is listed next to each entry word, as it is for the word *pronunciation*, above.

A **pronunciation key** helps you read the respelled pronunciations. In some dictionaries, the key appears at the bottom of every other page.

SAT-9

© McGraw-Hill School Division

# Paragraphs, Main Purpose and Audience, and Using a Dictionary

The skills on this page were originally covered in the On Your Mark! Get Set! Go! section. Refer to the following exercises as necessary:

## PARAGRAPHS

- Exercise 22      p. 182
- Exercise 23      p. 184
- Exercise 25      p. 188

## MAIN PURPOSE AND AUDIENCE

- Exercise 24      p. 186

## USING A DICTIONARY

- Exercise 27      p. 192
- Exercise 28      p. 194
- Exercise 29      p. 196

### TEACHING TIP

To help students become familiar with using a dictionary, spend five minutes each morning looking up a new word. You can call it "Word of the Day." Choose a new vocabulary word each day and pick a student to look it up in the dictionary. Record the meanings on the board, as well as the guide words and pronunciation key. Keep a running list of each new word and make sure each student gets a chance to read from the dictionary.

© McGraw-Hill School Division

# REVIEW

## Resources and Finding Information Inside a Book

The skills on this page were originally covered in the On Your Mark! Get Set! Go! section. Refer to the following exercises as necessary:

- Exercise 28    p. 194
- Exercise 29    p. 196

---

### Resources

A **dictionary** gives the meaning, spelling, and pronunciation of words.

A **thesaurus** helps you find words with similar meanings.

An **atlas** is a book of maps.

An **encyclopedia** is a set of books that tells you facts about people, places, and things.

An **almanac** gives general information using facts and numbers.

A **newspaper** tells about daily events.

A **textbook** has information about subjects studied in school. You can use history books, language books, spelling books, and math books to find information when you need it.

### Finding Information Inside a Book

An **index** is a list that usually appears at the back of a book. It is in alphabetical order. It tells you where to find all the important things in the book.

The exact words for the things you are looking for will not always be listed in the index. Sometimes they may be listed under a more **general name** or **category.** For example, information about *Earth*, *Jupiter*, and *Saturn* might be listed under the category *Planets*.

---

## TEACHING TIP

To help students become familiar with using information sources, spend five minutes each morning reading from different resources. For example, one morning you might read a page of an atlas and show students a map. Another morning you might have students pick a word and then read them the list of synonyms from a thesaurus. Another morning you might read an article from your local newspaper.

# TERRANOVA

# TEACHER
# INTRODUCTION

# WHY *PREPARATION AND PRACTICE FOR THE TERRANOVA* IS THE BEST PREPARATION FOR STUDENTS

Welcome to the Teacher Edition of *Preparation and Practice for the TerraNova* for grade 3!

By completing each section of this book, students will:

- Increase their knowledge and understanding of language arts skills
- Become familiar with the types of questions that will be asked on the test
- Become aware of and experience first-hand the amount of time they will have to complete the test
- Become accustomed to the style of the test
- Become better writers and speakers
- Learn test-taking techniques and tips that will help them on the TerraNova
- Feel comfortable on the day of the exam

# Parts of This Book

There are eight sections of this Teacher Edition:

## Teacher Introduction

The Teacher Introduction familiarizes you with the purpose and format of *Preparation and Practice for the TerraNova.* It also describes the TerraNova sections and questions on the test that pertain to language arts skills.

## Student and Class Diagnostic Charts

This section consists of two charts. A student and a class diagnostic chart are included for the Warm-Up Test. These charts may be used to gauge student performance and determine the skills with which students will need the most practice as they prepare for the TerraNova.

## Student Introduction

This section contains some tips and explanations for students as they begin their preparation for the TerraNova. Extra annotations are included for teachers to help you further explain what is expected of students and to encourage them as they begin their test preparation.

## Warm-Up Test

This diagnostic test reveals students' strengths and weaknesses so that you may customize your test preparation accordingly. The skill tested in each question on the Warm-Up Test directly correlates to a skill reviewed in one of the 30 On Your Mark! Get Set! Go! practice exercises.

## On Your Mark! Get Set! Go!

This section consists of 30 practice exercises. Each exercise focuses on a specific language arts skill or test-taking strategy. On Your Mark! introduces and explains the skill. Get Set! provides an example question that tests the skill. (You should go over the question as a class.) Go! contains questions that test the skills introduced in the exercise. Have students complete these questions on their own.

## Practice Test

The Practice Test is a replica of the TerraNova in style and format. The test contains the exact number of questions that will appear on the actual test so that students are given a realistic test-taking experience. The Practice Test includes questions from each section. *Note: The Practice Test contains reading comprehension passages and questions in addition to language arts questions. These were included because the actual TerraNova combines these two sections.*

## On Your Mark! Get Set! Go! Review

This review section is an overview of the skills contained in On Your Mark! Get Set! Go! Similar skills are grouped together and the On Your Mark! Get Set! Go! exercises to which the skills correspond are noted.

## Index

The index is a brief listing of where you can look to find exercises about specific skills.

# How to Use This Book

This book has been designed so that you may customize your TerraNova test preparation according to your class's needs and time frame. However, we do recommend that you begin your test preparation as early in the school year as possible. This book will yield your students' best TerraNova scores if you diagnose your students' strengths and weaknesses early and work toward helping them achieve their best performance. Please note that preparing students for a test such as the TerraNova is a process. As much preparation as possible should take place in the classroom and be discussed as a class.

## Warm-Up Test

Have students complete the Warm-Up Test in class. It should be administered as early in the school year as possible. By doing so, students will gain familiarity with the types of questions and the specific skills tested on the TerraNova *before* they begin working through the skill-specific exercises in this book. Use the student and class diagnostic charts to grade the tests. The results of the Warm-Up Test reveal students' strengths and weaknesses and allow you to focus your test preparation accordingly.

## On Your Mark! Get Set! Go!

We recommend that you review an On Your Mark! Get Set! Go! exercise after completing each chapter in your McGraw-Hill language arts textbook. It is best to go through the On Your Mark! Get Set! Go! section throughout the year so that students can digest the material properly. Consider reviewing On Your Mark! and Get Set! as a class. The Go! sections may be assigned as homework or completed by students individually in class. Having students complete Go! individually will provide the best simulated preparation for the TerraNova. After students have completed the Go! exercises, go over the correct answers as a class. The Princeton Review's research and experience shows this in-class work to be an essential element in effective test preparation.

## Practice Test

The Practice Test should be administered in the weeks prior to the actual exam. Testing conditions should be simulated. For example, no two desks should be placed directly next to each other, students should have two pencils at their disposal, the room should be quiet, and so on.

## On Your Mark! Get Set! Go! Review

Use this review in the few days leading up to the actual exam. Its purpose is to solidify the On Your Mark! Get Set! Go! skills students have learned throughout the school year. Answer any questions students might have and go over the specific exercises and skills with which students are the most concerned. You might want students to read over the section as homework and bring in a list of their questions to class the next day. Address as many of the students concerns as possible before the actual exam. If students need additional review, consult the On Your Mark! Get Set! Go! exercises that correlate to the skills.

# About the Teacher Pages

Each page of the Pupil Edition is reproduced in this Teacher Edition, either reduced or full-size. Each reduced Pupil Edition page has wrap-around teacher text that consists of a **column** and a **box**.

- The column serves as a guide for you as you present the material on the Pupil Edition page in an interactive way. Guiding prompts and notes are included to ensure that information pivotal to the exercise is covered.

- The gray box includes teaching tips and extra activities. The extra activities are often fun, game-like activities for your class. These activities give students the opportunity to learn or apply TerraNova-related skills in a variety of ways.

Teacher wrap pages are punctuated with five icon types that help guide you through the Pupil Edition.

 This icon correlates the teacher wrap to the information in the On Your Mark! section of the Pupil Edition page.

 This icon reminds you to go over the example question in the Get Set! section of the Pupil Edition page.

 This icon reminds you to go over each question on the Go! pages of the Pupil Edition.

 This icon provides a point of emphasis for you to make concerning the exercise on the Pupil Edition page.

 This icon identifies an extra activity.

# About the Annotated Pages

Some pages in the Teacher Edition include full-size Pupil Edition pages. These occur in the Student Introduction, the Warm-Up Test section, and the Practice Test section.

All of these full-size reproductions are highlighted with teacher annotations. These annotations, which appear in magenta ink, provide the following:

- **Correct Answers**

The correct answer to each question is circled in magenta ink.

- **Question Analyses**

Sometimes an annotation offers further explanation of a specific question.

- **Extra Tips**

Certain annotations provide you with extra teaching tips specific to the skill tested on the Pupil Edition page.

- **Hints**

Some annotations offer hints that you can give to your students when they are working through the questions in the exercise or test sections.

# Introduction to the TerraNova

The TerraNova is a standardized test taken every year by students throughout the country. Talk to your school's test administrator to get the exact testing date for this school year.

The TerraNova is a multiple-choice test that assesses students' skills in reading, language arts, mathematics, science, and social studies. This book covers the language arts section of the TerraNova. There are three sections of the TerraNova that incorporate language arts skills:

- **Reading and Language Arts**

- **Language Mechanics**

- **Spelling**

The specific number of questions for each section discussed above and the time allotted for it is broken down as follows on the actual TerraNova:

| Skill | Reading and Language Arts | Language Mechanics | Spelling |
|---|---|---|---|
| **Number of Items** | 70 | 20 | 20 |
| **Time** | 75 minutes | 15 minutes | 15 minutes |

# How Language Arts Skills Are Tested

## Reading and Language Arts

The reading and language arts section of the Terranova includes *both* reading comprehension questions and language skills questions. For the purposes of this book, you should only be concerned with the language skills questions.

There are several different types of language skills questions on the Terranova.

- **Word Usage:** Students are asked to pick the pronoun or form of a verb, adjective, or noun that best fits into the provided sentence.

- **Sentence Structure:** Students are asked to determine which sentence is complete or incomplete.

- **Punctuation:** Students are asked to choose the correctly punctuated sentence, address, date, or letter greeting and closing to replace an incorrect or blank section of a sentence or a paragraph.

- **Capitalization:** Students are asked to pick the sentence that has the correct capitalization.

- **Main and Supporting Ideas:** Students are asked to determine the topic of a paragraph or to pick out the sentence that does not match the theme of the paragraph.

## Language Mechanics

In this section, students are asked to identify a wide variety of punctuation and capitalization errors.

EXAMPLE

*Students must choose the sentence with the correct punctuation.*

**A**  How did you get all wet.

**B**  How did you get all wet?

**C**  How did you get all wet,

**D**  How did you get all wet

This question tests students' ability to pick out the correct punctuation for a question. Other language mechanics questions will address punctuation and capitalization rules for quotations, exclamations, proper nouns, and letter greetings and closings. There will also be questions about correct punctuation usage for addresses, dates, times, and commas in a series.

## Spelling

For this section, students are tested on their ability to recognize whether a word is misspelled. Students are required to choose the correct spelling of the word.

EXAMPLE

*Students must choose the sentence with the correctly spelled underlined word.*

○  I like him <u>because</u> he is nice.

○  I like him <u>becaze</u> he is nice.

○  I like him <u>becaws</u> he is nice.

○  I like him <u>becaus</u> he is nice.

For this question, students must choose the correctly spelled form of the underlined word. Other spelling questions contain sentences with several words underlined. Students much choose which of the underlined words, if any, is spelled incorrectly.

# STUDENT AND CLASS DIAGNOSTIC CHARTS

# How to Use the Student Diagnostic Chart

The Student Diagnostic Chart on page T55 should be used to score the Warm-Up Test in this book. The chart is designed to help you and your individual students determine the areas in which they need the most practice as they begin their preparation for the TerraNova. You will need to make enough copies of the chart for each of your students.

There are two ways to use the Student Diagnostic Chart:

- You can collect the finished Warm-Up Tests from each student and fill out one chart for each student as you grade the tests.

- You can give one copy of the Student Diagnostic Chart to each student and have students grade their own tests as you read aloud the correct answer choices.

*Note: Correct answer choices are marked in the Warm-Up Test of this Teacher Edition.*

## How to Fill Out the Student Diagnostic Chart

For each question number, there is a blank column labeled "Right or Wrong." An "R" or a "W" should be placed in that column for each question on the Warm-Up Test. By looking at the chart upon completion, students will understand which questions they answered incorrectly and to which skills these incorrect answers correspond. The exercise from the On Your Mark! Get Set! Go! section that teaches the skill is also noted. You should encourage students to spend extra time going over the corresponding exercises covering the skills with which they had the most trouble. The charts will also help you determine which students need the most practice and what skills gave the majority of the students trouble. This way, you can plan your students' TerraNova preparation schedule accordingly.

# How to Use the Class Diagnostic Chart

The Class Diagnostic Chart on page T56 should be used to record your class's performance on the Warm-Up Test in this book. The chart is designed to help you determine what areas your class needs to practice most as you begin their preparation for the TerraNova. The Class Diagnostic Chart is strictly for your own use. You should not share it with students.

## How to Fill Out the Class Diagnostic Chart

Under the "Name" column, you should write the names of each of your students. Then use the completed Student Diagnostic Charts to help you fill out the Class Diagnostic Chart. Fill out one row for each student.

For each question on the Warm-Up Test, there is a corresponding row in the Class Diagnostic Chart. The row is labeled with the question number and the exercise number of the correlating On Your Mark! Get Set! Go! exercise. If a student gets a question wrong, you should mark an "X" in the box underneath that question number. After completing a column for one student, add up all of the Xs and put a total for that student in the "Total" row on the top of the page. When you have filled out a row for each student, you should total up the Xs for each question. Put the totals in the "Total" column on the right-hand side of the page. Assessing both "Total" columns will help you determine two things: 1) which students are having the most trouble individually, and 2) which questions are giving the class as a whole the most trouble.

You should use the information gathered in the Class Diagnostic Chart to determine which skills to spend the most time reviewing and which students need the most individual practice and guidance.

# Student Diagnostic Chart

| Question # | Correct Answer | Right or Wrong | Exercise # | Skill |
|---|---|---|---|---|
| 1 | 2nd | | 1 | Spelling: Learn the Rules |
| 2 | 3rd | | 3 | Tricky Spellings |
| 3 | 2nd | | 2 | Spelling: Memorize |
| 4 | 3rd | | 5 | End Marks |
| 5 | 1st | | 6 | Commas |
| 6 | 2nd | | 7 | Commas in a Series |
| 7 | 2nd | | 8 | Quotations |
| 8 | 2nd | | 9 | Holidays |
| 9 | 2nd | | 10 | Titles of People |
| 10 | 3rd | | 11 | Writing Letters |
| 11 | 1st | | 12 | Capitalizing Places |
| 12 | 1st | | 13 | Capitalizing Sentences |
| 13 | 1st | | 15 | Parts of a Sentence |
| 14 | 2nd | | 16 | Verbs |
| 15 | 1st | | 17 | Verb Tense |
| 16 | 3rd | | 18 | Helping Verbs |
| 17 | 4th | | 19 | Subject-Verb Agreement |
| 18 | 1st | | 21 | Adjectives that Compare |
| 19 | 2nd | | 22 | Pronouns |
| 20 | 2nd | | 23 | Contractions |
| 21 | 3rd | | 25 | Complete Sentences |
| 22 | 2nd | | 26 | Run-Ons and Conjunctions |
| 23 | 3rd | | 27 | Topic Sentences |
| 24 | 1st | | 28 | Supporting a Topic Sentence |
| 25 | 4th | | 25 | Complete Sentences |

# Class Diagnostic Chart

| Name | Q1-Ex. 1 | Q2-Ex. 3 | Q3-Ex. 2 | Q4-Ex. 5 | Q5-Ex. 6 | Q6-Ex. 7 | Q7-Ex. 8 | Q8-Ex. 9 | Q9-Ex. 10 | Q10-Ex. 11 | Q11-Ex. 12 | Q12-Ex. 13 | Q13-Ex. 15 | Q14-Ex. 16 | Q15-Ex. 17 | Q16-Ex. 18 | Q17-Ex. 19 | Q18-Ex. 21 | Q19-Ex. 22 | Q20-Ex. 23 | Q21-Ex. 25 | Q22-Ex. 26 | Q23-Ex. 27 | Q24-Ex. 28 | Q25-Ex. 25 | Total |
|------|------|------|------|------|------|------|------|------|------|------|------|------|------|------|------|------|------|------|------|------|------|------|------|------|------|------|
| | | | | | | | | | | | | | | | | | | | | | | | | | | |
| | | | | | | | | | | | | | | | | | | | | | | | | | | |
| | | | | | | | | | | | | | | | | | | | | | | | | | | |
| | | | | | | | | | | | | | | | | | | | | | | | | | | |
| | | | | | | | | | | | | | | | | | | | | | | | | | | |
| | | | | | | | | | | | | | | | | | | | | | | | | | | |
| | | | | | | | | | | | | | | | | | | | | | | | | | | |
| | | | | | | | | | | | | | | | | | | | | | | | | | | |
| | | | | | | | | | | | | | | | | | | | | | | | | | | |
| | | | | | | | | | | | | | | | | | | | | | | | | | | |
| | | | | | | | | | | | | | | | | | | | | | | | | | | |
| | | | | | | | | | | | | | | | | | | | | | | | | | | |
| | | | | | | | | | | | | | | | | | | | | | | | | | | |
| | | | | | | | | | | | | | | | | | | | | | | | | | | |
| Total | | | | | | | | | | | | | | | | | | | | | | | | | | |

Introduction • Preparation and Practice for the ITBS, SAT-9, and TerraNova • Grade 3

# STUDENT
# INTRODUCTION

# INTRODUCTION TO THE TERRANOVA

## What is the TerraNova?

The TerraNova is a multiple-choice test that helps you and your teacher find out how much you have learned in school so far. Now's your chance to show off all that you learned about reading and writing this year!

## Does the TerraNova measure how smart I am?

No, not at all. The TerraNova only tests how well you can use the skills you've learned in class so far.

## How can I prepare for the TerraNova?

You can use this book to practice the types of questions you will see on the test. You can also use this book to learn some simple test-taking tips that will help you do your best. Just like riding a bike or playing the piano, studying for the TerraNova takes practice. The more you practice, the better you will do and the more confident you'll feel on the day of the test!

It's important to tell students that TerraNova measures the skills that they are learning in school. It's not a test of their intelligence. Therefore, the best way for them to prepare for the TerraNova is by using this book to familiarize themselves with the types of questions that will appear on the test, review skills they have already been practicing in school, and learn new test-taking strategies.

**TERRANOVA**

# There are four parts in this book.

1. **Warm-Up Test**—This test is shorter than the real TerraNova, but it will show you what you know—and what you need to practice.

2. **On Your Mark! Get Set! Go!**—Here's where you really get to roll up your sleeves! First, you will learn the skills that you'll need to know for the test. Then you will practice what you've learned on questions that are just like the ones on the real TerraNova. Trust us, this is the best part of the book!

3. **Practice Test**—This test is just like the real TerraNova.

4. **On Your Mark! Get Set! Go! Review**—This is a list of all the important things that you will learn in this book. Go back to this part when you need to review or study what you've learned.

You may want to write a timeline on the board to show students how much time you will spend using each part of this book and preparing for the test. This will keep students from feeling overwhelmed and help them maintain a positive attitude about preparing for and taking the TerraNova.

# USING THIS BOOK

Here's what you can do to help yourself while you use this book:

**Work carefully.**

Completing this book is not a race. Now is the time to work slowly and carefully and to really learn what you need to know. We'll teach you how to go faster later in the book, so you'll be ready to take the real TerraNova in the time your teacher will give you.

**Pay attention to the directions.**

Read all of the directions carefully. The directions tell you how to answer the questions. Always make sure you understand the directions before starting a new set of questions. Pretend you are driving a car, and the directions are the road signs that tell you what's ahead.

**Read the questions and answer choices carefully.**

Always read the *entire* question and *all* of the answer choices slowly and carefully. Make sure you've read through *all* of the answer choices before you make your choice, even if you think you have already found the correct answer. There might be a better one!

**TERRANOVA**

# Get Rid of the Wrong Answer Choices

This book prepares you for the multiple-choice questions on the TerraNova. On a multiple-choice question, you are given four or five answer choices to choose from. Only one of these choices is the best answer. Here's how to make sure you find it:

1. Read each answer choice, one by one.

2. Decide whether you think each answer choice is right or wrong.

3. Get rid of the answer choices you *know* are wrong.

4. Save the answer choices that might be right or that you aren't sure about.

5. Choose the best answer from the choices you think might be right.

6. If you don't know the answer, take your best guess.

> **Getting rid of wrong answer choices, even only one, makes your chances of picking the correct answer choice a lot better!**
>
> **So remember:**
>
> ✔ Get rid of what you can.
>
> ✔ See what you have left over.
>
> ✔ If you don't know the answer, make your best guess and move on.

POE is one of the most important strategies students can use to increase their success on standardized tests.

You may want to illustrate this concept by playing some form of a guessing game with your students. For example, write down four things (e.g., days of the week) on index cards. Share the items with your students, and then have one student choose one card. Ask the rest of the class to guess the chosen card. Keep track of the number of guesses. Repeat the game with three cards, two cards, and finally, one card. This should illustrate to students how the chances of guessing correctly increase as the number of choices decreases.

© McGraw-Hill School Division

# Pace Yourself

The TerraNova is a timed test. This means that your teacher is only allowed to let you work on it for a certain amount of time. While you take the test, remember to use your time wisely. Here's how:

### Don't spend too much time on one question.

Some questions on the TerraNova are harder than others. Don't get stuck on any questions you don't know the answer to. Just take your best guess and move on. You want to be sure that you will have enough time to answer the easier questions that come later.

### But don't rush, either!

Going too fast is not good—you will only make silly mistakes. If you don't waste time on difficult questions, you will have enough time to finish the test without rushing.

### Find your own steady pace.

Everyone works at a different pace. Don't compare yourself with others. Just try to answer as many of the questions as you can. Work carefully through each of them. Pick the best answer, and then move on to the next question. When the teacher says time is up, put your pencil down and feel good about all the hard work you have done.

Pacing is an important aspect of taking timed tests. Tell students that they need to strike a balance between working carefully and progressing efficiently through the questions. Remind students that by completing the exercises in this book, they will find a pace that works for them.

TERRANOVA

# MARK YOUR ANSWER CHOICES CORRECTLY

When you take the TerraNova, you will be given the test and an answer sheet. The answer sheet is where you mark your answer choices. Marking your answers is very simple. Here's how you should answer a question:

1. Read the question.

2. Decide which answer choice is correct. Each answer choice has a letter next to it. Remember the letter that is next to the answer you picked.

3. Find the question number on your answer sheet that is the same as the number of the question you are answering.

4. Fill in the bubble that has the same letter as your answer choice.

## Always make sure that you fill in the answer bubbles completely.

 Do NOT fill in half of the bubble. This is wrong.

 Do NOT put a checkmark over the bubble. This is wrong.

 Do NOT scribble inside the bubble. This is wrong.

 DO fill in the bubble completely. This is correct!

Then go on to the next question until you are done with the test. It's that easy!

Explain to students that it's important to fill in the bubbles correctly because the test is scored by a machine. If their bubbles are not filled in completely, students may not get credit for questions that they have answered correctly.

# Practice, Practice, Practice!

The more you practice, the more prepared you'll be for the actual test. Remember, the TerraNova tests what you already know. What you should practice is how to use what you know on the test. The more you practice, the more comfortable you will feel taking the test!

To help students understand the value of practice, lead a discussion about how practicing leads to improvements. For example, ask students to name several activities (e.g., sports, music, art) in which they participate. Then ask them to discuss how they practice for these activities. Has practice helped them improve their skills? How? In what ways can they see their progress?

**TERRANOVA**

# GETTING READY FOR THE TERRANOVA

You can practice for the TerraNova even when you're *not* using this book! Here's how:

**Read as much as you can.** Read everything and anything you can get your hands on. Of course, in class, you should read everything your teacher tells you to read. But outside of class, you get to choose what to read. Read comic books, magazines, and cereal boxes. Read signs as you pass by them. Read stories aloud. Listen to others read stories aloud to you. All reading is good reading.

**Play the word game.** When you come across a word you don't understand, play a game: try to figure out what the word could mean. Ask yourself, "If I had to guess, what do I think the definition of that word would be?"

1. Write down your best guess.

2. Look the word up in a dictionary, or if you're not near a dictionary, ask an adult.

3. Write the word and its correct definition down on an index card. This will help you remember it.

4. Later, go back and read your index cards to see how good your memory is.

Remind students how important it is to practice reading. Reading is exercise for the brain, and the more they exercise their brains—by reading all types of materials—the greater improvement they'll see in their overall reading comprehension and in their performance on the TerraNova.

**Pay attention in class.** Not only will you learn cool things, but you'll also spend less time wrestling with tricky homework after school and more time playing with your friends!

**Ask questions.** Ask your teacher if you don't understand why an answer is wrong. Other students probably have the same question.

**Learn from your mistakes.** Notice the questions you have trouble with. Find out why you answered them incorrectly. Ask your teacher to review the skills you need to brush up on.

**Pat yourself on the back.** Congratulate yourself on the things you know well, and keep up the good work!

Answering questions incorrectly can be as valuable as answering questions correctly in preparing for a standardized test. Make sure students understand that it is okay to make mistakes. The important thing is that students learn from their mistakes.

As students work through the tests and exercises in this book, provide them with positive feedback and encourage them with congratulations as they improve their skills. Allowing students to celebrate their progress will help them approach the TerraNova with confidence and a positive attitude.

**TERRANOVA**

# Warm-Up Test

## Directions

For Numbers 1 through 3, find the underlined word that is NOT spelled correctly. If all the words are spelled correctly, mark the last answer choice, "All correct."

**1**
- ○ The king <u>reigned</u> for twenty years.
- ● He was married to the queen for <u>eght</u> years.
- ○ The <u>chief</u> of the tribe welcomed us.
- ○ All correct

> eight

**2**
- ○ I sat in the <u>chair</u>.
- ○ My teacher <u>said</u> that I should eat more.
- ● This boat runs on a <u>moter</u>.
- ○ All correct

> motor

**3**
- ○ I like it <u>a lot</u>.
- ● I think that these cookies and those cookies look <u>a like</u>.
- ○ I <u>almost</u> forgot to clean my plate.
- ○ All correct

> *Alike* is one word, not two.

**TERRANOVA**

**Go On** ⇨

**For Numbers 4 through 9, find the answer choice with the correct punctuation and capitalization.**

Remind students that they are looking for the sentence that has the correct punctuation and capitalization.

**4**
- ○ How many dogs are in the house.
- ○ I thought I saw fifteen dogs
- ● She said there were at least ten dogs.

**5**
- ● Last summer, I was a lifeguard.
- ○ Excuse me Paula what time is the play?
- ○ I am short but, Hank is shorter.
- ○ My brother swims, runs, and, bikes in the triathlon.

**6**
- ○ I used my pail shovel and a cup to make the sand castle.
- ● She invited her brother, sister, and father to dinner.
- ○ The dog stepped on my roses tulips, and, pansies.
- ○ I dusted the chair, bookshelf, and, table.

The first answer choice is missing the commas necessary in a series. The third and fourth answer choices use a comma incorrectly: after *and*.

**7**
- ○ I asked, Do I have to do my chores?
- ● She said, "Yes."
- ○ He told me "that I could stay home".
- ○ Suzy said, "please pass the peas"

**8**
- ○ I have lived here since memorial Day.
- ● We rented a cabin for Labor Day.
- ○ She will move in on valentines day.

**9**
- ○ I have to go to the hospital to meet dr Juarez.
- ● The nurse was named Ms. Sullivan.
- ○ Most people call him Mr Biggerman.
- ○ I like mrs. Martin's cookies the best of them all.

**Directions**

For Numbers 10 through 12, find the answer choice that best completes the underlined sections of this letter.

_____**(10)**_____

I have never been to_____**(11)**_____

_____**(12)**_____

                                          Sincerely,
                                          Mary

**10**  ○  dear Kevin,

   ○  Dear Kevin

   ● Dear Kevin,

> The words in a letter greeting should always be capitalized.

**11**  ● Paris, France!

   ○  Paris france!

   ○  paris, france!

> The names of cities and countries are always capitalized.

**12**  ● May I visit you?

   ○  May I Visit you?

   ○  may I visit you?

> The first answer choice is the only one that correctly uses capital letters. The second answer choice incorrectly capitalizes *visit*. A verb in the middle of a sentence should never be capitalized. In the third answer choice, *may* needs a capital letter because the first word of a sentence is always capitalized.

TERRANOVA

Go On →

**13** Find the <u>subject</u> in the sentences below.

*I <u>saw a brown dog</u>. It <u>carried a bone in its mouth.</u>*

| | Only the first answer choice is a subject. The second and third answer choices are predicates. |

● It
○ saw a brown dog
○ carried a bone in its mouth

**14** Which word best completes the sentence?

*He _____ five books last summer.*

○ readed
● read
○ reading
○ reads

**For Numbers 15 through 18, find the sentence that is grammatically correct.**

**15**
● He finished his chores before he walked to the park.
○ He finishes his chores before he walked to the park.
○ He finish his chores before he walked to the park.

**16**
○ I had be playing the trombone for two years.
○ I have being playing the trombone for two years.
● I have been playing the trombone for two years.
○ I has been playing the trombone for two years.

The clue in the sentence, *for two years*, should help students understand that the verb must be in the past tense.

**17**
○ She are a good singer. *Are* should be *is*.
○ They sings often. *Sings* should be *sing*.
○ I likes to sing. *Likes* should be *like*.
● He sings everyday. This is correct.

**18**
● He has the bluest eyes I have ever seen.
○ His eyes are more bluest than yours.
○ Your eyes are the bluer of our whole family.
○ Her eyes are blue than mine.

# Directions

For questions 19 and 20, find the word that could go in place of the underlined words.

**19** _My dogs need to go for a walk._

- ○ Its
- ● They
- ○ He
- ○ We

> _My dogs_ is plural and must be replaced by a plural pronoun. Only _they_ is plural.

**20** _They are coming tomorrow!_

- ○ The'yre
- ● They're
- ○ They'are
- ○ Theyr'e

> The apostophe in a contraction replaces the missing letters.

# Directions

For questions 21 and 22, find the sentence that is complete and written correctly.

**21**
- ○ The soft summer breeze. | Fragment |
- ○ Brushed against my face. | Fragment |
- ● It was cold. | Complete |
- ○ When I felt the breeze on my neck. | Fragment |

**22**
- ○ My aunt took me sailing it was fun. | Run-on |
- ● I thought that we might tip over, but it was safe. | Complete |
- ○ She showed me how to tie the knots they go in certain places. | Run-on |
- ○ I liked sailing with my aunt she is nice. | Run-on |

TERRANOVA

Go On

**23** Which of these would be the best topic sentence for this paragraph?

_____. *When she throws the ball, Jenny never misses the basket. She knows how to dodge out of the way of the other players without losing the ball.*

- ○ Basketball is a fun game.
- ○ More people should try out for our basketball team.
- ● Jenny is the best player on our basketball team.
- ○ Sports are a good way to stay healthy.

> The paragraph is about Jenny, so the topic sentence should be about Jenny.

**24** Which sentence completes this paragraph the best?

*Spring has arrived! _____. They smell so pretty.*

- ● The flowers have bloomed.
- ○ Spring is my favorite season.
- ○ I'm glad that I can smell, even though I have a cold.

> The subject in the second sentence must agree with the subject *they* in the third sentence. *They* is plural, so the subject of the second sentence must also be plural. Only the first answer choice has a plural subject, *flowers.*

**25** Find the sentence that is complete.

- ○ The closest friend I have.
- ○ When you know you have a good friend.
- ○ Being nice to me.
- ● He is nice to me.

# On Your Mark, Get Set, Go!

## Exercise 1
# SPELLING

## Learn the Rules

 **Review the helpful spelling tips listed on the Pupil Edition page with your class.**

Ask students to name some more examples of *ie* and *ei* words. Write them on the board in two columns to differentiate them for the class. Some examples might be:

- *ie: relieve, belief, fierce, grief*
- *ei: receipt, deceive, reign, weight*

Have students give you examples of words that apply to the other rules listed on the Pupil Edition page and write them on the board. Remind students that understanding these unusual spelling rules will help them on the TerraNova.

 **Go over the example question as a class.**

---

 ## ON YOUR MARK!

### Spelling: Learn the Rules

Here are a few **spelling rules** you can learn to help you become a better speller.

***ie* and *ei* words:** *i* comes before *e* except after *c* or when it sounds like /ā/ as in *neighbor, freight,* and *sleigh.*

**The silent *e*:** When words end in silent *e*, drop the *e* when adding an ending that begins with a vowel, such as *-ing* or *-ed (chase + ed = chased, chase + ing = chasing).* When adding an ending that begins with a consonant, such as *-ly*, keep the silent *e*. *(sure + ly = surely)*

**The letter *q*:** The letter *q* is always followed by *u*. *(quick, quiz, quality)*

**The /f/ sound:** The /f/ sound may be spelled *f, ph,* or *gh. (fear, leaf; phone, graph; laugh)*

 ## GET SET!

One type of TerraNova spelling question asks you to choose the phrase that includes an underlined word that is not spelled correctly. Three of the choices are spelled correctly. Only one is spelled incorrectly. Choose the phrase with the incorrectly spelled word. If none of the choices are spelled incorrectly, choose the answer choice marked "All correct."

Let's look at an example.

Find the underlined word that is NOT spelled correctly.

- ○  a <u>money</u> clip
- ● <u>evry</u> penny counts
- ○  smile, be <u>happy</u>
- ○  All correct

(2nd) is **correct!** The correct spelling is *every.*

---

 ## TEACHING TIP

Go over the *All correct* choice with your students. Make sure that students know that this is always a possible answer choice in the spelling section of the TerraNova. Emphasize the importance of reading every answer choice before making a selection.

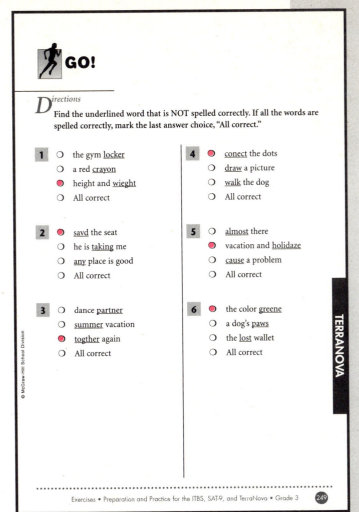

## GO!

**Directions**

Find the underlined word that is NOT spelled correctly. If all the words are spelled correctly, mark the last answer choice, "All correct."

**1**
- ○ the gym <u>locker</u>
- ○ a red <u>crayon</u>
- ● height and <u>wieght</u>
- ○ All correct

**2**
- ● <u>savd</u> the seat
- ○ he is <u>taking</u> me
- ○ <u>any</u> place is good
- ○ All correct

**3**
- ○ dance <u>partner</u>
- ○ <u>summer</u> vacation
- ● <u>togther</u> again
- ○ All correct

**4**
- ● <u>conect</u> the dots
- ○ <u>draw</u> a picture
- ○ <u>walk</u> the dog
- ○ All correct

**5**
- ○ <u>almost</u> there
- ● vacation and <u>holidaze</u>
- ○ <u>cause</u> a problem
- ○ All correct

**6**
- ● the color <u>greene</u>
- ○ a dog's <u>paws</u>
- ○ the <u>lost</u> wallet
- ○ All correct

TERRANOVA

---

 **Go over each question on the page as a class.**

### Question 1

Special rule: long /a/ sound gets *ei.*

### Question 2

saved

### Question 3

together

### Question 4

connect

### Question 5

holidays

### Question 6

green

Some of the spelling rules discussed on Pupil Edition page 248 are not tested on this page (*qu, ph, gh*). Provide students with extra questions that contain words with these sounds.

# SPELLING

## Memorize!

**Emphasize the importance of spelling memorization to your class.**

Remind students that each word is unique, just like each student is unique. Tell them to get familiar with the words they see and read. Encourage students to remember how a word looks, so that they can tell when a word "doesn't look right" and fix it.

**Go over the example question with your class.**

---

**Exercise 2**

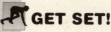

## ON YOUR MARK!

### Spelling: Memorize!

Some words can be tricky to spell because often there are many different ways to write the same sound. For example, the words *giant* and *jam* both have the same *j* sound at the beginning, but they use different letters to spell it.

There are many words that you need to **memorize** in order to know how to spell them. It will help to keep a **spelling journal** where you can keep a list of words that you often have trouble spelling. Also, become familiar with the **dictionary** and use it often.

**Tips for Memorizing Spelling Words**

✓ Make up **clues** to help you remember the spelling. (*u* and *i* build a house; a *pie*ce of *pie*; the princip*al* is your *pal*)

✓ Look for **word chunks** or smaller words that help you remember the spelling. (*hippopotamus = hippo pot am us*)

✓ **Visualize:** Think of a time you may have seen the word in a book, a magazine, on a sign, or in a textbook. Try to remember how it looked.

 GET SET!

Let's look at an example.

Find the underlined word that is NOT spelled correctly.

○ the pencil <u>point</u>

○ to <u>appear</u> nervous

● <u>abowt</u> thirty birds.

○ All correct

Think of where you have seen these words written before. Which spelling looks right?

(3rd) is **correct!** The correct spelling is *about*, with *-ou* in the middle.

---

 ★ **EXTRA ACTIVITY**

Have students think of ways that they can memorize tricky words. Some ways might be placing similar words together in groups (*cough, laugh*), making up rhymes or sayings (*We <u>ate eight</u> cookies and gained <u>weight</u>*), or even by simply keeping note cards and writing down all the tricky words they come across when reading.

Tell students to focus only on the underlined word when spelling is tested. Other words in each phrase are unimportant and distracting.

Remind students to read all of the answer choices carefully before choosing an answer.

**Question 1**

monkey

**Question 2**

tear

**Question 3**

thousands

**Question 4**

usually

**Question 6**

breakfast

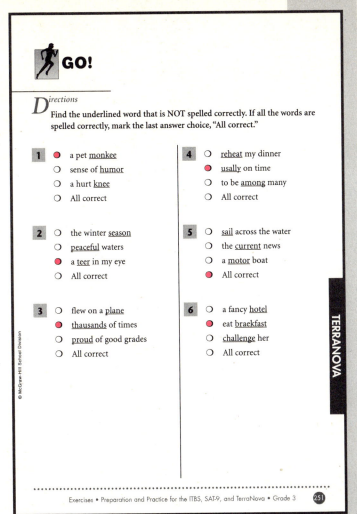

## GO!

*Directions*

Find the underlined word that is NOT spelled correctly. If all the words are spelled correctly, mark the last answer choice, "All correct."

**1**
- ● a pet <u>monkee</u>
- ○ sense of <u>humor</u>
- ○ a hurt <u>knee</u>
- ○ All correct

**2**
- ○ the winter <u>season</u>
- ○ <u>peaceful</u> waters
- ● a <u>teer</u> in my eye
- ○ All correct

**3**
- ○ flew on a <u>plane</u>
- ● <u>thausands</u> of times
- ○ <u>proud</u> of good grades
- ○ All correct

**4**
- ○ <u>reheat</u> my dinner
- ● <u>usally</u> on time
- ○ to be <u>among</u> many
- ○ All correct

**5**
- ○ <u>sail</u> across the water
- ○ the <u>current</u> news
- ○ a <u>motor</u> boat
- ● All correct

**6**
- ○ a fancy <u>hotel</u>
- ● eat <u>braekfast</u>
- ○ <u>challenge</u> her
- ○ All correct

**TERRANOVA**

# SPELLING

## Tricky Spellings

 **Review the difficult spellings shown on the Pupil Edition page.**

Explain that some words have groups of letters that may not look like they sound. Students have to memorize these tricky words.

On the board, write some other words that contain the confusing groups of letters. Some examples you might use are:

- *rough*
- *enough*
- *ghoul*
- *weight*
- *light*

 **Go over the example question as class.**

---

 ## ON YOUR MARK!

### Tricky Spellings

Some words have groups of letters that may not look like they sound.

> *Tough* is pronounced "tuhf."

In the word *tough*, the *gh* makes an *f* sound.

> *Eight* is pronounced "ate."

In the word *eight*, the *gh* is silent.

> *Ghost* is pronounced "gohst."

In the word *ghost*, the *gh* makes a hard *g* sound.

When you look at answer choices on the TerraNova, always remember that there is often more than one way to spell a sound.

> **TIP:** Some misspelled words on the test "look right." Some correctly spelled words "look wrong."
> Try writing the word on your own. Try spelling it a few ways. Choose the one that seems **correct!** Then compare your spelling to the answer choice.

 ## GET SET!

Let's look at an example.

Find the word that is spelled correctly and completes the sentence.

*Before you go to camp, put a _____ on your shirts.*

 ● label
○ labell
○ lable
○ laebl

(1st) is **correct!** The other answer choices are spelled incorrectly.

---

 ## EXTRA ACTIVITY

Ask students to name as many words as they can that contain the letter combinations mentioned on the Pupil Edition page. You might want to give students a set amount of time to write down as many of these words as they can. Make it a game. The student with the most correct words wins.

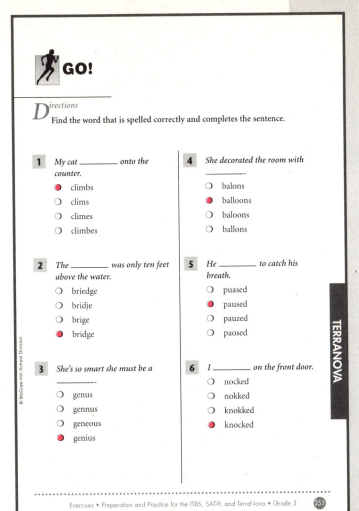

## GO!

*Directions*
Find the word that is spelled correctly and completes the sentence.

**1** My cat _____ onto the counter.
- ● climbs
- ○ clims
- ○ climes
- ○ climbes

**2** The _____ was only ten feet above the water.
- ○ briedge
- ○ bridje
- ○ brige
- ● bridge

**3** She's so smart she must be a _____.
- ○ genus
- ○ gennus
- ○ geneous
- ● genius

**4** She decorated the room with _____.
- ○ balons
- ● balloons
- ○ baloons
- ○ ballons

**5** He _____ to catch his breath.
- ○ puased
- ● paused
- ○ pauzed
- ○ paosed

**6** I _____ on the front door.
- ○ nocked
- ○ nokked
- ○ knokked
- ● knocked

**TERRANOVA**

### Go over each question on the page as a class.

Encourage students to pronounce each word to themselves. They then have two clues for removing the incorrect answer choices: those that don't look right and those that don't sound right.

### Question 1

Silent /b/

### Question 2

The letters *dge* often make the /j/ sound.

### Question 4

Every answer choice for this example is very similar. Students must read each answer choice carefully.

### Question 6

Remind students that *knocked* contains a silent /k/.

# Exercise 4

# RULING OUT WRONG ANSWER CHOICES

**Review the concept of ruling out wrong answer choices with the class.**

Explain that this approach is extremely important and beneficial when taking a multiple-choice test.

Go over the example question in the On Your Mark! section of the Pupil Edition page. Point out to students that they always have a one in four chance of answering a multiple-choice question correctly, even when they have no idea what the answer is.

If they can rule out just one answer choice, their chances of answering correctly go up to one in three. Ruling out two answer choices leaves them with a 50 percent chance of answering the question correctly.

For difficult questions, students should always rely on this test-taking strategy. Encourage them to cross out answer choice letters that they can rule out. They should do this on the actual test pages, not the answer sheet. If they cannot write on the test, tell them to record the answer choice letters that they are eliminating on scratch paper.

**Go over the example question as a class.** Make sure students rule out wrong answer choices.

---

## ON YOUR MARK!

### Ruling Out Wrong Answer Choices

Sometimes you can find the right answer to a question, even if you don't know the answer right away! All you have to do is rule out the answer choices you know are wrong.

**Where does your neighbor Mr. Johnson live?**

○ in a pond
○ in a library
● in a house
○ in a tree

You can answer this question even if you don't know Mr. Johnson.

- (1st) *in a pond.* Mr. Johnson cannot live in a pond! Rule this out.
- (2nd) *in a library.* Mr. Johnson cannot live in a library! Rule this out.
- (3rd) *in a house.* Mr. Johnson could definitely live in a house. Keep this one, and look at the last answer choice.
- (4th) *in a tree.* Mr. Johnson cannot live in a tree! Rule this out. The (3rd) Answer choice must be correct!

## GET SET!

Let's look at an example. Remember to rule out the wrong answer choices first.

Find the word that is spelled correctly and completes the sentence.

*He could run _____ the track for hours.*

● around
○ aruond
○ arownd

(1st) is **correct!** If you rule out the answer choices that you know are wrong, it makes finding the correct answer easier for you!

---

⭐ **EXTRA ACTIVITY**

Play *Twenty Questions* with students. Think of a person they would know, such as your school principal, and have them guess who you are thinking of by asking questions. After the game is over, point out to students that they were able to rule out incorrect answer choices with each question. For example, if one student asked, "Is this person a girl?" and you answered, "yes," they were able to rule out a huge number of people.

**Go over each question on the page as a class.**

The questions on this page test the spelling skills students learned in Exercises 1 through 3. Remind students to rule out answer choices that they know are wrong as they work through the questions on this page.

The words on this page do not follow any specific spelling rules. Their spellings must be memorized.

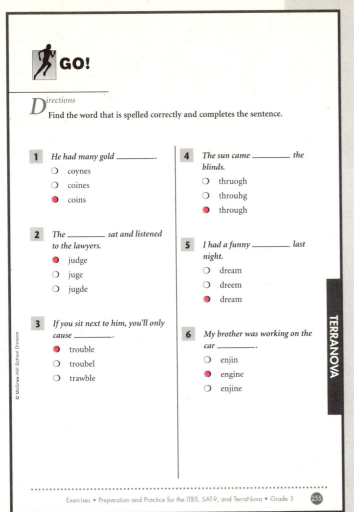

**GO!**

*Directions*
Find the word that is spelled correctly and completes the sentence.

**1** *He had many gold _____.*
- ○ coynes
- ○ coines
- ● coins

**2** *The _____ sat and listened to the lawyers.*
- ● judge
- ○ juge
- ○ jugde

**3** *If you sit next to him, you'll only cause _____.*
- ● trouble
- ○ troubel
- ○ trawble

**4** *The sun came _____ the blinds.*
- ○ thruogh
- ○ throuhg
- ● through

**5** *I had a funny _____ last night.*
- ○ dream
- ○ dreem
- ● dream

**6** *My brother was working on the car _____.*
- ○ enjin
- ● engine
- ○ enjine

**TERRANOVA**

## Exercise 5

# END MARKS

**Review the very important rules concerning end marks with your class.**

Remind students that every sentence must have a punctuation mark. Also, review with them the difference between periods, question marks, and exclamation marks so that they can place them accurately.

Write some sentences on the board and have students supply the end mark. Some examples you might use are:

- *Are you coming to my party (?)*
- *Watch out (!)*
- *I like to play basketball (.)*
- *My favorite teacher is Mrs (.) Lopez (.)*

## TEACHING TIP

Point out that using a period after an abbreviation is not the same type of end mark as the others discussed on the Pupil Edition page. This type of period can appear anywhere in a sentence—not just at the end.

**Go over the example question as a class.**

---

### Exercise 5

## ON YOUR MARK!

### End Marks

 **Use periods to end a statement.**
*Mustapha plays the trumpet.*

**Use periods at the end of an abbreviation.**
*I live next to Mrs. Matthews.*

 **Use question marks to end a question.**
*Do you like cheese?*

 **Use exclamation marks to end a statement of excitement.**
*Look out for that car!*

 **GET SET!**

Let's look at an example.

**Find the anser choice with the correct punctuation and capitalization.**

○ Have you seen my socks.
○ Wow, that's great?
○ I took my shoes off at the door
● I cannot remember where I put them.

(1st) is **wrong.** This sentence is a question. It must end with a question mark, not a period.

(2nd) is **wrong.** This sentence is a statement of excitement. It must end with an exclamation point, not a question mark.

(3rd) is **wrong.** This sentence has no punctuation at all. Every sentence needs a punctuation mark at the end of it.

(4th) is **correct!** It is a statement, so it should have a period.

---

### TEACHING TIP

Explain to students that question marks are only used with sentences that *ask* something. Familiarize students with the most common question words. Tell them to look for these words at the beginning of sentences. A question word at the beginning of a sentence is a clue to use a question mark at the end. Some examples: *Are, What, How, Who, When, Where, Which, Can, Is,* and *Did.*

**GO!**

Directions

For Numbers 1 through 6, find the answer choice with the correct punctuation and capitalization.

**1**
- ○ It was the last soccer game of the season
- ○ The game was tied with five minutes left to play?
- ○ She made the final goal with only seconds left in the game,
- ● It knocked me off my feet!

**2**
- ● I like math class.
- ○ We get to play games,
- ○ I like to solve problems?
- ○ I wish class was longer

**3**
- ● Quick!
- ○ Help me set the table for dinner?
- ○ They are tired after work!
- ○ I will help again tomorrow,

**4**
- ○ My dog Max is very sweet?
- ○ He meets me at the door when I come home from school
- ○ He licks my face and wags his tail,
- ● Max makes me feel loved.

**5**
- ○ The birds sing every morning:
- ● Do you like to hear them sing?
- ○ It seems to change every day
- ○ It is a nice way to start the day

**6**
- ○ My class has a pet hamster?
- ● His name is Albert.
- ○ We got to vote on the name!
- ○ Albert is fuzzy and friendly?

**TERRANOVA**

---

 **Go over each question on the page as a class.**

## Question 1

1st choice: Missing an end mark

2nd choice: Not a question

3rd choice: Commas never go at the end of a sentence.

4th choice: Correct

## Question 2

1st choice: Correct

2nd choice: Commas never go at the end of a sentence.

3rd choice: Not a question

4th choice: Missing an end mark

## Question 5

There is a colon in the first answer choice. Explain to students what a colon is and when it is used in writing.

None of the correct answers on this page involves a question. Give students an extra example that uses a question as the correct answer.

## Exercise 6

# COMMAS

 **Review the rules for using commas with your students.**

Explain to students that commas are only used within sentences, not at the end like an end mark. Using examples on the board, show students that commas are used at natural pauses in a sentence. Only end marks should be used to finish a sentence.

Write some sentences on the board and have students insert commas in the proper places. Some examples you might use are:

- *No I don't want to go.*
- *Once upon a time there was a dog named Sandy.*
- *Sara what are you doing?*
- *I went to the park but I didn't stay long.*
- *Juan likes to play basketball and he is very tall.*

 **Go over the example question as a class.**

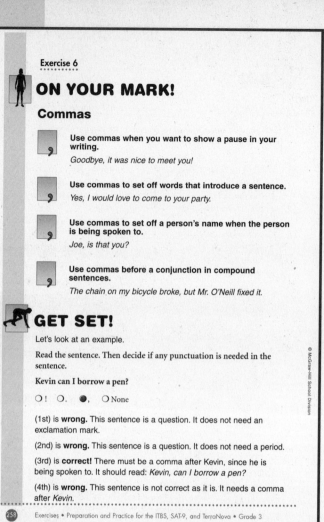

### Exercise 6

## ON YOUR MARK!

### Commas

**,** Use commas when you want to show a pause in your writing.
*Goodbye, it was nice to meet you!*

**,** Use commas to set off words that introduce a sentence.
*Yes, I would love to come to your party.*

**,** Use commas to set off a person's name when the person is being spoken to.
*Joe, is that you?*

**,** Use commas before a conjunction in compound sentences.
*The chain on my bicycle broke, but Mr. O'Neill fixed it.*

## GET SET!

Let's look at an example.

Read the sentence. Then decide if any punctuation is needed in the sentence.

Kevin can I borrow a pen?

○ !    ○ .    ● ,    ○ None

(1st) is **wrong.** This sentence is a question. It does not need an exclamation mark.

(2nd) is **wrong.** This sentence is a question. It does not need a period.

(3rd) is **correct!** There must be a comma after Kevin, since he is being spoken to. It should read: *Kevin, can I borrow a pen?*

(4th) is **wrong.** This sentence is not correct as it is. It needs a comma after *Kevin.*

 **TEACHING TIP**

Review the conjunctions that students will see most often. Quick recognition of conjunctions will help students identify the need for a comma. Some familiar conjunctions are: *but, because, and, since, despite, yet, although, though,* and *however.*

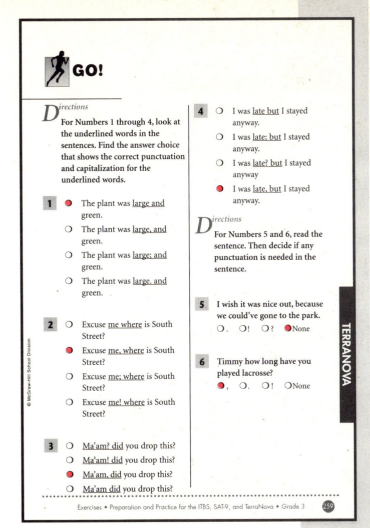

**GO!**

*Directions*
For Numbers 1 through 4, look at the underlined words in the sentences. Find the answer choice that shows the correct punctuation and capitalization for the underlined words.

**1** ● The plant was <u>large and</u> green.
   ○ The plant was <u>large, and</u> green.
   ○ The plant was <u>large; and</u> green.
   ○ The plant was <u>large. and</u> green.

**2** ○ Excuse <u>me where</u> is South Street?
   ● Excuse <u>me, where</u> is South Street?
   ○ Excuse <u>me; where</u> is South Street?
   ○ Excuse <u>me! where</u> is South Street?

**3** ○ <u>Ma'am? did</u> you drop this?
   ○ <u>Ma'am! did</u> you drop this?
   ● <u>Ma'am, did</u> you drop this?
   ○ <u>Ma'am did</u> you drop this?

**4** ○ I was <u>late but</u> I stayed anyway.
   ○ I was <u>late; but</u> I stayed anyway.
   ○ I was <u>late? but</u> I stayed anyway
   ● I was <u>late, but</u> I stayed anyway.

*Directions*
For Numbers 5 and 6, read the sentence. Then decide if any punctuation is needed in the sentence.

**5** I wish it was nice out, because we could've gone to the park.
   ○ .   ○ !   ○ ?   ● None

**6** Timmy how long have you played lacrosse?
   ● ,   ○ .   ○ !   ○ None

**TERRANOVA**

**Go over each question on the page as a class.**

## Question 1

Two adjectives connected by *and* do not require a comma.

## Question 2

*Excuse me* is set off from the rest of the sentence with a comma.

## Question 3

Commas always follow a direct address such as *Ma'am*.

## Question 4

A comma always comes before a conjunction in a compound sentence.

## Question 6

A comma should follow a direct address.

# COMMAS IN A SERIES

 **Review the proper usage of commas in a series.**

Point out to your students that commas in a series are often used with the word *and.* The last comma in the series precedes the word *and.*

Write some sentences on the board that contain series but no commas. Have students come to the board and insert commas where appropriate. Some examples you might use are:

- *I like to eat apples oranges and mangos.*
- *I put away my toys my clothes my books and my games.*
- *My three sisters are named Sally Patricia and Jordan.*

 **Go over the example question as a class.**

---

Exercise 7

 ## ON YOUR MARK!

### Commas in a Series

 Use commas between items in a series.

*He likes cats, dogs, and fish.*

*I mopped the floor, washed the dishes, and swept the porch.*

*We studied French, math, and science.*

*She went out to dinner with her mother, uncle, and brother.*

 ## GET SET!

Let's look at an example.

**Find the answer choice with the correct punctuation and capitalization.**

- ○ He bought carrots apples and bagels at the store.
- ● I folded my shirts, pants, and sweaters.
- ○ She drank milk, apple juice, and, water.
- ○ They painted the rooms red green, and blue.

(1st) is **wrong.** A comma must be between each item on the list: *carrots, apples, and bagels.*

(2nd) is **correct!** There is a comma between each item on the list.

(3rd) is **wrong.** There are commas after every item on the list, but no comma is needed after *and.*

(4th) is **wrong.** A comma must come after *red,* since that is an item on the list.

---

  ## EXTRA ACTIVITY

Give students some prompting sentences that need lists to be completed.

The names of my friends are...

My five favorite foods are...

Under my bed you can find...

When I go on vacation, I bring with me...

**GO!**

*Directions*

For Numbers 1 and 2, find the answer choice with the correct punctuation and capitalization.

**1**
- ● I like to ski, hike, and rock climb.
- ❍ Last year, I hiked in Arizona, Colorado and, Utah.
- ❍ I rock climb with Eric, Greg, and, Steve.
- ❍ When I ski, I bring my boots skis, and poles.

**2**
- ❍ I went shopping at the toy store, the music store and, the bookstore.
- ❍ I needed to buy presents for my friend my teacher, and, my aunt.
- ● I bought a toy boat, a tape, and a cookbook.
- ❍ I wrapped tied and delivered each gift.

*Directions*

For Numbers 3 through 5, look at the underlined words in the sentences. Find the answer choice that shows the correct punctuation and capitalization for the underlined words.

**3**
- ❍ I have lived in <u>Washington Oregon and California</u>.
- ● I have lived in <u>Washington, Oregon, and California</u>.
- ❍ I have lived in <u>Washington, Oregon, and, California</u>.
- ❍ I have lived in <u>Washington Oregon, and California</u>.

**4**
- ● In track club, we <u>stretch, jog, and run</u>.
- ❍ In track club, we <u>stretch jog, and run</u>.
- ❍ In track club, we <u>stretch, jog, and, run</u>.
- ❍ In track club, we <u>stretch jog and run</u>.

**5**
- ❍ I learn <u>math science and English</u> every day at school.
- ❍ I learn <u>math, science, and, English</u>, every day at school.
- ● I learn <u>math, science, and English</u> every day at school.

Exercises • Preparation and Practice for the ITBS, SAT-9, and TerraNova • Grade 3  261

**TERRANOVA**

© McGraw-Hill School Division

 **Go over each question on the page as a class.**

Tell students that incorrect punctuation on the TerraNova could mean too much punctuation as well as too little.

For each question on this page, remind students that a comma always goes after each item in a series, except the last one. A comma never should go after *and* when it is used to describe a series.

# QUOTATIONS

## Capitalization and Punctuation

 Go over the important rules regarding writing quotations discussed on the Pupil Edition page.

Write some quotations on the board, but include several errors. Have students come to the board and fix the errors. Some examples you might use are:

- *"Jackie said, I'm tired."*
- *My brother said that I should, "leave him alone."*
- *Mom said "Hello."*
- *I asked, "What are you doing"*

When students fix the errors, have them point out which rule each error applies to.

 Go over the example question as a class.

---

## ON YOUR MARK!

### Quotations: Capitalization and Punctuation

Quotation marks show that someone is speaking.

*Linda said, "Let's go to a movie."*
*"These cookies are great!" shouted Claire.*

> **Remember these important rules about writing quotations:**
>
> - Quotation marks come at the beginning and end of a person's exact words.
> - The first letter inside a quotation is *always* capitalized.
>   *My sister said, "**Y**our room looks great now!"*
> - Put a comma before the quote.
>   *Dad said**,** "I think it's clean enough."*
> - Put punctuation at the end of the quote.
>   *He asked, "Can I borrow your vacuum cleaner**?**"*

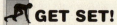 ## GET SET!

Let's look at an example.

Read the sentence. Then decide if any punctuation is needed in the sentence.

"Good morning, Ms. Hommes, the student said.

● "    ○ !    ○ ,    ○ None

(1st) is **correct!** A quotation mark must come before and after a person's exact words. *"Good morning, Ms. Hommes," the students said.*

(2nd) is **wrong.** This statement is not an exclamation. It does not need an exclamation point.

(3rd) is **wrong.** There are commas everywhere there should be in this sentence, after *good morning,* and after *Ms. Hommes.*

(4th) is **wrong.** The sentence is missing a quotation mark.

---

 ## TEACHING TIP

Remind students that quotation marks are placed outside the end marks. This is an unusual situation since students are taught to end every sentence with the appropriate end mark. Emphasize that using the correct end mark (question mark, exclamation mark, and period) is still important even though, in this instance, they do not occur at the end of the sentence.

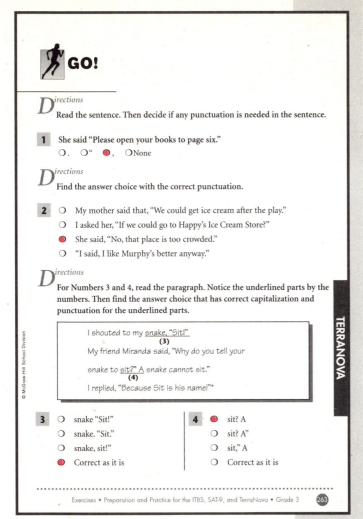

### GO!

*Directions*
Read the sentence. Then decide if any punctuation is needed in the sentence.

**1** She said "Please open your books to page six."
○ .   ○ "   ● ,   ○None

*Directions*
Find the answer choice with the correct punctuation.

**2**
○ My mother said that, "We could get ice cream after the play."
○ I asked her, "If we could go to Happy's Ice Cream Store?"
● She said, "No, that place is too crowded."
○ "I said, I like Murphy's better anyway."

*Directions*
For Numbers 3 and 4, read the paragraph. Notice the underlined parts by the numbers. Then find the answer choice that has correct capitalization and punctuation for the underlined parts.

> I shouted to my <u>snake, "Sit!"</u>
>           **(3)**
> My friend Miranda said, "Why do you tell your
>
> snake to <u>sit?" A</u> snake cannot sit."
>       **(4)**
> I replied, "Because Sit is his name!"*

**3**
○ snake "Sit!"
○ snake. "Sit."
○ snake, sit!"
● Correct as it is

**4**
● sit? A
○ sit? A"
○ sit," A
○ Correct as it is

**TERRANOVA**

© McGraw-Hill School Division

 **Go over each question on the page as a class.**

### Question 1

Comma required after *said.*

### Question 2

Quotation marks should only be placed around direct quotations—a speaker's exact words.

### Question 3

This example is *Correct as it is* because it follows all the rules noted on Pupil Edition page 262. Point out how each of the rules was followed.

### Question 4

Quotation marks should never be placed in the middle of a direct quotation.

# DATES AND HOLIDAYS

**Go over the rules regarding the correct punctuation and capitalization of dates and holidays.**

Remind students that days of the week are capitalized, as are months. In addition to the examples in the Pupil Edition book, give students examples of dates and holidays within sentences. Leave out some necessary capitalization and punctuation and have students correct the errors. Some examples you might use are:

- *I will be nine years old on january, 7 2002.*

- *We met on October 5 1995.*

- *St. patrick's day is March 17th.*

- *Where were you on the night of december 8 2000?*

## TEACHING TIP

The term "proper noun" is introduced on the Pupil Edition page. Make sure your students understand what a proper noun is before completing this exercise.

**Go over the example question as a class.**

---

## ON YOUR MARK!

### Dates and Holidays

A **date** lists a specific month, date, and year.

*October 11, 1973*

When writing a date, a **comma** is placed between the day and the year only. Never place a comma between the month and date.

*July 1, 1970*       *February 14, 2000*

**Months** are proper nouns and are always capitalized.

*January, April, July, December*

A **holiday** is a name that describes a specific date. A holiday may include more than one word.

*Labor Day*       *Fourth of July*       *St. Patrick's Day*

## GET SET!

Let's look at an example.

**Find the answer choice with the correct punctuation and capitalization.**

- ○  School ends just after memorial day.
- ○  The exact date is june 2 2000.
- ●  We are leaving for vacation on June 12, 2001.
- ○  I love the Summer.

(1st) is **wrong.** *Memorial Day* must be capitalized. It is a holiday.

(2nd) is **wrong.** A comma must come between the date and the year, and the month must be capitalized.

(3rd) is **correct!** The month is capitalized, and there is a comma between the day and year.

(4th) is **wrong.** *Summer* should not be capitalized. It is not a month or a holiday.

264    Exercises • Preparation and Practice for the ITBS, SAT-9, and TerraNova • Grade 3

---

## EXTRA ACTIVITY

Have students write a paragraph about their favorite holiday. Before they begin writing, have them look at a calendar to determine the date when that holiday will take place next. Make sure they include the name of the holiday and the date in their paragraphs. Check their paragraphs for correct punctuation and capitalization.

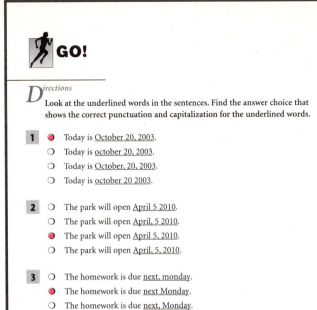

# GO!

**Directions**

Look at the underlined words in the sentences. Find the answer choice that shows the correct punctuation and capitalization for the underlined words.

**1**
- ● Today is <u>October 20, 2003</u>.
- ○ Today is <u>october 20, 2003</u>.
- ○ Today is <u>October, 20, 2003</u>.
- ○ Today is <u>october 20 2003</u>.

**2**
- ○ The park will open <u>April 5 2010</u>.
- ○ The park will open <u>April, 5 2010</u>.
- ● The park will open <u>April 5, 2010</u>.
- ○ The park will open <u>April, 5, 2010</u>.

**3**
- ○ The homework is due <u>next, monday</u>.
- ● The homework is due <u>next Monday</u>.
- ○ The homework is due <u>next, Monday</u>.
- ○ The homework is due <u>next monday</u>.

**4**
- ○ Every <u>sunday of the summer</u>, we go out for dinner.
- ○ Every <u>sunday of the Summer</u>, we go out for dinner.
- ● Every <u>Sunday of the summer</u>, we go out for dinner.
- ○ Every <u>Sunday of the Summer</u>, we go out for dinner.

**5**
- ● I made my mother a card for <u>Mother's Day</u>.
- ○ I made my mother a card for <u>Mother's day</u>.
- ○ I made my mother a card for <u>mother's Day</u>.
- ○ I made my mother a card for <u>mother's day</u>.

**TERRANOVA**

## Go over each question on the page as a class.

### Question 1

Months are always capitalized. A comma goes between the day and the year.

### Question 2

A comma goes between the day and the year.

### Question 3

Point out to students that the last answer choice has the correct punctuation, but *monday* should be capitalized. Students must look over sentences carefully for both punctuation and capitalization errors.

### Question 4

The word *summer* is not capitalized because it is not a proper noun. Days of the week are always capitalized.

### Question 5

All important words in a holiday are capitalized.

# TITLES OF PEOPLE

 **Review with students the meaning of the word *title*.**

Go over the different titles explained on the Pupil Edition page. Ask students to name some other titles they know that can be applied to people. Some examples are:

- *Miss*
- *King*
- *Queen*
- *Emperor*
- *Professor*

Go over the tip box on the Pupil Edition page that differentiates titles from common nouns. Make sure students understand this. Provide examples if necessary.

 ## TEACHING TIP

Make sure students know that a period always follow a title abbreviation.

 **Go over the example question as a class.**

---

 ## ON YOUR MARK!

### Titles of People

A **title** is a term of respect for someone. Capitalize titles and names.

*President Washington*

*Principal Adam Skinner*

> **TIP:** Do not capitalize words for jobs if they do not show a specific person's position. *The first* **president**, **President** *Washington, is my favorite* **president***.*

A title can be abbreviated in some cases. Remember to capitalize them and place a period at the end of the title.

*I like Mr. Forrester.*

*He is taller than Mrs. Forrester.*

*I call their daughter Ms. Forrester.*

*Their son, Dr. Forrester, is my doctor.*

 ## GET SET!

Let's look at an example.

**Find the answer choice with the correct punctuation and capitalization.**

- ● She mowed all of the yards, starting with Mr. Harrison's house.
- ○ Next, she went to mrs black's house.
- ○ It didn't seem like Ms Wu was home.
- ○ Finally, she dropped by dr. Nelson's house.

(1st) is **correct!** *Mr.* is capitalized and is followed by a period.

(2nd) is **wrong.** *Mrs.* is not capitalized and it is not followed by a period. Also, *Black*, a proper noun, must be capitalized.

(3rd) is **wrong.** *Ms.* is capitalized, but it is not followed by a period.

(4th) is **wrong.** *Dr.* is not capitalized.

---

 ## EXTRA ACTIVITY

To give students practice with titles as common versus proper nouns, make a worksheet containing several sentences for students and tell them to pick out the words that do and do not need to be capitalized. Some examples you might use are:

- *She is the best principal I've ever had.*
- *I'm going to see principal Smith.*
- *Some day I will be king.*
- *I think king arthur is wonderful.*

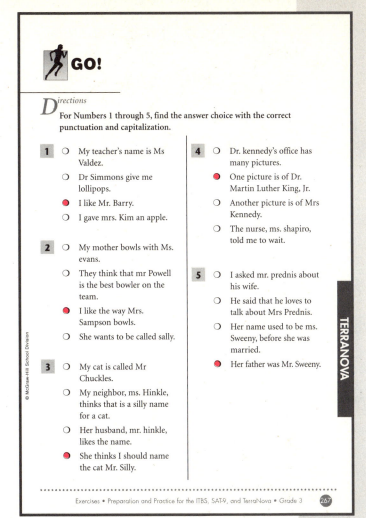

## GO!

*Directions*

For Numbers 1 through 5, find the answer choice with the correct punctuation and capitalization.

**1**
- ○ My teacher's name is Ms Valdez.
- ○ Dr Simmons give me lollipops.
- ● I like Mr. Barry.
- ○ I gave mrs. Kim an apple.

**2**
- ○ My mother bowls with Ms. evans.
- ○ They think that mr Powell is the best bowler on the team.
- ● I like the way Mrs. Sampson bowls.
- ○ She wants to be called sally.

**3**
- ○ My cat is called Mr Chuckles.
- ○ My neighbor, ms. Hinkle, thinks that is a silly name for a cat.
- ○ Her husband, mr. hinkle, likes the name.
- ● She thinks I should name the cat Mr. Silly.

**4**
- ○ Dr. kennedy's office has many pictures.
- ● One picture is of Dr. Martin Luther King, Jr.
- ○ Another picture is of Mrs Kennedy.
- ○ The nurse, ms. shapiro, told me to wait.

**5**
- ○ I asked mr. prednis about his wife.
- ○ He said that he loves to talk about Mrs Prednis.
- ○ Her name used to be ms. Sweeny, before she was married.
- ● Her father was Mr. Sweeny.

TERRANOVA

© McGraw-Hill School Division

 **Go over each question on the page as a class.**

### Question 1

Abbreviated titles must be capitalized and followed by a period.

### Question 2

First names, last names, and titles of specific people must be capitalized.

### Question 3

Pet names, like other names, are capitalized.

### Question 4

Only the second choice uses correct capitalization and punctuation of titles.

### Question 5

Abbreviated titles must be capitalized and followed by a period. Last names must be capitalized.

The only titles tested on this page involve abbreviations. Assign the exercise in the gray box on Teacher Edition page 266 to give students practice with titles that are not abbreviations.

© McGraw-Hill School Division

## Exercise 11
# WRITING LETTERS

**Go over the rules for writing letter greetings and closings with the class.**

Explain that the first word of a greeting or closing is always capitalized.

## TEACHING TIP

Remind students that names and titles in greetings and closings should be capitalized as always. They are still proper nouns.

Write examples of greeting and closings on the board so students become familiar with them. Some examples you might use are:

- *Sincerely*
- *Regards*
- *Love always*
- *To Whom it May Concern*
- *Dear Sirs*
- *Dear Mrs. Smith*
- *Hello*
- *Yours truly*
- *Your friend*

**Go over the example question as a class.**

---

### Exercise 11

# ON YOUR MARK!

## Writing Letters

All letters contain a greeting at the beginning and a closing at the end.

The **greeting** usually starts with *Dear* followed by the name of the person who will receive the letter.

   *Dear Joey,*      *Dear Monica,*      *Dear Mr. Chandler,*

The first word in the greeting and the name should both be **capitalized**.

Use a **comma** after the end of the greeting.

The **closing** tells the reader that the letter is about to end.

   *Sincerely,*     *Your friend,*     *Best wishes,*
   *Ross*        *Rachel*       *Phoebe*

Only the first word in the closing should be **capitalized**.

Use a **comma** after the end of the closing.

# GET SET!

Let's look at an example.

**Read the letter. Then find the answer choice that shows the correct punctuation and capitalization.**

Thanks for returning my hat. I was so upset that I left it in the store.

                    Sincerely,
                    Ramona

○  Dear Felix
●  Dear Felix,
○  dear Felix
○  dear Felix,

(2nd) is **correct!** The greeting is capitalized and the greeting ends with a comma.

---

## EXTRA ACTIVITY

Have students write letters as an extra activity to help them understand capitalization and punctuation. Tell them to choose one person to whom they would like to write a letter. Have them write a short note to the person. They should open the letter with a greeting and end with a closing. Emphasize the importance of using correct capitalization and punctuation.

## GO!

*Directions*

Read the letter. Then find the answer choice that best completes the underlined sections of this letter.

---

**(1)**

I'll be home late. Start dinner without me.

**(2)**

Margery

---

**1**
- ○ Dear Larry
- ○ dear Larry
- ● Dear Larry,
- ○ dear Larry,

**2**
- ○ love
- ● Love,
- ○ Love
- ○ love,

---

**(3)**

My plane arrives at 10:30 P.M. I look forward to seeing you.

**(4)**

Maxine

---

**3**
- ○ dear raul
- ○ dear Raul
- ○ Dear, Raul,
- ● Dear Raul,

**4**
- ○ sincerely,
- ○ sincerely
- ● Sincerely,
- ○ Sincerely

**TERRANOVA**

---

**Go over each question on the page as a class.**

### Question 1 and 3

Capitalize all important words in a letter greeting. This includes both the salutation and any names. The greeting should be followed by a comma.

### Question 2 and 4

The first word in a letter closing must be capitalized and the closing should be followed by a comma.

# Exercise 12

# CAPITALIZATION

## Places

 **Go over the specific place names that require capitalization.**

Ask students for their own examples of each type of place. Write their suggestions on the board. Some examples might be:

- *Detroit, Michigan, Spain, South America*

- *Mississippi River, Smokey Mountains*

- *Puritan Avenue, Interstate 54*

- *Museum of Natural History, Brooklyn Bridge, Sears Tower*

 **Go over the example question as a class.**

---

 **Exercise 12**

## ON YOUR MARK!

### Capitalization: Places

Capitalize names of specific places.

**Cities, States, Countries, Continents**
*Dallas, Washington, France, Asia*

**Geographical Features**
*Rocky Mountains, Snake River*

**Streets and Highways**
*Elm Street, Highway 66*

**Buildings and Bridges**
*Museum of Modern Art, Empire State Building, Golden Gate Bridge*

> **TIP:** Capitalize the name of a specific place:
> ***Bob's Coffee Store***
> Do NOT capitalize a word that does not name a specific place:
> the **store**

 **GET SET!**

Let's look at an example.

**Find the answer choice with the correct punctuation and capitalization.**

○ We're going on vacation to norway.

○ I live at 40 South harbor drive.

● They're hiking in the Sierra Mountains.

○ The smithsonian museum closes at 4:30.

(1st) is **wrong.** *Norway* is the name of a country. It must be capitalized.

(2nd) is **wrong.** *South Harbor Drive* must be capitalized. It is a specific road.

(3rd) is **correct!** *Sierra Mountains* is a specific place. It must be capitalized.

(4th) is **wrong.** *The Smithsonian Museum* is a specific place. It must be capitalized.

© McGraw-Hill School Division

---

## TEACHING TIP

Remind students that the names of specific places are capitalized. Similar words that do not name a particular place are not capitalized. Give students examples that show this difference.

- *Do you see that bridge over there?*

- *It is the Betsy Ross Bridge.*

- *My favorite museum is the Guggenheim Museum.*

- *I live on Oak Street. It is the prettiest street in the neighborhood.*

© McGraw-Hill School Division

**GO!**

*Directions*

For Numbers 1 through 3, choose find the answer choice with the correct punctuation and capitalization.

**1** ● We saw pictures of Puerto Rico.
○ I liked them better than the ones of tokyo, japan.
○ My mother thought that Rome, italy looked the most beautiful.
○ My father asked us if we wanted to see pictures of Mexico city, Mexico next.

**2** ○ My trip started in washington d.c.
○ I went to New haven, connecticut next.
● After that, I traveled to Boston, Massachusetts.
○ Finally, I went to Freeport maine.

**3** ○ Fans came from all over the country to Madison wisconsin.
○ Most of the fans came from minneapolis minnesota.
● Several fans came from Savannah, Georgia.
○ The fans who had traveled the farthest came from Juneau, alaska.

**TERRANOVA**

*Directions*

For Number 4, look at the underlined words in the sentences. Find the answer choice that shows the punctuation and capitalization for the underlined words.

**4** My favorite place to go on a sunny day is <u>Golden Gardens Park</u>.
○ golden Gardens park.
○ golden gardens park.
○ Golden gardens park.
● Correct as it is

 **Go over each question on the page as a class.**

## Questions 1, 2, and 3

The names of cities, states, and countries are always capitalized.

## Question 4

All of the important words in the name of a specific place must be capitalized.

# CAPITALIZATION

## Beginning of a Sentence

 **Go over the rule for using capital letters at the beginning of a sentence.**

Remind students that this rule applies to any word that begins any sentence. This includes both proper nouns that are normally capitalized and common nouns that are not.

 **Go over the example question as a class.**

---

 **Exercise 13**

### ON YOUR MARK!

**Capitalization: Beginning of a Sentence**

The first letter in a sentence must be capitalized.

**Incorrect:**
*mom got us a bird to keep us company in our new house.*
*we named the bird "Newcomer."*
*the bird sings "Row, Row, Row Your Boat."*

**Correct:**
*Mom got us a bird to keep us company in our new house.*
*We named the bird "Newcomer."*
*The bird sings "Row, Row, Row Your Boat."*

 ### GET SET!

Let's look at an example.

**Which sentence has correct punctuation and capitalization?**

○   she walked to Suzanne's house.

○   coffee tastes better at City Diner.

●   The mug was too hot to hold.

○   it cooled quickly!

(1st) is **wrong.** *Suzanne* is capitalized because it is the name of a specific person, but the first word in the sentence is not capitalized.

(2nd) is **wrong.** *City Diner* is capitalized because it is the name of a specific place, but the first word in the sentence is not capitalized.

(3rd) is **correct!** It is the only sentence that begins with a capitalized word.

(4th) is **wrong.** The first word in the sentence is not capitalized.

---

### TEACHING TIP

When practice sentences are isolated by error types, students are quicker to notice incorrect capitalization. On the TerraNova, students will have to recognize incorrect capitalization in sentences that are mixed with other sentences.

### Questions 1 and 2

An end mark must go at the end of a sentence, and the first word of a new sentence is always capitalized.

### Question 4

All of the incorrect answer choices have incorrect capitalization at the beginning of the sentence.

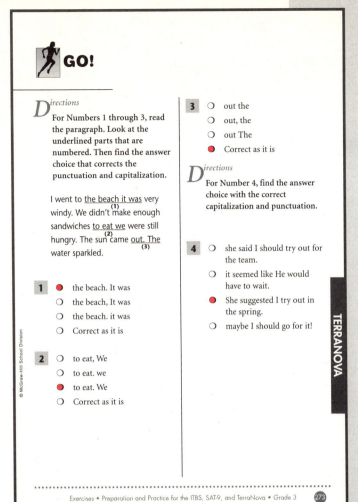

## GO!

*D*irections

For Numbers 1 through 3, read the paragraph. Look at the underlined parts that are numbered. Then find the answer choice that corrects the punctuation and capitalization.

I went to the beach it was very
                   (1)
windy. We didn't make enough sandwiches to eat we were still
              (2)
hungry. The sun came out. The
                      (3)
water sparkled.

**1**  ● the beach. It was
   ○ the beach, It was
   ○ the beach. it was
   ○ Correct as it is

**2**  ○ to eat, We
   ○ to eat. we
   ● to eat. We
   ○ Correct as it is

**3**  ○ out the
   ○ out, the
   ○ out The
   ● Correct as it is

*D*irections

For Number 4, find the answer choice with the correct capitalization and punctuation.

**4**  ○ she said I should try out for the team.
   ○ it seemed like He would have to wait.
   ● She suggested I try out in the spring.
   ○ maybe I should go for it!

**TERRANOVA**

© McGraw-Hill School Division

© McGraw-Hill School Division

# LANGUAGE MECHANICS

**Emphasize to students the importance of recognizing proper capitalization and punctuation in sentences.**

Explain that the TerraNova tests all the rules they have learned in Exercises 1 through 13 in a specific section called Language Mechanics.

Tell students that on the TerraNova, capitalization and punctuation rules may be tested together on the same question. Students will need to identify both types of mistakes.

**Go over the example question as a class.**

---

**Exercise 14**

## ON YOUR MARK!

### Language Mechanics

On the Language Mechanics section of the TerraNova, you will have to answer questions about **punctuation** and **capitalization**.

The questions test different rules. For example, one question might be about using quotation marks correctly, while another question might be about using commas correctly.

Figure out what each question is asking before you try to answer it. That way, you will know what mistakes to look for.

## GET SET!

Let's look at an example.

**Choose the answer choice that is written correctly and shows the correct capitalization and punctuation.**

○ How does my costume look!
○ Wow, I can't believe it?
○ You look exactly like the cartoon character
● The costume party will be fun.

*What is this question testing?*

The question is asking you to choose the sentence that uses correct punctuation at the end. It helps to know this because then you can focus on that specific error. Let's see which choice is correct.

(1st) is **wrong.** This sentence is a question, so it needs a question mark at the end.

(2nd) is **wrong.** This sentence is an exclamation, so it needs an exclamation mark at the end.

(3rd) is **wrong.** This sentence has no punctuation at all at the end. It needs a period.

(4th) is **correct!** This sentence makes a statement. The period at the end is correct.

---

## EXTRA ACTIVITY

To familiarize students with the Language Mechanics section of the TerraNova, make a mini-test for them, including questions that test the *skills* learned in Exercises 1 through 13 of this book. Mix up the skills and have students complete the worksheet in a set amount of time. You can use some of the questions already printed on the Go! pages in Exercises 1 through 13.

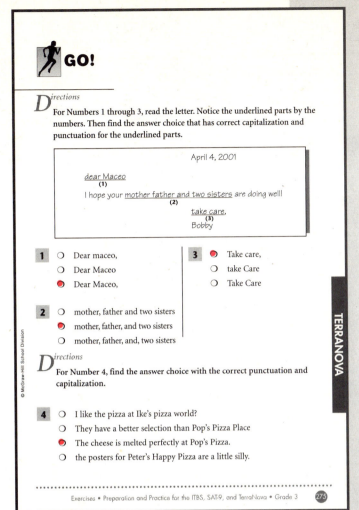

## GO!

*Directions*

For Numbers 1 through 3, read the letter. Notice the underlined parts by the numbers. Then find the answer choice that has correct capitalization and punctuation for the underlined parts.

April 4, 2001

<u>dear Maceo</u>
**(1)**
I hope your <u>mother father and two sisters</u> are doing well!
**(2)**

<u>take care,</u>
**(3)**
Bobby

**1**  ○ Dear maceo,
    ○ Dear Maceo
    ● Dear Maceo,

**2**  ○ mother, father and two sisters
    ● mother, father, and two sisters
    ○ mother, father, and, two sisters

**3**  ● Take care,
    ○ take Care
    ○ Take Care

*Directions*

For Number 4, find the answer choice with the correct punctuation and capitalization.

**4**  ○ I like the pizza at Ike's pizza world?
    ○ They have a better selection than Pop's Pizza Place
    ● The cheese is melted perfectly at Pop's Pizza.
    ○ the posters for Peter's Happy Pizza are a little silly.

TERRANOVA

Exercises • Preparation and Practice for the ITBS, SAT-9, and TerraNova • Grade 3   275

### Question 1

The first word and any names in a letter greeting must be capitalized, and the greeting should be followed by a comma.

### Question 2

A comma goes after each item in a series except the last one. A comma never follows *and* when it is used to separate items in a series.

### Question 3

Always capitalize the first word only in a letter closing.

### Question 4

1st choice: *pizza world* should be capitalized.

2nd choice: A period is needed at the end.

3rd choice: Correct

4th choice: The first word should be capitalized.

# PARTS OF A SENTENCE

 **Go over the two important parts of a sentence with students.**

Tell students that a sentence is incomplete if it is missing one of the two parts. Remind students that the predicate of a sentence must include a verb.

Write some sentences on the board and have students tell you the subject and the predicate of each sentence. Some examples you might use are:

- *Barney jumped up and down.*
- *Paco likes ice cream*
- *The salamander ran away.*
- *The football team is winning.*

 **Go over the example question as a class.**

---

 Exercise 15

## ON YOUR MARK!

### Parts of a Sentence

There are two parts of a sentence.

The **subject** of a sentence tells what or whom the sentence is about.

*Mice do not like cats.*

Sometimes the subject is more than one word.

*My cat jumped on a small mouse.*

The **predicate** of a sentence tells what the subject does or is.

*Mona is an old friend.*

*Mona writes me letters.*

 **GET SET!**

Let's look at an example.

Read the two sentences. Which underlined part is the predicate?

*She made me a huge dinner. The dinner was delicious.*

○  She
●  made me a huge dinner
○  The dinner

(1st) is **wrong.** *She* is the subject. It tells you what or who made a huge dinner.

(2nd) is **correct!** *Made me a huge dinner* tells what the subject, *she*, did.

(3rd) is **wrong.** *The dinner* is the subject. It tells what was delicious.

---

  ### TEACHING TIP

Remind students to read sentences carefully in order to find the predicate. Sentence fragments that seem wrong do not necessarily contain a predicate. Give students examples of sentence fragments without a predicate.

- *Josef and his playful dog, Whiskers.*
- *According to many people.*
- *Last Friday, at the beginning of the day.*

## GO!

**1** Find the underlined part that is the subject.

*The leaves <u>fell from the tree</u>. The <u>tree</u> <u>is in my backyard</u>.*

- ○ fell from the tree
- ● tree
- ○ is in my backyard

**2** Find the underlined part that is the predicate.

*The <u>jacket and shirt</u> <u>match</u>. <u>They</u> are blue and tan.*

- ○ jacket and shirt
- ● match
- ○ They

**3** Find the underlined part that is the subject.

*<u>The clouds in the sky</u> <u>are dark</u>. A storm <u>is coming</u>.*

- ● The clouds in the sky
- ○ are dark
- ○ is coming

**4** Find the underlined part that is the predicate.

*<u>Dad</u> made a fire. <u>The coals</u> <u>are very hot</u>.*

- ○ Dad
- ○ The coals
- ● are very hot

**5** Find the underlined part that is the subject.

*My <u>cat</u> <u>sheds her fur</u>. Her fur <u>keeps her warm</u>.*

- ● cat
- ○ sheds her fur
- ○ keeps her warm

Exercises • Preparation and Practice for the ITBS, SAT-9, and TerraNova • Grade 3  (277)

## Go over each question on the page as a class.

Remind students of the following before they answer the questions on this page:

- *The subject of a sentence tells who or what the sentence is about.*

- *Subjects are always nouns.*

- *Subjects can be more than one word.*

- *The predicate of a sentence tells what the subject does or did.*

- *Predicates always contain verbs.*

## Exercise 16
# VERBS

**Go over the definition of present tense and past tense with students.**

Explain how these tenses apply to verbs.

Discuss how to add -*ed* to verbs to make them past tense. Once you are sure students have grasped how and when to add -*ed*, point out the irregular verbs listed on the Pupil Edition page. Remind students that they must be able to recognize verbs that take an irregular past tense. Ask them to name some extra examples. List them on the board. The list might include:

- *think*⟶*thought*
- *bring*⟶*brought*
- *sing*⟶*sang*
- *take*⟶*took*
- *sleep*⟶*slept*
- *see*⟶*saw*

**Go over the example question as a class.**

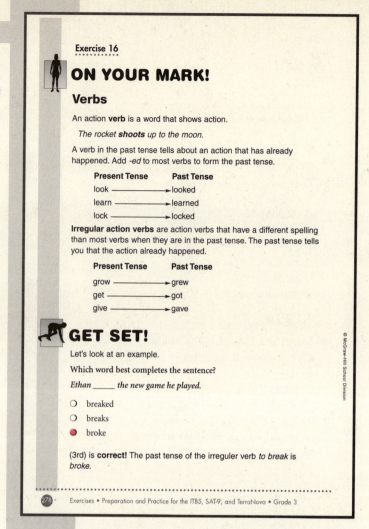

### Exercise 16

# ON YOUR MARK!

## Verbs

An action **verb** is a word that shows action.

*The rocket **shoots** up to the moon.*

A verb in the past tense tells about an action that has already happened. Add -*ed* to most verbs to form the past tense.

| Present Tense | Past Tense |
|---|---|
| look ⟶ | looked |
| learn ⟶ | learned |
| lock ⟶ | locked |

**Irregular action verbs** are action verbs that have a different spelling than most verbs when they are in the past tense. The past tense tells you that the action already happened.

| Present Tense | Past Tense |
|---|---|
| grow ⟶ | grew |
| get ⟶ | got |
| give ⟶ | gave |

# GET SET!

Let's look at an example.

Which word best completes the sentence?

*Ethan _____ the new game he played.*

○ breaked
○ breaks
● broke

(3rd) is **correct!** The past tense of the irreguler verb *to break* is *broke*.

---

⭐ **EXTRA ACTIVITY**

Perform an activity at the front of the class. You might play with two puppets and have them talk to each other. Or you could pretend to get ready in front of an imaginary mirror, donning a coat, combing your hair, and adjusting a hat. Or you might pretend to paint an arrangement of flowers. Try to vary your movements and include as much action as possible. When you are finished, have students write a description of what you did. They should use past-tense verbs to describe your actions.

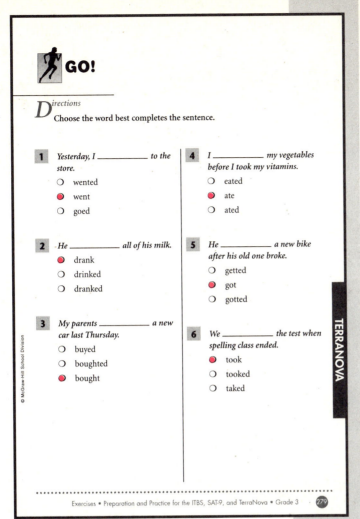

## GO!

**Directions**

Choose the word best completes the sentence.

**1** *Yesterday, I _____ to the store.*
- ○ wented
- ● went
- ○ goed

**2** *He _____ all of his milk.*
- ● drank
- ○ drinked
- ○ dranked

**3** *My parents _____ a new car last Thursday.*
- ○ buyed
- ○ boughted
- ● bought

**4** *I _____ my vegetables before I took my vitamins.*
- ○ eated
- ● ate
- ○ ated

**5** *He _____ a new bike after his old one broke.*
- ○ getted
- ● got
- ○ gotted

**6** *We _____ the test when spelling class ended.*
- ● took
- ○ tooked
- ○ taked

**TERRANOVA**

 **Go over each question on the page as a class.**

Every question on this page tests the past tense of an irregular verb. Give students extra questions about verbs with regular past tense spellings.

# VERB TENSE

 **Go over the different verb tenses—past, present, and future—with the class.**

Have students write three sentences. They should use a different verb tense in each sentence. For example:

- *She played with the dog.*
- *She plays with the dog.*
- *She will play with the dog.*

 ## TEACHING TIP

Explain to students that verbs must always agree with the subjects of sentences. Explain this concept with extra example sentences.

 **Go over the example question as a class.**

---

Exercise 17

 ## ON YOUR MARK!

### Verb Tense

Use the **past tense** of a verb for an action that happened *before* now.

   He **danced** well yesterday.

Use the **present tense** for an action that is happening now.

   He **dances** well.

Use the **future tense** for an action that will happen *after* now.

   He **will dance** well tomorrow night.

**A verb must agree with the rest of the sentence.** That means all verbs must be in the same tense.

   **Past:** *When my grandfather **was** a boy, there **was** no television.*

   **Future:** *When I **get** to school, I **will** ask the teacher a question.*

 ## GET SET!

Let's look at an example.

Which word or words complete the sentence correctly?

*Yesterday, I _____ out my window.*

- ● looked
- ○ looks
- ○ will look

(1st) is **correct!** *Yesterday* tells us this event happened in the past. That means the verb should be in the past tense.

(2nd) is **wrong.** If the sentence takes place in the past, the present tense of *to look* is wrong.

(3rd) is **wrong.** This sentence did not take place in the future. It's in the past.

*© McGraw-Hill School Division*

---

 ## EXTRA ACTIVITY

Play charades with students. Have one student perform an action verb (e.g., skiing, jumping, running). Have the class guess what the student is doing. When a student guesses correctly, have that student go to the board and write the present-tense form of the verb. Then have two more students come to the board. One should write the past tense of the verb, and the other should write the future tense of the verb. Then have students volunteer sentences that include one of the three verb forms.

*© McGraw-Hill School Division*

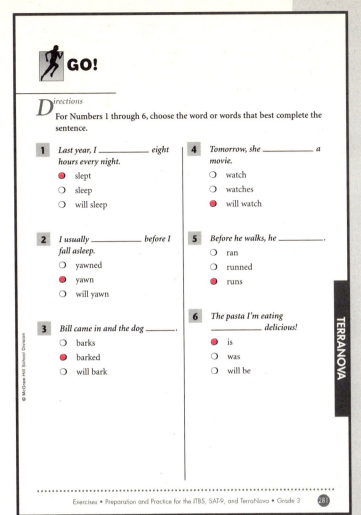

 **GO!**

### Directions

For Numbers 1 through 6, choose the word or words that best complete the sentence.

**1** *Last year, I _____ eight hours every night.*
- ● slept
- ○ sleep
- ○ will sleep

**2** *I usually _____ before I fall asleep.*
- ○ yawned
- ● yawn
- ○ will yawn

**3** *Bill came in and the dog _____.*
- ○ barks
- ● barked
- ○ will bark

**4** *Tomorrow, she _____ a movie.*
- ○ watch
- ○ watches
- ● will watch

**5** *Before he walks, he _____.*
- ○ ran
- ○ runned
- ● runs

**6** *The pasta I'm eating _____ delicious!*
- ● is
- ○ was
- ○ will be

TERRANOVA

© McGraw-Hill School Division

## Go over each question on the page as a class.

### Question 1

*Last year* is a clue that the past tense is required.

### Question 2

*Usually* is a clue that the present tense is required.

### Question 3

*Came* is a clue that the past tense is required. All verbs must agree in tense.

### Question 4

*Tomorrow* is a clue that the future tense is required.

### Question 5

There are no clear clues in this sentence.

### Question 6

*Eating* is a clue that the present tense is required.

© McGraw-Hill School Division

# HELPING VERBS

**Go over the definition of helping verbs with students.**

Review the most common helping verbs listed on the Pupil Edition page.

Write some sentences on the board, excluding the helping verb. Have students help you decide which helping verb to insert in the blank. Some examples you might use are:

- *They (were) going to the store yesterday when it started raining.*

- *I (am) playing soccer right now.*

- *Jenna (will) wake up early tomorrow morning.*

Explain to students why these helping verbs are the correct ones and how both verbs agree in their tense.

**Go over the example question as a class.**

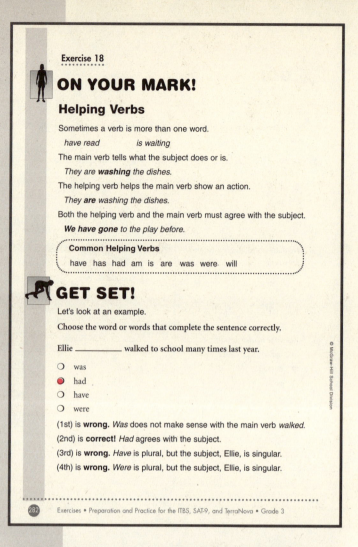

Exercise 18

## ON YOUR MARK!

### Helping Verbs

Sometimes a verb is more than one word.

*have read*          *is waiting*

The main verb tells what the subject does or is.

*They are **washing** the dishes.*

The helping verb helps the main verb show an action.

*They **are** washing the dishes.*

Both the helping verb and the main verb must agree with the subject.

***We have gone** to the play before.*

> **Common Helping Verbs**
>
> have  has  had  am  is  are  was  were  will

## GET SET!

Let's look at an example.

Choose the word or words that complete the sentence correctly.

Ellie _____ walked to school many times last year.

- ○ was
- ● had
- ○ have
- ○ were

(1st) is **wrong.** *Was* does not make sense with the main verb *walked.*

(2nd) is **correct!** *Had* agrees with the subject.

(3rd) is **wrong.** *Have* is plural, but the subject, Ellie, is singular.

(4th) is **wrong.** *Were* is plural, but the subject, Ellie, is singular.

## ⭐ EXTRA ACTIVITY

Have students write nine sentences—each including one of the helping verbs listed on the Pupil Edition page. Have students volunteer to read their sentences to the class. Encourage them by congratulating proper usage.

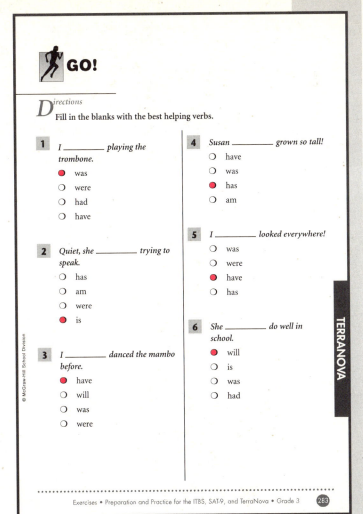

## GO!

*Directions*

Fill in the blanks with the best helping verbs.

**1** *I _____ playing the trombone.*
- ● was
- ○ were
- ○ had
- ○ have

**2** *Quiet, she _____ trying to speak.*
- ○ has
- ○ am
- ○ were
- ● is

**3** *I _____ danced the mambo before.*
- ● have
- ○ will
- ○ was
- ○ were

**4** *Susan _____ grown so tall!*
- ○ have
- ○ was
- ● has
- ○ am

**5** *I _____ looked everywhere!*
- ○ was
- ○ were
- ● have
- ○ has

**6** *She _____ do well in school.*
- ● will
- ○ is
- ○ was
- ○ had

TERRANOVA

© McGraw-Hill School Division

 **Go over each question on the page as a class.**

### Question 1
Past tense helping verb

### Question 2
Present tense helping verb

### Question 3
Past tense helping verb

### Question 4
Present tense helping verb

### Question 5
Past tense helping verb

### Question 6
Future tense helping verb

# SUBJECT-VERB AGREEMENT

 **Go over the meaning of subject-verb agreement with your class.**

Make sure students understand the terms *singular* and *plural*. Write a list of sentences on the board and have students tell you if the subjects and verbs agree or disagree. Some examples you might use are:

- *The dog sit on my lap.*
- *Jamie waits by the pool.*
- *The athlete play tennis.*
- *The frog jumps on the lily pad.*
- *Francis and Danny like each other.*

For each incorrect example, have students raise their hands and offer suggestions to fix the error. Explain that the subject and verb must agree for the sentence to be correct.

 **Go over the example question as a class.**

---

 ## ON YOUR MARK!

### Subject-Verb Agreement

A verb must always **agree** with the subject of a sentence.

If the subject is **singular** (if there is only one of something), then the verb must also be singular.

The *artist paints* on the canvas.        Your *baby-sitter lives* nearby.

If the subject is **plural** (if there is more than one of something), then the verb must also be plural.

The *artists paint* on the canvas.        Your *baby-sitters live* nearby.

> **TIP:** The subject *you* always takes a plural verb, even though it may refer to one person or many people.

 ## GET SET!

Let's look at an example.

Choose the sentence that is written correctly.

- ● The flowers smell pretty.
- ○ My nose are running.
- ○ The dancers spins often.
- ○ The duck land in the lake.

(1st) is **correct!** The word *flowers* is plural, and *smell* is plural, too.

(2nd) is **wrong.** *Nose* is singular, but *are* is plural.

(3rd) is **wrong.** The word *dancers* is plural, but *spins* is singlar.

(4th) is **wrong.** The word *duck* is singular, but *land* is plural.

---

## TEACHING TIP

Emphasize the tip box on the Pupil Edition page. Remind students of the difference between singular *you* and plural *you*. Both require a plural verb, but students should still know the distinction when *you* is used as the subject.

**Go over each question on the page as a class.**

Go over each answer choice in question 3 with the class. In the first and second answer choices, the subjects, *we* and *janitors*, are plural and require plural verbs. *Works* is singular. The third answer choice is correct because *Mr. Vansiclen* and *works* are both singular. The last answer choice is incorrect because *I*, like *you*, often takes a plural verb even though it is a singular subject.

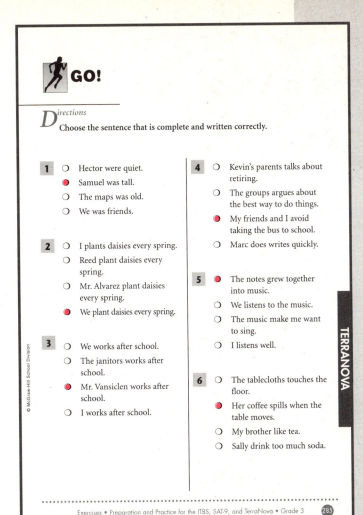

# GO!

*Directions*

Choose the sentence that is complete and written correctly.

**1**
- ○ Hector were quiet.
- ● Samuel was tall.
- ○ The maps was old.
- ○ We was friends.

**2**
- ○ I plants daisies every spring.
- ○ Reed plant daisies every spring.
- ○ Mr. Alvarez plant daisies every spring.
- ● We plant daisies every spring.

**3**
- ○ We works after school.
- ○ The janitors works after school.
- ● Mr. Vansiclen works after school.
- ○ I works after school.

**4**
- ○ Kevin's parents talks about retiring.
- ○ The groups argues about the best way to do things.
- ● My friends and I avoid taking the bus to school.
- ○ Marc does writes quickly.

**5**
- ● The notes grew together into music.
- ○ We listens to the music.
- ○ The music make me want to sing.
- ○ I listens well.

**6**
- ○ The tablecloths touches the floor.
- ● Her coffee spills when the table moves.
- ○ My brother like tea.
- ○ Sally drink too much soda.

**TERRANOVA**

© McGraw-Hill School Division

# LISTEN TO YOURSELF

**Review with students the importance of "hearing" the sentences they are reading.**

Encourage students to listen to how sentences sound in their heads as they read them in order to find errors. Advise students that this technique can work on many questions on the TerraNova. Remind them, however, that they should not read anything aloud when taking the test.

**Go over the example question as a class.**

---

### Exercise 20

# ON YOUR MARK!

## Listen to Yourself

Don't forget to **listen to yourself** when you answer the grammar questions on the TerraNova.

Read the answer choices to yourself. Imagine that you are listening to someone say what you are reading. Does it sound right? Or does it sound funny? If it sounds funny, then it's probably not written correctly.

Read these sentences out loud. How do they sound?

*I sits down.*          *We has time.*          *They am together.*

They sound funny, don't they? They sound funny because they are not correctly written. They have mistakes in them. Here are the sentences written correctly. Read them out loud. Don't they sound better?

*I sit down.*          *We have time.*          *They are together.*

# GET SET!

Let's look at another example. Listen to yourself as you read each answer choice. Does it sound right or wrong?

**Which sentence is complete and written correctly?**

○    Baseball players has to practice a lot.
○    Bob's favorite bat will be used last game.
●    The baseballs are small and hard.
○    Dirt get into player's cleats.

(1st) is **wrong.** *Has* is singular, but *players* is plural.

(2nd) is **wrong.** *Will be* is future tense, but *last game* tells you it happened in the past.

(3rd) is **correct!** The subject and verb agree. The verb is in the correct tense.

(4th) is **wrong.** *Dirt* is singular, but *get* is plural.

---

## TEACHING TIP

Advise students that reading to themselves is a skill that they can use often. Encourage them to "hear" themselves as they read stories and books for pleasure.

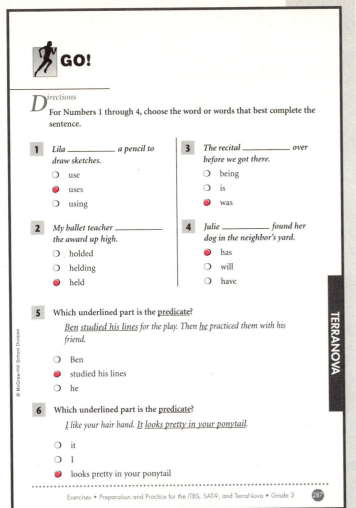

## GO!

*Directions*

For Numbers 1 through 4, choose the word or words that best complete the sentence.

**1** Lila _____ a pencil to draw sketches.

- ○ use
- ● uses
- ○ using

**2** My ballet teacher _____ the award up high.

- ○ holded
- ○ helding
- ● held

**3** The recital _____ over before we got there.

- ○ being
- ○ is
- ● was

**4** Julie _____ found her dog in the neighbor's yard.

- ● has
- ○ will
- ○ have

**5** Which underlined part is the predicate?

*Ben studied his lines for the play. Then he practiced them with his friend.*

- ○ Ben
- ● studied his lines
- ○ he

**6** Which underlined part is the predicate?

*I like your hair band. It looks pretty in your ponytail.*

- ○ it
- ○ I
- ● looks pretty in your ponytail

© McGraw-Hill School Division

**TERRANOVA**

 **Go over each question on the page as a class.**

Remind students to "say" the answer choices in their heads and listen to how they sound. This will help them determine which answer choice is correct.

### Questions 1, 2, and 3

Verb tense questions

### Question 4

Helping verb question

### Questions 5 and 6

The predicate always contains a verb.

© McGraw-Hill School Division

# ADJECTIVES THAT COMPARE

**Explain what an adjective is to students, and then go over the difference between a comparative adjective and a superlative adjective.**

On the board, create two columns: comparative adjectives (compare two nouns) and superlative adjectives (compare more than two nouns). Using the examples on the Pupil Edition page as guides, ask students for additional examples. Write their examples in the appropriate columns.

Explain that some adjectives that are used to compare do not follow the usual pattern (-*er, -est*). Go over the examples provided on the Pupil Edition page. Call on students to create sentences with each of the words. Answer any questions students have.

## TEACHING TIP

Go over the tip box on the Pupil Edition page with the class. Make sure students are comfortable with adding endings to words like *silly*, *funny*, and *sunny*.

**Go over the example question as a class.**

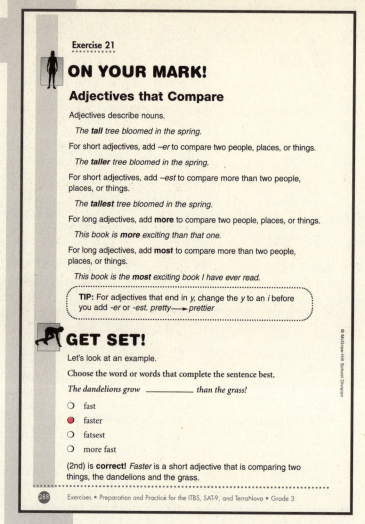

Exercise 21

## ON YOUR MARK!

### Adjectives that Compare

Adjectives describe nouns.

*The **tall** tree bloomed in the spring.*

For short adjectives, add –*er* to compare two people, places, or things.

*The **taller** tree bloomed in the spring.*

For short adjectives, add –*est* to compare more than two people, places, or things.

*The **tallest** tree bloomed in the spring.*

For long adjectives, add **more** to compare two people, places, or things.

*This book is **more** exciting than that one.*

For long adjectives, add **most** to compare more than two people, places, or things.

*This book is the **most** exciting book I have ever read.*

**TIP:** For adjectives that end in *y*, change the *y* to an *i* before you add -*er* or -*est*. *pretty* ⟶ *prettier*

## GET SET!

Let's look at an example.

Choose the word or words that complete the sentence best.

*The dandelions grow _____ than the grass!*

○ fast

● faster

○ fatsest

○ more fast

(2nd) is **correct!** *Faster* is a short adjective that is comparing two things, the dandelions and the grass.

288 Exercises • Preparation and Practice for the ITBS, SAT-9, and TerraNova • Grade 3

## EXTRA ACTIVITY

Have two students come to the front of the class. Ask the students who are seated to create sentences that compare the two students. You might start with an example, such as "Marta has shorter hair than Jacob." After students have created a few sentences involving comparative adjectives, have a third student join them. Have the students who are seated create sentences comparing all three of the standing students. You might start with an example, such as "Jacob's shirt is the most colorful of all." Write some of the students' sentences on the board and circle the comparative and superlative adjectives.

**Go over each question on the page as a class.**

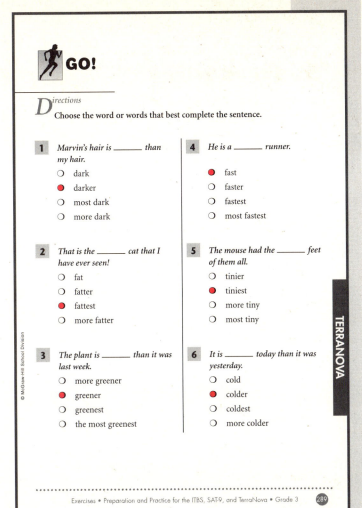

## GO!

*Directions*

Choose the word or words that best complete the sentence.

**1** *Marvin's hair is _____ than my hair.*
- ○ dark
- ● darker
- ○ most dark
- ○ more dark

**2** *That is the _____ cat that I have ever seen!*
- ○ fat
- ○ fatter
- ● fattest
- ○ more fatter

**3** *The plant is _____ than it was last week.*
- ○ more greener
- ● greener
- ○ greenest
- ○ the most greenest

**4** *He is a _____ runner.*
- ● fast
- ○ faster
- ○ fastest
- ○ most fastest

**5** *The mouse had the _____ feet of them all.*
- ○ tinier
- ● tiniest
- ○ more tiny
- ○ most tiny

**6** *It is _____ today than it was yesterday.*
- ○ cold
- ● colder
- ○ coldest
- ○ more colder

**TERRANOVA**

Exercises • Preparation and Practice for the ITBS, SAT-9, and TerraNova • Grade 3  289

### Question 1

Comparative adjective—comparing two things

### Question 2

Superlative adjective—comparing more than two things

### Question 3

Comparative adjective is needed. Never use -*er* and *more* together.

### Question 4

Regular adjective is needed. No comparison is being made.

### Question 5

*Them all* is the clue that a superlative adjective is needed.

### Question 6

*Today* is being compared to *yesterday*. Two things are being compared.

# PRONOUNS

**Explain to students that pronouns are special words that take the place of nouns in a sentence.**

Go over the two types of pronouns, object and subject, thoroughly with your class. Write sentences on the board and have students tell you which pronouns are object pronouns and which are subject pronouns. Some examples you might use are:

- *She likes to eat macaroni. (subject)*
- *Jenny is friends with her. (object)*
- *Where are you going with them? (object)*
- *We are not having fun. (subject)*
- *It is great. (subject)*

## TEACHING TIP

Go over the box on the Pupil Edition page with your class. Make sure students are familiar with the difference between singular and plural pronouns.

**Go over the example question as a class.**

---

**Exercise 22**

## ON YOUR MARK!

### Pronouns

A **pronoun** is a word that takes the place of a noun.

A **subject pronoun** is used as the subject of a sentence. It tells whom or what the sentence is about.

*The classrooms* are empty.      *They* are empty.

An **object pronoun** is never the subject. It follows an action verb or a word such as *for, at, of, with,* or *to.*

*Vince met **Alice**.*      *Vince met **her**.*

> A pronoun *must* match the noun it refers to. Singular pronouns take the place of singular nouns. Plural pronouns take the place of plural nouns.
>
> **Subject Pronouns**      **Object Pronouns**
> **Singular:** *I, you, he, she, it*    **Singular:** *me, you, him, her, it*
> **Plural:** *we, you, they*       **Plural:** *us, you, them*

 **GET SET!**

Let's look at an example.

Which word could go in place of the underlined words in the sentence?

<u>The cars</u> are rusty.

- ○ It
- ● They
- ○ He
- ○ She

(2nd) is **correct!** *The cars* is a plural noun. It must be replced by a plural pronun. *They* is the only plural pronoun listed in the answer choices.

---

 ⭐ **EXTRA ACTIVITY**

Prepare a list of sentences for the class using the following format: *Tamika and Valerie are friends. (They, Them) both have brown hair.* Students must circle the pronoun that correctly fits into the sentence. Prepare at least two sentences for each possible pronoun. For extra credit, have students label the correct pronouns as subject or object pronouns.

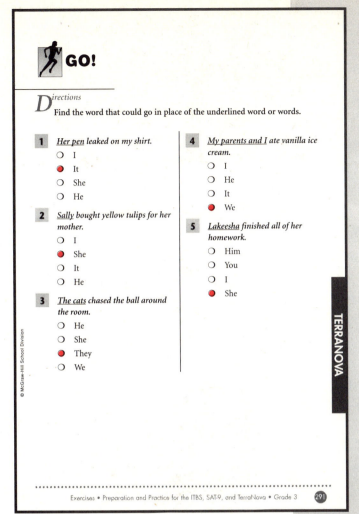

### GO!

**Directions**

Find the word that could go in place of the underlined word or words.

**1** _Her pen_ leaked on my shirt.
- ○ I
- ● It
- ○ She
- ○ He

**2** _Sally_ bought yellow tulips for her mother.
- ○ I
- ● She
- ○ It
- ○ He

**3** _The cats_ chased the ball around the room.
- ○ He
- ○ She
- ● They
- ○ We

**4** _My parents and I_ ate vanilla ice cream.
- ○ I
- ○ He
- ○ It
- ● We

**5** _Lakeesha_ finished all of her homework.
- ○ Him
- ○ You
- ○ I
- ● She

**TERRANOVA**

© McGraw-Hill School Division

### Go over each question on the page as a class.

None of the questions on this page tests students' knowledge of object pronouns. Provide them with extra questions to test this skill. Some examples you can use are:

I told <u>David</u> not to come over.
- ○ he
- ○ it
- ○ him*
- ○ her

James ate all of <u>the leftovers</u>.
- ○ they
- ○ them*
- ○ him
- ○ we

Cassandra is going to see <u>the play</u>.
- ○ it*
- ○ her
- ○ them
- ○ she

# CONTRACTIONS

**Go over with students how contractions are formed, and explain the proper placement of the apostrophe.**

Ask students to offer extra examples of each type of pronoun. Some examples might be:

## PRONOUN CONTRACTIONS

- *she's*
- *we've*
- *he'd*
- *I'll*

## CONTRACTIONS WITH "NOT"

- *won't*
- *hadn't*
- *don't*
- *couldn't*
- *shouldn't*

For each pronoun students offer, ask them to tell you the two words from which the contraction was made.

**Go over the example question as a class.**

---

**Exercise 23**

## ON YOUR MARK!

### Contractions

A **contraction** combines two words into one word. An **apostrophe** (') is used to show where letters are left out.

*He is playing lacrosse.* ⟶ *He's playing lacrosse.*

*She was not going home.* ⟶ *She wasn't going home.*

There are two kinds of contractions: pronouns joined with verbs, and verbs joined with "not." Here are some common examples:

| Pronoun Contractions | | Contractions with Not | |
|---|---|---|---|
| I am | → I'm | cannot | → can't |
| he is/he has | → he's | did not | → didn't |
| you are | → you're | does not | → doesn't |
| it is/it has | → it's | were not | → weren't |
| we are | → we're | have not | → haven't |
| they have | → they've | is not | → isn't |
| | | are not | → aren't |

## GET SET!

Let's look at an example.

Which of the following has correct punctuation?

- ● You shouldn't cross the street without looking both ways.
- ○ Hes going to buy some fishing bait.
- ○ Wev'e planned on taking a trip for weeks.
- ○ They said theyll bring the books I forgot.

(1st) is **correct!** *Shouldn't* is a contraction of *should not.*

(2nd) is **wrong.** The apostrophe is missing in *he's.* It's a contraction for *he is.*

(3rd) is **wrong.** The apostrophe is misplaced in *we've.* It's a contraction for *we have.*

(4th) is **wrong.** The apostrophe is missing altogether in *they'll.* It's a contraction for *they will.*

---

## TEACHING TIP

Reiterate to students that the apostrophe belongs wherever a letter or letters have been removed. To properly spell a contraction, or to spot a contraction error on the TerraNova, students should look for the missing letters from the combined words.

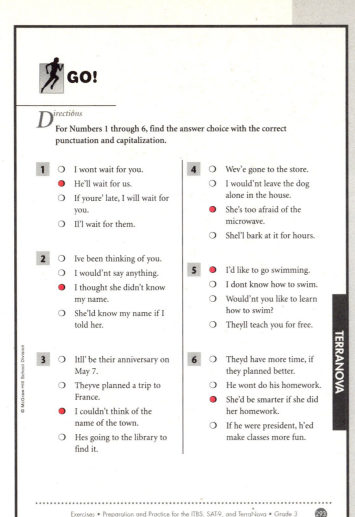

# GO!

**Directions**

For Numbers 1 through 6, find the answer choice with the correct punctuation and capitalization.

**1**
- ○ I wont wait for you.
- ● He'll wait for us.
- ○ If youre' late, I will wait for you.
- ○ Il'l wait for them.

**2**
- ○ Ive been thinking of you.
- ○ I would'nt say anything.
- ● I thought she didn't know my name.
- ○ She'ld know my name if I told her.

**3**
- ○ Itll' be their anniversary on May 7.
- ○ Theyve planned a trip to France.
- ● I couldn't think of the name of the town.
- ○ Hes going to the library to find it.

**4**
- ○ Wev'e gone to the store.
- ○ I would'nt leave the dog alone in the house.
- ● She's too afraid of the microwave.
- ○ Shel'l bark at it for hours.

**5**
- ● I'd like to go swimming.
- ○ I dont know how to swim.
- ○ Would'nt you like to learn how to swim?
- ○ Theyll teach you for free.

**6**
- ○ Theyd have more time, if they planned better.
- ○ He wont do his homework.
- ● She'd be smarter if she did her homework.
- ○ If he were president, h'ed make classes more fun.

TERRANOVA

© McGraw-Hill School Division

Exercises • Preparation and Practice for the ITBS, SAT-9, and TerraNova • Grade 3    293

 **Go over each question on the page as a class.**

On the TerraNova, incorrect usage of contractions includes either incorrect placement of an apostrophe or no apostrophe at all. Students must not only check to see if a word requires an apostrophe but also if the apostrophe is in the right place.

Before students begin working on the questions on this page, remind them of the following:

- *All contractions need an apostrophe.*

- *Apostrophes take the place of the missing words in a contraction.*

- *There are pronoun contractions*

- *There are contractions with "not."*

© McGraw-Hill School Division

# PACING YOURSELF

**Go over the importance of pacing while taking the TerraNova.**

Tell students that performing well on the test involves more than just having strong grammar skills. Test-taking skills are important, too. Efficient use of time will help students perform well. Remind students that relaxing will also help them concentrate.

**Go over the example question as a class.**

---

**Exercise 24**

## ON YOUR MARK!

### Pacing Yourself

It is important to take time to answer each TerraNova question carefully. But you also don't want to spend so much time on a question that you cannot finish the test. That is why *pacing yourself* is important. **Pacing yourself** means completing as many questions as you can without rushing or spending too much time on one question.

- **Do not let yourself get stuck on one question.** If you have been trying to answer a question for a while, take your best guess and move on.
- **Relax as best you can.** Don't worry if you don't know an answer. The TerraNova is just one way to measure your skills. You'll have plenty of other chances to show what you have learned. Besides, the calmer you are, the more likely you are to answer the questions correctly!

## GET SET!

Let's look at another example. Choose the word or words that complete the sentence best. Do you know the answer right away? If not, you shouldn't spend too much time trying to figure it out. You should get rid of answer choices you know are wrong, take your best guess, and then move on.

*Patrick and Elizabeth _____ next August.*

  will move

○  has moved

○  moved

○  is moving

(1st) is **correct!** *Next August* tells you the verb must be in the future tense.

(2nd) is **wrong.** *Has moved* is in the past tense.

(3rd) is **wrong.** *Moved* is in the past tense, too.

(4th) is **wrong.** *Is* is a singular verb. But Elizabeth and Patrick are two people. A plural noun must take a plural verb.

---

## EXTRA ACTIVITY

This activity requires a watch and a few fun and silly quiz questions. Make a sheet full of fun questions. Questions can be about anything students might enjoy. Label the sheet "Quiz." Give half the class the quiz. Have the other half of the class help you yell "Stop!" after one minute. Collect the quizzes. Then give the second half of the class five minutes for the same quiz. Count the scores. Show students that time affects how well they perform. On a timed test, a good pace is as important as strong grammar skills.

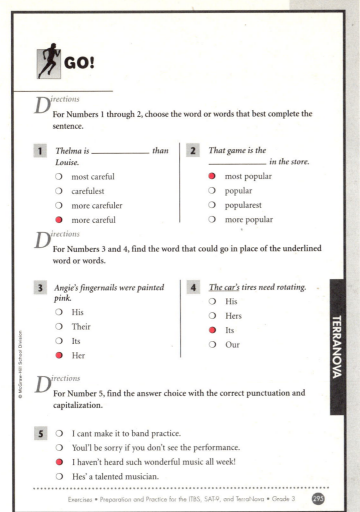

## GO!

*Directions*

For Numbers 1 through 2, choose the word or words that best complete the sentence.

**1** Thelma is _____ than Louise.
- ○ most careful
- ○ carefulest
- ○ more carefuler
- ● more careful

**2** That game is the _____ in the store.
- ● most popular
- ○ popular
- ○ popularest
- ○ more popular

*Directions*

For Numbers 3 and 4, find the word that could go in place of the underlined word or words.

**3** *Angie's* fingernails were painted pink.
- ○ His
- ○ Their
- ○ Its
- ● Her

**4** *The car's* tires need rotating.
- ○ His
- ○ Hers
- ● Its
- ○ Our

*Directions*

For Number 5, find the answer choice with the correct punctuation and capitalization.

**5**
- ○ I cant make it to band practice.
- ○ Youl'l be sorry if you don't see the performance.
- ● I haven't heard such wonderful music all week!
- ○ Hes' a talented musician.

**TERRANOVA**

 **Go over each question on the page as a class.**

The questions on this page test skills learned in the previous exercises of this book. You might want to give students a set amount of time to complete the questions so they can pace themselves as they go along.

### Questions 1 and 2

These are adjective questions.

### Questions 3 and 4

These are pronoun questions.

### Question 5

This is a contraction question.

## Exercise 25

# COMPLETE SENTENCES

 **Go over the difference between a complete sentence and a sentence fragment.**

On the board, show students how a long fragment can look like a complete sentence, yet still lack either a subject or a verb.

**Example:** *Eating with my older brother, my little sister, and the rest of my cousins. (There is no subject.)*

Write some sentences and some fragments on the board, and have students decide which ones are complete sentences. Make sure they can tell you *why* a sentence is or isn't complete.

 **Go over the example question as a class.**

---

 **Exercise 25**

# ON YOUR MARK!

### Complete Sentences

A **sentence** is a group of words that expresses a complete thought. It should contain a noun (a subject) and a verb (a predicate) that goes with it. It must name a person or thing, and it must tell what happens.

*The purple **balloon blew** away.*

A **sentence fragment** is a group of words that does not express a complete thought. It contains only a subject or only a predicate, but not both.

*The purple balloon.          Blew away.*

You should write only in complete sentences!

Some sentences contain *both* a complete thought and an incomplete thought. These are also considered sentence fragments. If a sentence contains two subjects, then both subjects must have an action that goes with them.

*Incorrect:* My sister always sings, and my brother.

*Correct:* My sister always sings, and my brother always whistles.

 **GET SET!**

Let's look at an example.

Which sentence is complete and correct?

- ○ My older brother.
- ○ Plays chess every Thursday.
- ● The dog stinks!
- ○ Her very ugly cat.

(1st) is **wrong.** The predicate is missing. *My older brother* does what?

(2nd) is **wrong.** The subject is missing. Who *plays chess every day?*

(3rd) is **correct!** The subject is *the dog* and the verb is *stinks.* This sentence is complete.

(4th) is **wrong.** The predicate is missing. The *cat* does what?

*© McGraw-Hill School Division*

(296) Exercises • Preparation and Practice for the ITBS, SAT-9, and TerraNova • Grade 3

---

 ⭐ **EXTRA ACTIVITY**

Play a game with students. Write different fragments on several index cards. Some should include a subject with no verb. Others should include a verb with no subject. Hand out one card to each student. Start a stopwatch and give students one minute to find a partner whose fragment can begin or end their sentence. The first pair to complete a sentence wins a prize.

*© McGraw-Hill School Division*

## Go over each question on the page as a class.

### Question 1

The answer must be a complete predicate with verb.

### Question 2

The sentence requires a subject.

### Questions 3, 4, 5, and 6

Explain that long answer choices are not necessarily complete sentences. A complete sentence must have a subject and predicate.

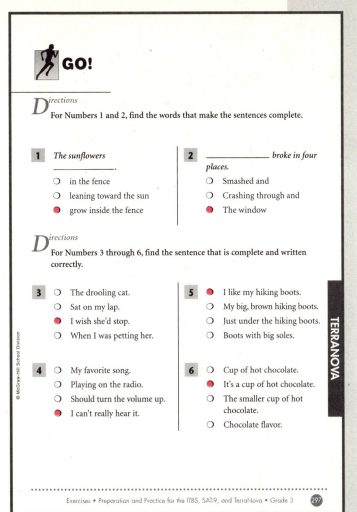

**GO!**

*Directions*

For Numbers 1 and 2, find the words that make the sentences complete.

**1** *The sunflowers*
_____.

○ in the fence
○ leaning toward the sun
● grow inside the fence

**2** _____ *broke in four places.*

○ Smashed and
○ Crashing through and
● The window

*Directions*

For Numbers 3 through 6, find the sentence that is complete and written correctly.

**3** ○ The drooling cat.
○ Sat on my lap.
● I wish she'd stop.
○ When I was petting her.

**4** ○ My favorite song.
○ Playing on the radio.
○ Should turn the volume up.
● I can't really hear it.

**5** ● I like my hiking boots.
○ My big, brown hiking boots.
○ Just under the hiking boots.
○ Boots with big soles.

**6** ○ Cup of hot chocolate.
● It's a cup of hot chocolate.
○ The smaller cup of hot chocolate.
○ Chocolate flavor.

**TERRANOVA**

# RUN-ON SENTENCES AND CONJUNCTIONS

 **Go over the examples of run-on sentences and conjunctions with students.**

Emphasize that conjunctions—such as *and*, *but*, *because*, *so*, and *if*—can often fix run-on sentences.

On the board, write several run-on sentences and ask students to fix them by inserting conjunctions. Some examples of run-on sentences you might use are

- *I like to play baseball I'm not a very fast runner. (but)*

- *I will go to the pool it is sunny. (if)*

- *Lizards are slimy they are interesting to look at. (and)*

- *I'm tired I didn't sleep well last night. (because)*

- *Rudy is studying hard he will do well on the test. (so)*

Point out that commas usually go before the conjunction in a sentence.

 **Go over the example question as a class.**

---

 **Exercise 26**

# ON YOUR MARK!

## Run-On Sentences and Conjunctions

A **run-on sentence** joins together two or more sentences that should be written separately.

*Let's go to the car wash it will be fun to sit inside the car.*

*Grammy's molasses cookies are the best in my neighborhood she uses a special recipe.*

A **conjunction** is a word that joins two ideas together. *And, but, because, so,* and *if* are all conjunctions.

Conjunctions can fix run on sentences.

**Run-on:** *I love Saturdays, I get to stay up late.*

**Complete Sentence:** *I love Saturdays **because** I get to stay up late.*

 # GET SET!

Let's look at an example.

Which sentence is complete and correctly written?

○  I like my shoes, they are very comfortable.

○  I walk to school it is not far.

○  I like to walk and I see people and I feel calm.

●  It takes me ten minutes to walk to school.

(1st) is **wrong.** This sentence is a run-on. It is really two sentences joined by a comma.

(2nd) is **wrong.** This sentence is really two sentences.

(3rd) is **wrong.** This sentence is really three sentences joined by *and*.

(4th) is **correct!** It has one subject and one verb, and it is one complete idea.

---

  ## EXTRA ACTIVITY

Write a short story using one very long run-on sentence. Hand out copies to students and have them read along as you read to them. Have students correct your story. (They can be the teacher and use a red pen!) Tell them to use commas and conjunctions in their corrections.

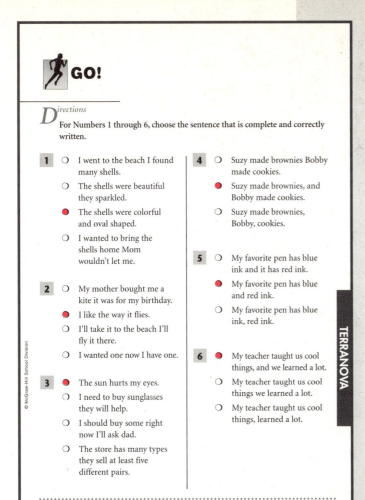

## GO!

*Directions*

For Numbers 1 through 6, choose the sentence that is complete and correctly written.

**1**
- ○ I went to the beach I found many shells.
- ○ The shells were beautiful they sparkled.
- ● The shells were colorful and oval shaped.
- ○ I wanted to bring the shells home Mom wouldn't let me.

**2**
- ○ My mother bought me a kite it was for my birthday.
- ● I like the way it flies.
- ○ I'll take it to the beach I'll fly it there.
- ○ I wanted one now I have one.

**3**
- ● The sun hurts my eyes.
- ○ I need to buy sunglasses they will help.
- ○ I should buy some right now I'll ask dad.
- ○ The store has many types they sell at least five different pairs.

**4**
- ○ Suzy made brownies Bobby made cookies.
- ● Suzy made brownies, and Bobby made cookies.
- ○ Suzy made brownies, Bobby, cookies.

**5**
- ○ My favorite pen has blue ink and it has red ink.
- ● My favorite pen has blue and red ink.
- ○ My favorite pen has blue ink, red ink.

**6**
- ● My teacher taught us cool things, and we learned a lot.
- ○ My teacher taught us cool things we learned a lot.
- ○ My teacher taught us cool things, learned a lot.

**TERRANOVA**

## Go over each question on the page as a class.

### Question 1

Only the third answer choice uses a conjunction correctly.

### Question 2

All the incorrect answer choices are run-on sentences.

### Question 4

Commas usually precede a conjunction that connects two complete sentences.

# TOPIC SENTENCES

**Go over the importance of topic sentences with students.**

Review the steps for finding the topic sentence.

Explain that all paragraphs have a main idea. To enforce this concept, clip some paragraphs from stories or articles and read them to students. Ask them to tell you the main idea of each paragraph you read. You might want to leave out the topic sentence and have students offer suggestions. Write their suggestions on the board.

**Go over the example question as a class.**

---

Exercise 27

## ON YOUR MARK!

### Topic Sentences

Writers use **paragraphs** to organize their ideas. A paragraph should have one **main idea**. This idea is usually stated in a topic sentence, the first sentence in the paragraph. The rest of the sentences should work together to tell about the main idea.

> On the TerraNova, some questions ask you to read a paragraph and then choose the sentence that would make the best topic sentence for the paragraph. In order to find the topic sentence, you should:
>
> 1. Read the rest of the paragraph.
> 2. Decide what the paragraph is mostly about.
> 3. Choose the sentence that tells what the paragraph is mostly about.

## GET SET!

Let's look at an example.

Choose the sentence that should come first in this paragraph.

_____. *His mother told him that they are good for him. His favorite vegetables are carrots and tomatoes.*

○   Pierce eats a piece of fruit for lunch.

●   Pierce eats a lot of vegetables.

○   Pierce doesn't listen to his mother.

○   Pierce wants to get a pet hamster.

(1st) is **wrong.** The paragraph does not mention fruit.

(2nd) is **correct!** The paragraph is mostly about vegetables. It makes sense that the topic sentence is about eating a lot of vegetables.

(3rd) is **wrong.** The topic sentence should talk about vegetables, not his mother.

(4th) is **wrong.** The paragraph does not mention hamsters.

---

### TEACHING TIP

To encourage students to look for topic sentences in their reading, ask them to bring their favorite stories to class. Have them choose a few paragraphs from each story and write down the topic sentences. Check to see if they are copying their sentences correctly. For fun, choose a few of the stories and read them aloud to the class.

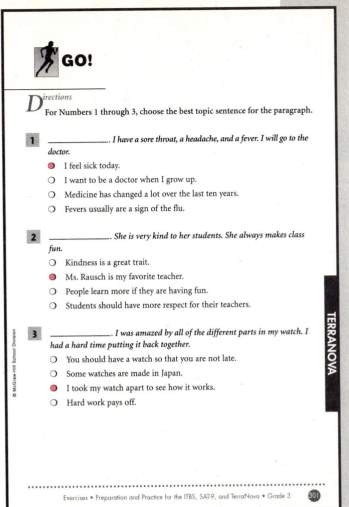

### GO!

*Directions*

For Numbers 1 through 3, choose the best topic sentence for the paragraph.

**1** _____. *I have a sore throat, a headache, and a fever. I will go to the doctor.*

- ● I feel sick today.
- ○ I want to be a doctor when I grow up.
- ○ Medicine has changed a lot over the last ten years.
- ○ Fevers usually are a sign of the flu.

**2** _____. *She is very kind to her students. She always makes class fun.*

- ○ Kindness is a great trait.
- ● Ms. Rausch is my favorite teacher.
- ○ People learn more if they are having fun.
- ○ Students should have more respect for their teachers.

**3** _____. *I was amazed by all of the different parts in my watch. I had a hard time putting it back together.*

- ○ You should have a watch so that you are not late.
- ○ Some watches are made in Japan.
- ● I took my watch apart to see how it works.
- ○ Hard work pays off.

TERRANOVA

 **Go over each question on the page as a class.**

### Question 1

Only the first answer choice logically leads to the second sentence.

### Question 2

Only the second answer choice tells who *she* is in the second sentence.

### Question 3

Only the third answer choice introduces the narrator's actual watch.

# Exercise 28

## SUPPORTING A TOPIC SENTENCE

 **Go over the information regarding supporting sentences.**

Read with students the important details located in the box on the Pupil Edition page.

Explain to students the difference between a general idea and a specific idea. Make a list on the board of topics and explain why each is general or specific. Some examples you might use are:

- *cat*
- *Siamese cat*
- *athletes*
- *tennis players*
- *food*
- *macaroni and cheese*

 **Go over the example question as a class.**

 **ON YOUR MARK!**

### Supporting a Topic Sentence

You have learned that a **topic sentence** of a paragraph introduces what the paragraph is about. The sentences that follow should **support** the topic sentence. They should not just talk about the general topic. They should prove or give details about what the topic sentence says.

> On the TerraNova, some questions ask you to read a topic sentence and then choose the sentence that best supports it. Find the sentence that talks about the **specific idea** in the topic sentence, not just the general idea.

 **GET SET!**

Let's look at an example.

Choose the sentences that best supports this topic sentence.

*My favorite sport is tennis. _____. I also like to hit the ball with my racket.*

- ○ Football is my favorite sport.
- ○ I don't like to hit the ball into the net though.
- ● I like to run around the court.
- ○ I like sports.

(A) is **wrong.** The topic sentence and the last sentence are both about *tennis*. The middle sentence must be about tennis, too.

(B) is **wrong.** The last sentence states that the author *also* likes something about tennis. Therefore, the middle sentence must state that the author likes something about tennis, too.

(C) is **correct!** The topic sentence is about *tennis*. The last sentence is about what the author *likes*. It makes sense that the middle sentence is also about something the author *likes about tennis*.

(D) is **wrong.** The topic sentence already tells us that the author likes a sport. The middle sentence should not repeat what the topic sentence has already said.

302  Exercises • Preparation and Practice for the ITBS, SAT-9, and TerraNova • Grade 3

© McGraw-Hill School Division

  **TEACHING TIP**

Every good paragraph will only contain information necessary to the story. Still, there are sentences that carry greater importance than others. Tell students that they must recognize which sentences are topic sentences, which are supporting the topic, and which simply make the passage readable by connecting all of the writer's ideas.

© McGraw-Hill School Division

**GO!**

*Directions*

For Numbers 1 through 3, choose the sentence or sentences that best fit in the story.

**1** *My dog is very friendly. _____. I'm glad she plays well with people.*

- ● She'll run up to people and lick their faces.
- ○ I am friendly, too.
- ○ I also have a friendly cat.
- ○ My favorite dog is a golden retriever.

**2** *She is a fast reader. _____. She can also remember it all.*

- ○ She types quickly, as well.
- ● She read the whole book in one day.
- ○ Reading is important.

**3** *This set of markers is the most complete of all of the ones in the art room. _____.*

- ● It has one of every color. None of the markers in this set have run out of ink.
- ○ I like to draw with markers. It is more fun than making pictures with paint.
- ○ Markers come in many different styles. You should check the box before you buy a set.
- ○ Art is a great escape. Whenever I feel stressed, I always use art to calm down.

**TERRANOVA**

 **Go over each question on the page as a class.**

Students must read each answer choice carefully in order to determine which choice fits the best with the example sentences. More than one answer choice might seem correct, but only one sentence fits best with the story.

## Exercise 29

# KEY WORDS

 **Go over the concept of key words with students.**

Advise students that they need to be able to recognize key words within sentences and paragraphs. Key words in sentences will help them find topic sentences. Key words in paragraphs will help them find the main idea of the paragraph.

 **Go over the example question as a class.**

---

### Exercise 29

# ON YOUR MARK!

## Key Words

As you know, **understanding the main idea** of a paragraph is very important when answering some TerraNova questions. A good way to help you figure out the main idea of a paragraph or sentence is to look for key words. Key words are the most important words in a sentence.

*Pamela went to the **store** and bought some **ice cream**.*

The key words of this sentence are *store* and *ice cream*. More than any other words in the sentence, *store* and *ice cream* tell you what the sentence is about.

Whenever the TerraNova asks you about a topic sentence or to fill in a blank in a paragraph, pick out the key words to make it easier to compare the answer choices.

 # GET SET!

Let's look at an example. Finding the key words will help you understand what information the missing sentence should be about.

**Which sentence best completes the paragraph?**

*There is just one problem with my favorite pair of shoes. _____ . I haven't figured out how to get the stains out.*

- ○ Shoes are really important.
- ○ I like shoes, especially when walking on rocky beaches.
- ○ My mother uses detergent to get stains out.
- ● They stain my socks brown.

(4th) is **correct!** The key words are *shoes* and *stain*. The answer must link the shoes to the stain.

---

## TEACHING TIP

The TerraNova tests language arts skills that are best improved through practice. Advise students that they should read as much as they can in order to improve their knowledge of language arts concepts. In general, reading is a beneficial habit. For the TerraNova, it will enable students to read and understand questions better, as well as make them more skilled at handling information found in paragraphs.

Tell students to read the entire question before looking at the answer choices. The correct answer choice will agree in meaning and content with the other sentences. Remind students to look for key words when answering the questions on this page.

### Question 1

This is a question about complete sentences.

### Question 2

This is a supporting sentences question.

### Question 3

This is a topic sentence question.

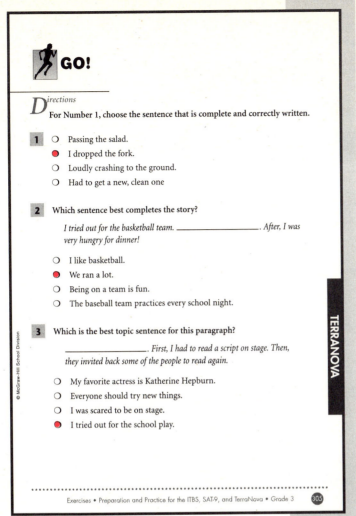

**GO!**

*Directions*
For Number 1, choose the sentence that is complete and correctly written.

**1**
- ○ Passing the salad.
- ● I dropped the fork.
- ○ Loudly crashing to the ground.
- ○ Had to get a new, clean one

**2** Which sentence best completes the story?

*I tried out for the basketball team. _____. After, I was very hungry for dinner!*

- ○ I like basketball.
- ● We ran a lot.
- ○ Being on a team is fun.
- ○ The baseball team practices every school night.

**3** Which is the best topic sentence for this paragraph?

*_____. First, I had to read a script on stage. Then, they invited back some of the people to read again.*

- ○ My favorite actress is Katherine Hepburn.
- ○ Everyone should try new things.
- ○ I was scared to be on stage.
- ● I tried out for the school play.

TERRANOVA

## Exercise 30

# PREPARING FOR THE TERRANOVA

Go over the tips for preparing for the TerraNova discussed on the Pupil Edition page.

Remind students that the TerraNova is a test, not a class. It will simply ask them what they know, not teach them something new. They shouldn't worry. Encourage students as the test approaches by assuring them that they will be prepared after completing the exercises in this book.

Go over the example question as a class.

---

### Exercise 30

## ON YOUR MARK!

### Preparing for the TerraNova

Sometimes when you read a question, you might think the first answer choice you read is correct. It may be correct, but always read all of the answer choices before you decide. If you mark the first answer choice you think is correct, you might miss a better answer that comes later.

> **Remember:** Always get rid of the wrong answer choices first. Put a finger over the wrong answers as you rule out each wrong answer choice. It will help you remember to read all of the answer choices before you mark your answer.

## GET SET!

The tips above will help you feel at ease when answering questions like this one and those on the next page on the day of the real test. Let's look at another example.

Which sentence is complete and correct?

- ○ They will go to the movie yesterday.
- ○ Loving the month of September!
- ● My father is taller than my mother.
- ○ He sitted on the ground after he saw there were no seets.

(1st) is **wrong.** The verb is in the future tense, but the word *yesterday* tells you it already happened. The verb *will go* should be *went*.

(2nd) is **wrong.** This is not a complete sentence. It's a fragment.

(3rd) is **correct!** The subject and the verb agree, the adjective, *taller*, is correct, and the sentence is complete.

(4th) is **wrong.** The past tense of *to sit* is *sat*, not *sitted*.

---

## TEACHING TIP

The information in the Remember box on the Pupil Edition page is useful for any test, including the TerraNova. Eliminating incorrect answer choices is a good test-taking habit. Using the process of elimination will help students focus on their skills rather than the superfluous test answers. Reinforce the idea of eliminating wrong answer choices with students.

## Go over each question on the page as a class.

### Question 1

This is an adjective question.

### Question 2

This is a subject-predicate question.

### Question 3

This is a supporting sentences question.

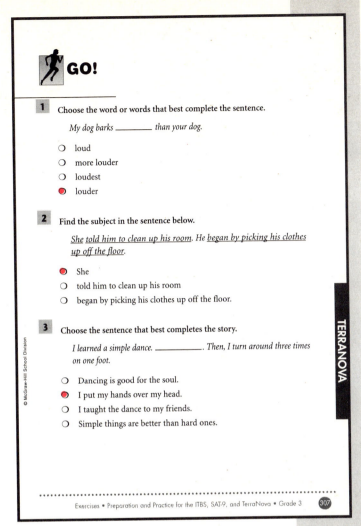

**GO!**

**1** Choose the word or words that best complete the sentence.

*My dog barks _____ than your dog.*

○ loud
○ more louder
○ loudest
● louder

**2** Find the subject in the sentence below.

*She told him to clean up his room. He began by picking his clothes up off the floor.*

● She
○ told him to clean up his room
○ began by picking his clothes up off the floor.

**3** Choose the sentence that best completes the story.

*I learned a simple dance. _____. Then, I turn around three times on one foot.*

○ Dancing is good for the soul.
● I put my hands over my head.
○ I taught the dance to my friends.
○ Simple things are better than hard ones.

TERRANOVA

# Practice
# Test

# Reading and Language Arts

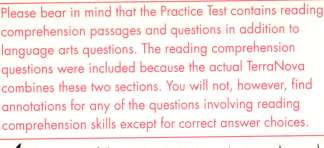

Robert needed money to buy a toy. He saw a sign that said the newspaper needed people to deliverer papers.

## Sample A

Robert probably ＿＿＿＿＿＿＿＿＿＿.

- ○ gave up on the idea of buying the toy
- ○ put an advertisement in the paper that he wanted the toy
- ● called the newspaper about the delivery job

## Sample B

Find the word or words that best complete the sentence.

*Sample questions help make test directions ＿＿＿＿＿＿ to understand.*

- ○ more easier
- ○ most easiest
- ● easier
- ○ least easiest

**Go On** →

**TERRANOVA**

# Section 1

What makes you feel good about yourself? Helping others? Helping others when you do not want anything in return is called a good deed. The stories in this section all have to do with doing good deeds.

"Smile!" is a poem about a girl who helps people cheer up by smiling at them. Read the poem, then answer Numbers 1 through 8.

## Smile!

Why are people so glum?
I should help them out some.
When I take a look around,
Just frowning faces are found.
So I should let my joy show
In every situation, wherever I go.
If someone looks sad,
I'll show them I'm glad.
Across my face,
On my happy space,
I'll let a huge smile grow,
And then for sure, I know,
A little joy will spread
Instead of this dread!

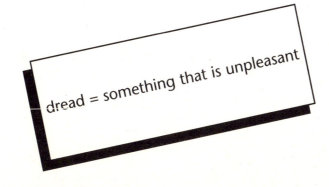

dread = something that is unpleasant

Go On →

**1**  The people that the girl smiled at will probably

- ○ hate the girl for being so happy
- ○ be sadder than before
- ● smile back

**2**  The girl says the smile grows on her <u>happy space</u>. Which of these is probably her <u>happy space</u>?

- ○ the street where she sees sad people
- ● her mouth
- ○ her favorite park

**3**  Which of the following is NOT a way that the girl tries to cheer up people?

- ○ She smiles at them.
- ○ She lets people see that she is happy.
- ● She tells them jokes.

**4**  The girl in the poem wonders, "Why are people so <u>glum</u>?" <u>Glum</u> probably means

- ○ happy
- ○ helpful
- ● sad

© McGraw-Hill School Division

**5** Why does the girl smile at people?

○ She hopes that they will give her toys.

● She wants to make them happy.

○ She doesn't want them to know that she is sad.

**6** The words "glad" and "joy" are both words that mean happiness. Which of these words also means happiness?

○ dread

● cheer

○ fear

**7** Choose the word that best completes this sentence.

*After she smiled at them, they were less _____ than they were before she smiled.*

● sad

○ sadder

○ saddest

> Never use the word *less* and an *-er* or *-est* ending with the same adjective.

**8** Find the sentence that is complete and written correctly.

● I like to smile.

○ As she smiles at them.

> Without the *as* this would be a complete sentence. With the *as* it becomes part of a larger sentence.

○ My smile larger than yours.

> No verb

TERRANOVA

**Go On** →

Read this story about how Bobby helped a man walk his dogs. Then answer Numbers 9 through 15.

# Furry Friends

Bobby usually jogged about three times a week. But lately, he didn't look forward to running. He started to feel bored and lonely on his long jogs.

One day, Bobby decided that he needed to stretch out a bit before he started running, so he walked around the block. Mr. Bland, Bobby's neighbor, was sitting on his porch in his wheelchair, staring at Bobby's running shoes with a far-away look in his eyes.

"What a fine day to go for a nice run, especially if you're a dog," Mr. Bland remarked.

Bobby had no idea what Mr. Bland was trying to say, and it must have shown on his face. Mr. Bland explained that he used to run every day with his dogs, but ever since his accident, the dogs did not get to run at all.

"I would love to run with your dogs, but, um, what kind of dogs are they?" said Bobby.

"Oh, they're golden retrievers that are just as sweet as can be. I didn't mean to bother you, it's just that you're wearing the same pair of running shoes that I used to wear."

"I'd love to have some company," Bobby said to Mr. Bland. "And I'd probably get a lot more exercise with a running partner or two."

Mr. Bland's face beamed as he called for his dogs. The dogs ran out of the house and jumped up on Bobby, licking his face and wagging their tails like mad. Bobby laughed at the dogs' excitement. They almost knocked him over! Mr. Bland gave a whistle like he used to before he took the dogs for a run. The dogs' ears perked at the first sound of the whistle. They both ran back into the house, and each came out with a leash in his mouth.

Bobby was amazed, and said to Mr. Bland with a laugh, "Wow, it looks like we're ready to go!"

**9** Why did the dogs grab their leashes?

○ Bobby shouted, "Let's go!"

● Mr. Bland whistled.

○ Bobby laughed at how happy the dogs were.

**10** The dogs ears "<u>perked</u> up at the first sound of the whistle." Which of these means about the same thing as <u>perked</u>?

○ drooped down

○ hurt a lot

● pointed up

**11** Mr. Bland was first reminded of his running days when —

● he saw Bobby's shoes

○ the dogs came out with their leashes

○ he whistled

**12** Which of these pictures best shows what the dogs look like?

●　　　　　　　　　○　　　　　　　　　○

Go On

TERRANOVA

**13** Why does Bobby ask what type of dogs Mr. Bland has?

○   He is allergic to certain types of dogs.

●   He wants to know if the dogs are friendly and fun.

○   He likes to run alone.

**14** Find the word or words that best complete the sentence.

*Mr. Bland and his dogs _____ and stretched every day.*

○   run

●   ran      This verb must be the same tense as "stretched."

○   are running

**15** Which of these is a complete and correctly written sentence?

●   Dogs are terrific.

○   Running with dogs.

○   To get in shape.

© McGraw-Hill School Division

**D**irections

Here is a story about how Juan helped a woman cross a street. Read the story, then answer Numbers 16 through 22.

# Crossing the Street

**J**uan was walking towards Chavez Street. The street was hard to cross, because the light changed very quickly. He never thought much about it. Today, however, he saw an elderly woman waiting at the corner. The light had changed several times, but she had missed it each time.

"Hello," Juan said.

"Yes? What?" the woman replied.

"I said Hello."

"Oh," said the woman.

"How are you?" he asked.

"Well, I'd be much better if I could get across this street!"

"What's the problem?" Juan asked.

"I can't really see when the walk sign lights up," the woman answered.

Juan agreed, "Oh. Yes, it is rather dim."

"By the time I see it change," the woman continued, "it's too late for me to start walking. I'm rather slow. I'm afraid that I'll twist an ankle on the potholes."

"Could I help?" Juan asked.

"Oh, I don't mean to trouble you."

"I'm in no rush. My name is Juan."

"Hi Juan. You're a very sweet boy. I'm Anna."

TERRANOVA

"I could hold your arm," Juan suggested.

"Okay," said the woman.

"You could put your other hand on my shoulder."

"Gotcha."

"The light is about to change. Are you ready to walk?"

"Yes."

"Okay, here we go," said Juan.

"Oh, this is so much easier."

"We're almost across. Step up over the curb."

"Thank you so much," Anna said gratefully.

"No need to thank me. It was nice to meet you."

"It was nice to meet you, too," said Anna. "Hope to see you again soon."

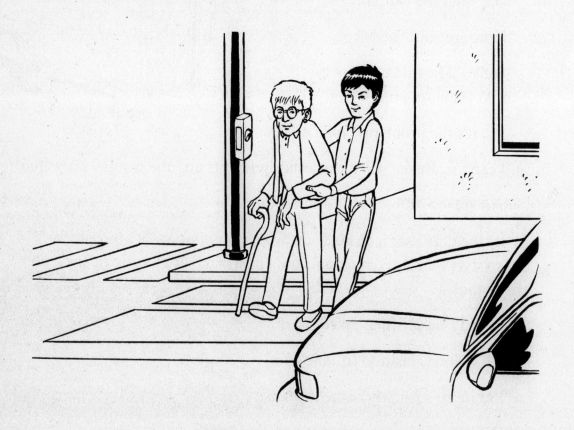

**16** How does Juan know that the woman needs help?

- ◯ He introduces himself.
- ● The woman has missed the light several times.
- ◯ She twisted her ankle and called out to people around her for help.
- ◯ He holds her arm.

**17** The story says that Juan never realized how quickly the light changes. Why do you think that is?

- ◯ He is scared of the street and doesn't like to think about it.
- ● He can walk across the street quickly, so he never noticed it.
- ◯ He does not drive yet, so he doesn't think about lights.
- ◯ He has too much homework to have time to worry about the lights.

**18** Which of these is NOT a reason the woman had trouble crossing the street?

- ◯ She moved slowly.
- ◯ She couldn't quite see when the light changed.
- ◯ She was afraid of the potholes.
- ● She couldn't hear when the cars where coming.

**19** How is Juan similar to the woman?

- ◯ He has trouble crossing the street.
- ◯ He doesn't hear very well, especially near streets.
- ● He also needs help from time to time.
- ◯ He is afraid of the potholes.

TERRANOVA

Go On

**20**  Anna's name is spelled the same when you write it backwards. If you write the letters of her name in reverse order, they still spell Anna. Some other words that are spelled the same when you write the letters in reverse order are mom, level, and radar. The word "apple" is NOT. It spells "elppa" backwards. Which of these words is spelled the same when you write it backwards?

○  never

●  racecar

○  bad

○  backwards

**21**  Find the word or words that best complete the sentence.

*The woman, with Juan's help, could cross the street _____ than without his help.*

○  quickly

●  more quickly     Use *more* to compare the two different things.

○  most quickly

○  quickliest

**22**  Find the word that best completes the sentence.

*I would like to help _____ when we cross the street.*

○  he

●  him     This must be a non-possessive object pronoun.

○  himself

○  his

# Section 2

Sometimes people discover great things by accident. In this section, you will read about some discoveries that people made without meaning to.

Go On

*Directions*

Read this passage about the invention of cheese. Then answer Numbers 23 through 32.

# By Golly, It's Cheese!

An Arabian man set out to travel across the hot desert. He left behind practically all of his belongings but took some food and a pouch made of a sheep's stomach for storing milk.

After traveling for a while, he opened the pouch of milk. But he found that the milk was no longer milk! It had separated into two forms. The first was thick chunks. We now call this cheese curd. The second was a watery fluid. We now call this whey. These are the basic forms of cheese. The Arabian traveler had accidentally discovered cheese!

Don't try this experiment at home. If you left some milk sitting around your house, it would not magically turn into cheese. The traveler had the two necessary things to make cheese; heat, and digestive juices. The heat of the sun slowly warmed his milk, and the digestive juices from his sheep's stomach pouch helped turn the milk into cheese. The Arabian's journey across the desert turned into a great discovery!

**23** The passage says that when the traveler looked at his milk, it "had separated into two forms." This probably means that

- ● the milk split into two different parts
- ○ the pouch ripped in half
- ○ the milk divided itself into two pouches
- ○ the milk combined with the pouch

**24** The traveler discovered the milk had become cheese when

- ○ he separated out the two forms with his fingers
- ○ he warmed the milk
- ○ he digested it
- ● he opened his pouch

**25** The passage states that the traveler had the two <u>necessary</u> things to make cheese. The OPPOSITE of <u>necessary</u> is

- ○ trouble
- ○ needed
- ● unwanted
- ○ smallest

**26** The traveler's milk became cheese because of the sun and the digestive juices. How did digestive juices get in his milk?

- ○ The traveler ate the milk.
- ● The traveler's pouch was made of a sheep's stomach.
- ○ The traveler put whey in with the milk.
- ○ When the traveler opened the pouch, some camel spit got in the milk.

Go On →

TERRANOVA

**27** The passage describes <u>whey</u> as

- ● watery
- ○ thick
- ○ chunky
- ○ warm

**28** Dan wrote a paragraph about food after reading the passage about cheese. Which of these is the best topic sentence for the paragraph?

_____. *Cheddar melted on broccoli is my favorite snack to eat while watching television. Fried mozzarella tastes delicious on a sandwich.*

- ○ There are several types of cheese sold in America today.
- ○ Cheese is a good source of calcium.
- ● I like to eat different types of cheese.
- ○ There are two basic forms of cheese.

Only the third choice logically connects to the word *my* in the paragraph.

**29** Which word in the following sentence is the <u>predicate</u> of the sentence?

*I like blue cheese.*

- ○ I   Subject
- ● like
- ○ blue   Adjective
- ○ cheese   Object

**30** Which sentence is complete and written correctly?

- ○ They was eating cheese.
- ○ We wasn't able to eat the cheese.
- ○ I have eated cheese that was bad.
- ● I ate some of the cheese.

**31**  Find the sentence that best completes the story.

*We made some cheese in science class. _____. Then we added some special ingredients.*

● First, we stirred the milk.

○ We do many different experiments at school.

○ Sometimes science experiments are hard.

○ I like science class the best.

*Only the first choice logically connects to the word then in the paragraph.*

**32**  Find the answer choice with the correct punctuation and capitalization.

○ How do you make cheese.  *Needs question mark*

○ There are two things that need to happen to make cheese  *Needs period*

○ first, you need to warm the milk.  *Capitalize first word*

● The milk should separate into two parts.

**TERRANOVA**

Go On

Read the story below. It explains how dogs came to lead the blind. Read the passage, then answer Numbers 33 through 35.

# Guide Dogs for the Blind

World War I left millions of people wounded. Many soldiers were blinded.

At a German hospital for soldiers, a doctor took a blind solider for a walk. The doctor's dog came along for the walk. At one point, someone called the doctor into a building to help. The doctor left the soldier alone with his dog.

By the time the doctor came back, the soldier and dog were gone. The doctor found that his dog had led the blind soldier safely across the hospital grounds.

The doctor was surprised that his untrained dog could lead a man. The doctor thought that if an untrained dog could lead so well, a dog with some training could be very helpful to a blind person.

**33** The picture next to the passage shows

○ how the soldier became blind

○ the way the dog was trained to help blind people

● what helped the doctor get the idea for seeing eye dogs

○ why the doctor was called away

**34** Here is a time line for the events in the passage. Which of the following should go in the blank spot?

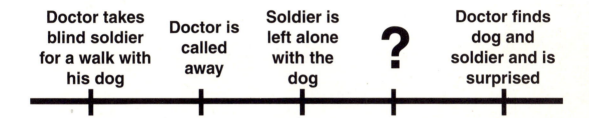

| Doctor takes blind soldier for a walk with his dog | Doctor is called away | Soldier is left alone with the dog | ? | Doctor finds dog and soldier and is surprised |

○ Doctor decides to try to train dogs to help blind people

○ World War I ends

● Dog safely leads the soldier across the hospital grounds

○ Seeing Eye dogs are used all over Germany and then the United States

**35** Which of these is probably the reason that the doctor wants to train dogs?

○ He likes being around dogs.

○ He wants to make lots of money.

● He wants to help blind people.

○ He wants to become famous.

Go On

TERRANOVA

# Directions

Josh wrote a story about a time when his dog helped him. For Numbers 36 and 37, find the word that best completes this story.

Once, I went ice skating. I fell ____**(36)**____ the thin ice. My dog ____**(37)**____ me out of the water.

**36**
- ○ into
- ○ to
- ● through
- ○ on

**37**
- ○ skated
- ● pulled
- ○ wagged
- ○ froze

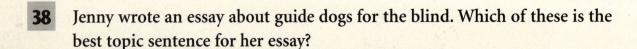

**38** Jenny wrote an essay about guide dogs for the blind. Which of these is the best topic sentence for her essay?

_____. *Once the German doctor had trained a few dogs, guide dogs were used all over Germany. Soon, an American heard of the great help dogs were to blind people, and began an American training center for dogs.*

- ● It did not take long for the idea of guide dogs to catch on.
- ○ The doctor should not have left a wounded soldier alone with just a dog.
- ○ There are thousands of blind Americans in the United States today.
- ○ Dogs can be trained to do a variety of tricks.

> The correct answer choice should mention the subject of the sentences that follow. The subject is *guide dogs.*

**39** Find the sentence that has the correct punctuation and capitalization.

○ There is a training center for dogs in stamford, connecticut.

○ Another training center is in Annapolis Maryland.

○ I worked at the center for dogs in Philadelphia, pennsylvania.

● I think the best center is in Chicago, Illinois.

Always capitalize the names of cities and states, and separate them with a comma.

**40** Find the sentence that is complete and written correctly.

○ Training dogs at the center.

○ The dog and the training.

● The dog was trained well. ◄ This is the only answer choice with a complete subject and a complete predicate.

○ The dog walking.

**41** Find the sentence that best completes this story.

*Guide dogs have a special harness that has a handle. _____. That way, when the dog walks, the person can feel where the dog is going.*

○ They have collars with dog tags, too.

● The person that the dog leads holds onto the handle.

○ Then, the person can follow along without being pulled.

○ There are lots of different harnesses for dogs.

Only the second choice is a logical supporting detail.

TERRANOVA

Go On

For Numbers 42 and 43, find the answer with the correct punctuation and capitalization for each underlined part of this letter.

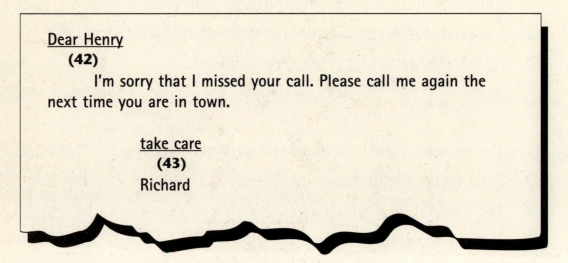

Dear Henry
(42)

    I'm sorry that I missed your call. Please call me again the next time you are in town.

take care
(43)
Richard

**42**
- ● Dear Henry,
- ○ dear Henry
- ○ dear Henry,
- ○ Correct as it is

Always capitalize the first word and the names in a letter greeting, and follow them with a comma.

**43**
- ○ take care,
- ● Take care,
- ○ Take Care
- ○ Correct as it is

Always capitalize the first word of a letter closing, and follow the closing with a comma.

**44** Find the word that best fits <u>both</u> sentences below.

*Don't climb too high, you might _____ down.*

*Next _____, I'm moving to a new town.*

- ○ slip
- ○ week
- ○ spring
- ● fall

**D**irections

For Numbers 45 and 46, choose the sentence that best fits in the blank.

I was a little nervous to move to a new town. I had to go to a new school. _____ **(45)** _____. Would they like me? But after only a week, it was as if I had always lived there. I had plenty of new friends. _____ **(46)** _____. I'm glad we moved here.

**45** ○ I didn't want to do my homework.
- ● I was scared to try to make new friends at the school.
- ○ I liked the new town's park better than my old town's park.
- ○ I get tired easily.

The correct answer choice must introduce a subject that will correspond to the *they* in the next sentence.

**46** ○ I am not familiar with our neighbors.
- ● I even knew the best path to take to walk to school.
- ○ My family moves too often.
- ○ I walk many places.

TERRANOVA

**Go On** ➡

**47** **Which of the following is NOT a complete sentence?**

- ● When I was walking to school. ◄ This is only part of a sentence. It does not express a complete thought.
- ○ I like to walk.
- ○ The school is not far from my house.
- ○ Walking is good for you.

# Spelling

## Directions

For all the spelling questions on this test, tell students they should rule out the spellings that they know are wrong. They should then take their best guess from the remaining selections.

**For Numbers 1 through 9, find the sentence in which the underlined word is spelled correctly.**

**1**
- ● I like him <u>because</u> he is nice.
- ○ I like him <u>becaze</u> he is nice.
- ○ I like him <u>becaws</u> he is nice.
- ○ I like him <u>becaus</u> he is nice.

**2**
- ○ I <u>sed</u> that I would do it.
- ○ I <u>saed</u> that I would do it.
- ○ I <u>sead</u> that I would do it.
- ● I <u>said</u> that I would do it.

**3**
- ○ I asked where he had <u>bine</u>.
- ○ I asked where he had <u>ben</u>.
- ○ I asked where he had <u>bene</u>.
- ● I asked where he had <u>been</u>.

**4**
- ○ Do I <u>noe</u> you?
- ○ Do I <u>kno</u> you?
- ● Do I <u>know</u> you?
- ○ Do I <u>knoe</u> you?

**5**
- ○ You are my <u>favorate</u> teacher.
- ● You are my <u>favorite</u> teacher.
- ○ You are my <u>favorete</u> teacher.
- ○ You are my <u>favorote</u> teacher.

**6**
- ○ She is quite <u>suceful</u>.
- ● She is quite <u>successful</u>.
- ○ She is quite <u>sucessfle</u>.
- ○ She is quite <u>successfle</u>.

**7**
- ○ <u>Finnally</u>, the test was finished.
- ○ <u>Finnaly</u>, the test was finished.
- ○ <u>Finaly</u>, the test was finished.
- ● <u>Finally</u>, the test was finished.

**8**
- ○ They put <u>thayer</u> shoes away.
- ○ They put <u>ther</u> shoes away.
- ● They put <u>their</u> shoes away.
- ○ They put <u>thair</u> shoes away.

**9**
- ○ I'm glad that we are <u>frends</u>.
- ○ I'm glad that we are <u>freinds</u>.
- ● I'm glad that we are <u>friends</u>.
- ○ I'm glad that we are <u>friands</u>.

Remind students of this quote: "A friend to the end." Tell them they can use this to help themselves remember the spelling of the word *friend*.

TERRANOVA

© McGraw-Hill School Division

Go On

**For Numbers 10 through 20, find the underlined word that is NOT spelled correctly. If there are none, mark the last answer choice, "All correct."**

**10** ○ He <u>held</u> my hand.

○ The <u>cabin</u> is close by.

● The shoreline is on the <u>edje</u> of the lake.

○ Grandma has a huge <u>attic</u>.

○ All correct

edge

**11** ● I like skiing <u>beter</u>.

○ The scarf keeps my <u>neck</u> warm.

○ They are big <u>cliffs</u>.

○ Skiing is <u>safe</u>.

○ All correct

better

**12** ○ I took a <u>bath</u>.

● It was <u>dificult</u> because the water was cold.

○ I <u>checked</u> it to see if it was warmer.

○ I didn't have any <u>luck</u>.

○ All correct

difficult

**13** ○ I visited a <u>rain forest</u>.

● I ate many <u>pinapples</u>.

○ I saw many birds, including <u>parrots</u>.

○ They flew around the <u>treetops</u>.

○ All correct

pineapples

© McGraw-Hill School Division

**14**
- ○ I have an important <u>job</u>.
- ○ Please <u>shut</u> the door.
- ○ We <u>painted</u> the room last spring.
- ○ The restaurant is <u>closed</u>.
- ● All correct

**15**
- ○ I heard a <u>strange</u> noise.
- ● It sounded like a person <u>screeming</u>.
- ○ I thought I was <u>imagining</u> it.
- ○ Then I saw <u>someone</u> shouting to me.
- ○ All correct

Screaming, root word: scream

**16**
- ○ She needs to clean up all of her <u>junk</u>.
- ● She can barely find the <u>fone</u> when it rings.
- ○ I bet she finds coins and <u>money</u> in the couch.
- ○ I found almost <u>twenty</u> cents when I cleaned my room!
- ○ All correct

phone

**17**
- ○ She has a very loud <u>laugh</u>.
- ○ The sandpaper is <u>rough</u>.
- ● I <u>nocked</u> three times.
- ○ The math problem was <u>wrong</u>.
- ○ All correct

Silent /k /in knocked

**18**
- ○ He ran very <u>quickly</u> in the race.
- ○ He usually has a lot of <u>speed</u>.
- ● He came in <u>eigth</u>.
- ○ He said that he felt <u>nervous</u> before the race started.
- ○ All correct

This is a tricky spelling. Remind students how *eight* is spelled. Tell them they only need to add an *h* to the end, not a *th*.

**19**
- ○ I <u>disguised</u> myself as my sister.
- ○ My mother was <u>furious</u> that I tricked her.
- ● She wanted to know the <u>reeson</u> I dressed up.
- ○ I said I just wanted to <u>tease</u> her.
- ○ All correct

reason

**20**
- ○ I <u>discovered</u> a new bird.
- ○ It was in my <u>backyard</u>.
- ○ It <u>expects</u> me to feed it.
- ○ My father taught us an important <u>lesson</u>.
- ● All correct

Go On

TERRANOVA

# Language Mechanics

*Directions*

Read the passage and notice the underlined words. For Numbers 1 through 4, find the answer choice with correct punctuation and capitalization. If there is no error in the underlined words, mark the last answer choice, "Correct as it is."

Sasha had <u>ballet, basketball and choir,</u> after school. <u>"Her mother</u>
(1)
<u>said, It's been a busy day."</u> <u>Sasha asked can we meet my friends for</u>
(2)                                                     (3)
<u>some ice cream?"</u> Her mother said, "Sure. <u>There</u> already at the
(4)
store."

**1**
- ○ ballet basketball and choir
- ○ ballet, basketball, and, choir
- ● ballet, basketball, and choir
- ○ Correct as it is

Commas in a series follow each item except the last and never follow the *and*.

**2**
- ● Her mother said, "It's been a busy day."
- ○ "Her mother said," It's been a busy day.
- ○ Her mother said, "It's been a busy day.
- ○ Correct as it is

Quotation marks come directly before and after a speaker's exact words.

**3**
- ○ "Sasha asked can we meet my friends for some ice cream?"
- ○ Sasha asked, Can we meet my friends for some ice cream?"
- ● Sasha asked, "Can we meet my friends for some ice cream?"
- ○ Correct as it is

**4**
- ● They're
- ○ Theyre
- ○ Their
- ○ Correct as it is

Explain the difference between the words *there*, *their*, and *they're*. Stress that *they're* is the only contraction, and all contractions are punctuated with an apostrophe.

For Numbers 5 through 8, read the paragraph. Notice the underlined parts by the numbers. Then find the answer choice with the best capitalization and punctuation for the underlined parts.

I went to the store called <u>happiness is ice cream.</u> I bought
**(5)**
<u>an ice cream cone, a cookie, and a cup</u> of hot chocolate. My friends
**(6)**
<u>arrived they were</u> very hungry. Mark <u>said, "let's</u> go get a hamburger!"
**(7)** **(8)**
I took my ice cream with me to the hamburger store.

**5**
- ○ happiness is Ice cream
- ● Happiness Is Ice Cream
- ○ happiness is ice cream"
- ○ Correct as it is

> Each word in the store's name must be capitalized.

**6**
- ○ an ice cream cone a cookie and a cup
- ○ an ice cream, cone, a cookie and a cup
- ○ an ice cream cone, a cookie and, a cup
- ● Correct as it is

**7**
- ○ arrived. they were
- ○ arrived, They were
- ● arrived. They were
- ○ Correct as it is

> The sentence contains two complete ideas and should be split into two sentences.

**8**
- ● said, "Let's
- ○ said "Let's
- ○ said "let's
- ○ Correct as it is

> A comma must separate a phrase from a quotation, and the first word in a quotation must be capitalized.

TERRANOVA

Go On →

**For Numbers 9 and 10, choose the answer with correct punctuation.**

**9** ● "You're standing on my foot!"

○ "You're standing on my foot"

○ "You're standing on my foot"!

○ "You're standing on my foot,"

**10** ○ How did you get all wet.

● How did you get all wet?

○ How did you get all wet,

○ How did you get all wet

**For Numbers 11 through 16, find the answer choice that has correct capitalization and punctuation.**

**11** ○ The show is on June 4 2003.

○ I want to finish school by July, 20 2002.

● I'll be there on May 3, 2001.

○ I'll 19 years old on November, 30, 2008.

**12** ○ I was not very hungry but I finished all of the food on my plate.

● I was very tired, but I finished my homework.

○ I was bored. but I listened to the speech quietly.

○ I did not like her: but I was still nice to her.

**13**
- ○ She visited Richmond Virginia.
- ○ I flew to dallas, texas.
- ● He lives in Seattle, Washington.
- ○ They work in san francisco california.

Cities and states must be capitalized and separated by a comma.

**14**
- ○ Jenny; why aren't you ready to go?
- ○ Hank did you see my shoes?
- ○ Dad: when did you arrive home?
- ● Mom, where are my socks?

Use a comma to separate the name of the person being addressed from the question they are asked.

**15**
- ○ I spoke with, Frank Evelyn and Sarah.
- ○ She invited Dan Steve, and Tom.
- ○ He danced with Jenny Suzy and Mary.
- ● Jim was faster than Kevin, Tom, and Brian.

Commas go after each item in a series.

**16**
- ● I screamed, "Go team!"
- ○ He yelled, nice play!"
- ○ She hollered "get the ball!"
- ○ We cheered Let's go team!"

No beginning quotation marks

No comma, first word of quote not capitalized

No comma, no beginning quotation marks

TERRANOVA

STOP

# On Your Mark, Get Set, Go! Review

# REVIEW

## Spelling

The spelling skills on this page were originally covered in the On Your Mark! Get Set! Go! section. Refer to the following exercises as necessary:

- Exercise 1        p. 248
- Exercise 2        p. 250
- Exericse 3        p. 252

---

## ON YOUR MARK! GET SET! GO! REVIEW

### Spelling: Learn the Rules

*ie* and *ei* words: *i* comes before *e* except after *c* or when it sounds like /ā/ as in *neighbor*, *freight*, and *sleigh*.

**The silent *e*:** When words **end in silent *e*,** drop the *e* when adding an ending that begins with a vowel, such as *-ing* or *-ed* (*chase* + *ed* = *chased*, *chase* + *ing* = *chasing*). When adding an ending that begins with a consonant, such as *-ly*, keep the silent *e*. (*sure* + *ly* = *surely*)

**The letter *q*:** The letter *q* is always followed by *u*. (*quick*, *quiz*, *quality*)

**The /f/ sound:** The /f/ sound may be spelled *f*, *ph*, or *gh*. (*fear, leaf; phone, graph; laugh*)

### Tips for Memorizing Spelling Words

- Make up **clues** to help you remember the spelling.

  *u* and *i* b<u>ui</u>ld a house; a p<u>ie</u>ce of p<u>ie</u>; the princip<u>al</u> is your p<u>al</u>

- Look for **word chunks** or smaller words that help you remember the spelling. (*hippopotamus = hippo pot am us*)

- **Visualize:** Think of a time you may have seen the word in a book, a magazine, on a sign, or in a textbook. Try to remember how it looked.

### Tricky Spellings

Try writing the word on your own. Try spelling it a few ways. Choose the one that seems correct. Then compare your spelling to the answer choice.

---

### EXTRA ACTIVITY

By now, students have probably realized that there are certain words they always seem to spell incorrectly. Have each student make a list of the "Top Five Suspects." Collect each student's list, and read the difficult words on each of their lists. After you have read each word, have the students write it down on a sheet of paper. When you have read all the words, write each correctly spelled word on the board, and find the number of students who spelled it incorrectly. Write that number next to the word. At the end, the words that were misspelled by the most students are the "Main Suspects." For especially tricky words, try to come up with a good trick for remembering how to spell them.

### End Marks

 **Use periods to end a statement.**
*Mustapha plays the trumpet.*

**Use periods at the end of an abbreviation.**
*I live next to Mrs. Matthews.*

 **Use question marks to end a question.**
*Do you like cheese?*

 **Use exclamation points to end a statement of excitement.**
*Look out for that car!*

 **Use commas when you want to show a pause in your writing.**
*Goodbye, it was nice to meet you!*

**Use commas to set off words that introduce a sentence.**
*Yes, I would love to come to your party.*

**Use commas to set off a person's name when the person is being spoken to.**
*Joe, is that you?*

**Use commas before a conjunction in compound sentences.**
*The chain on my bicycle broke, but Mr. O'Neill fixed it.*

**Use commas between items in a series.**
*He likes cats, dogs, and fish.*

**TERRANOVA**

## End Marks and Commas

The punctuation skills on this page were originally covered in the On Your Mark! Get Set! Go! section. Refer to the following exercises as necessary:

- Exercise 5          p. 256
- Exercise 6          p. 258
- Exercise 7          p. 260

 ### EXTRA ACTIVITY

Divide students into two teams. Play a punctuation game! Write a sentence with at least two missing punctuation marks on the board. Team 1 gets the chance to correct your errors. If they do, they get one point. Then it is Team 2's turn to try another sentence and so on back and forth. If a team is not able to fix both errors in the sentence, the other team gets a chance. If they successfully correct the sentence, then they get two points. Play up to twenty and reward the winning team with five minutes of extra recess.

# REVIEW

## Quotation Marks, Dates and Holidays, and Titles of People

The skills on this page were originally covered in the On Your Mark! Get Set! Go! section. Refer to the following exercises as necessary:

### QUOTATION MARKS

- Exercise 8      p. 262

### DATES AND HOLIDAYS

- Exercise 9      p. 264

### TITLES OF PEOPLE

- Exercise 10     p. 266

---

### Quotation Marks

Quotation marks show that someone is speaking.

*Linda said, "Let's go to a movie."*

**Remember these important rules about writing quotations:**

- Quotation marks come at the beginning and end of a person's exact words.
- The first letter inside a quotation is always capitalized.
  *My sister said, "Your room looks great now!"*
- Put a comma before the quote.
  *Dad said, "I think it's clean enough."*
- Put punctuation at the end of the quote.
  *"I already have," she answered.*

### Dates and Holidays

A **date** lists a specific month, day, and year. A **comma** is placed between the day and the year only. **Months** are proper nouns and are always capitalized.

*October 11, 1973*

A **holiday** is a name that describes a specific date. A holiday may include more than one word.

*St. Patrick's Day*

### Titles of People

A **title** is a term of respect for someone. Capitalize titles and names.

*Principal Adam Skinner*

A title can be abbreviated in some cases.
*Mr., Mrs., Ms., Dr.*

Do not capitalize words for jobs if they do not show a specific person's position.

*The first **president**, **President** Washington, is my favorite **president**.*

---

## EXTRA ACTIVITY

For extra practice with rules for writing dates and holidays, have students write an invitation to a holiday party. The party can be for any holiday, and it can be any type of party. Encourage students to be creative. Remind them that the text of their invitation must include the date of the event and the holiday that the party is in honor of.

### Letters

The **greeting** usually starts with *Dear* followed by the name of the person who will receive the letter. The first word in the greeting and the name should both be **capitalized**. Use a **comma** after the end of the greeting.

> *Dear Joey,*

The **closing** tells that the letter is about to end. Only the first word in the closing should be **capitalized**. Use a **comma** after the end of the closing.

> *Sincerely,*
>
> *Ross*

### Capitalization

**Cities, States, Countries, Continents**
> *Dallas, Washington, France, Asia*

**Geographical Places**
> *Rocky Mountains, Snake River*

**Streets and Highways**
> *Elm Street, Highway 66*

**Buildings and Bridges**
> *Museum of Modern Art, Empire State Building, Golden Gate Bridge*

**Beginning of a Sentence**
> *My mother makes me clothing.*

**TERRANOVA**

## Letters and Capitalization

The skills on this page were originally covered in the On Your Mark! Get Set! Go! section. Refer to the following exercises as necessary:

### LETTERS

- Exercise 11    p. 268

### CAPITALIZATION

- Exercise 12    p. 270
- Exercise 13    p. 272

## EXTRA ACTIVITY

For extra practice with capitalization, write a long paragraph, perhaps in the form of a letter, with 25–30 capitalization mistakes. Include several proper nouns including names of people, places, buildings, and so on. Make a copy for each student, and write the paragraph up on the board. Give the students time to find all the mistakes, and mark them on their copies. Then, go around the room in a circle, asking each student to pick out the very next mistake and explain why it is wrong. Count the number of mistakes that are corrected before one is missed, then either start from the beginning or continue from the next mistake, and praise the students for having gotten that far.

# REVIEW

## Subject and Predicate, Verbs, and Verb Tense

The skills on this page were originally covered in the On Your Mark! Get Set! Go! section. Refer to the following exercises as necessary:

### SUBJECT AND PREDICATE

- Exercise 15     p. 276

### VERBS

- Exercise 16     p. 278

### VERB TENSE

- Exercise 17     p. 280

---

### Parts of a Sentence: Subject and Predicate

The **subject** of a sentence tells what or whom the sentence is about.

    *Mice do not like cats.*

The **predicate** of a sentence tells what the subject does or is.

    *Mona **is an old friend.***

### Verbs

An action **verb** is a word that shows action.

    *The rocket **shoots** up to the moon.*

A verb in the past tense tells about an action that has already happened. Add *-ed* to most verbs to form the past tense.

    look——▸ looked

**Irregular action verbs** are action verbs that have a different spelling than most verbs when they are in the past tense.

    grow——▸ grew

### Verb Tense

Use the **past tense** of a verb for an action that happened *before* now.

    *He **danced** well yesterday.*

Use the **present tense** for an action that is happening now.

    *He **dances** well.*

Use the **future tense** for an action that will happen *after* now.

    *He **will dance** well tomorrow night.*

---

## EXTRA ACTIVITY

For extra practice with verb tense, have students write three short paragraphs. You might want to do this over a period of three days so as not to overwhelm students with too much writing. One paragraph should be about something from their past. One should be about something from their present life. The last paragraph should be about something they want to do or plan to do in the future. Students should use the appropriate verb tenses for each paragraph. Review their work for correct usage and ask some students to read one of their paragraphs to the class.

### Verb Tense Agreement

**A verb must agree with the rest of the sentence.** If part of a sentence talks about the **past**, then the rest of the sentence will most likely be in the past tense, too.

> *When my grandfather was a boy*, *there **was** no television.*

The same is true if a sentence is talking about the **future.** Use the **future** tense of the verb.

> *When I get to school*, *I **will ask** the teacher a question.*

### Helping Verbs

The **main verb** tells what the subject does or is.

> *They are **washing** the dishes.*

The **helping verb** helps the main verb show an action.

> *They **are** washing the dishes.*

### Subject-Verb Agreement

A verb must always **agree** with the subject of a sentence.

If the subject is **singular** (if there is only one of something), then the verb must also be singular.

> *The **artist paints** on the canvas.*

If the subject is **plural** (if there is more than one of something), then the verb must also be plural.

> *The **artists paint** on the canvas.*

**TERRANOVA**

# Verb Tense Agreement, Helping Verbs, and Subject-Verb Agreement

The skills on this page were originally covered in the On Your Mark! Get Set! Go! section. Refer to the following exercises as necessary:

**VERB TENSE AGREEMENT**

- Exercise 17    p. 280

**HELPING VERBS**

- Exercise 18    p. 282

**SUBJECT-VERB AGREEMENT**

- Exercise 19    p. 284

## TEACHING TIP

Understanding verbs is extremely important to success on the TerraNova. Throughout the preparation process, spend a lot of time working with your students on their understanding of verbs, verb tense, and so on. You might want to lead a five-minute verb lesson each week, focusing on a different aspect of verbs (e.g., tense agreement, helping verbs) each week.

# REVIEW

## Adjectives that Compare and Pronouns

The skills on this page were originally covered in the On Your Mark! Get Set! Go! section. Refer to the following exercises as necessary:

### ADJECTIVES THAT COMPARE

- Exercise 21     p. 288

### PRONOUNS

- Exercise 22     p. 290

---

### Adjectives that Compare

Add *–er* to short adjectives that compare two nouns.

> The **taller** tree bloomed in the spring.

Add *–est* to short adjectives that compare more than two nouns.

> The **tallest** tree bloomed in the spring.

Add *more* to adjectives that compare two people, places, or things.

> This book is **more** exciting than that one.

Add *most* to adjectives that compare more than two nouns.

> This book is the **most** exciting book I have ever read.

### Pronouns

A **pronoun** is a word that takes the place of a noun.

> **Nicholas** opened the gift.      **He** opened the gift.

A **subject pronoun** is used as the subject of a sentence. It tells whom or what the sentence is about.

> **The classrooms** are empty.      **They** are empty.

**Singular Subject Pronouns:** *I, you, he, she, it*

**Plural Subject Pronouns:** *we, you, they*

An **object pronoun** follows an action verb or a word such as *for, at, of, with,* or *to.*

> Vince met **Alice**.      Vince met **her**.

**Singular Object Pronouns:** *me, you, him, her, it*

**Plural Object Pronouns:** *us, you, them*

---

 **EXTRA ACTIVITY**

To practice using comparative adjectives, have students think of two people that they know well. It could be their parents, their siblings, their friends, or their relatives. Have students write a short paragraph comparing the two people. Check their paragraphs for correct use of comparative and superlative adjectives.

### Contractions

A **contraction** combines two words into one word. An **apostrophe (')** is used to show where letters are left out. There are two kinds of contractions: pronouns joined with verbs, and verbs joined with *not*.

*He is* playing lacrosse. ————→ *He's* playing lacrosse.

*She was not* going home. ————→ *She wasn't* going home.

### Complete Sentences

A **sentence** is a group of words that expresses a complete thought. It should contain a **subject** (a noun) and a **predicate** (a verb) that goes with it. It must name a person or thing, and it must tell what happens.

*The purple **balloon blew** away.*

A **sentence fragment** is a group of words that does not express a complete thought. It contains **only** a subject or **only** an action, but not both.

*The purple balloon.*          *Blew away.*

**TERRANOVA**

© McGraw-Hill School Division

## Contractions and Complete Sentences

**The skills on this page were originally covered in the On Your Mark! Get Set! Go! section. Refer to the following exercises as necessary:**

### CONTRACTIONS

- Exercise 23     p. 292

### COMPLETE SENTENCES

- Exercise 25     p. 296

⭐ **EXTRA ACTIVITY**

For extra practice with contractions, have students get into groups of three or four. Hand each of them a list of ten contractions that do not include the apostrophe. Start a stopwatch and give students a set amount of time to insert the apostrophes in the correct places and write down the two words that the contraction comes from.

© McGraw-Hill School Division

# REVIEW

## Run-On Sentences, Conjunctions, and Paragraphs

The skills on this page were originally covered in the On Your Mark! Get Set! Go! section. Refer to the following exercises as necessary:

### RUN-ON SENTENCES AND CONJUNCTIONS

- Exercise 26    p. 298

### PARAGRAPHS

- Exercise 27    p. 300
- Exercise 28    p. 302
- Exercise 29    p. 304

---

### Run-On Sentences and Conjunctions

A **run-on sentence** joins together two or more sentences that should be written separately.

*I love Saturdays, I get to stay up late.*

A **conjunction** is a word that joins two ideas together. *And, but, because, so,* and *if* are all conjunctions.

*I love Saturdays, **because** I get to stay up late.*

### Paragraphs

Writers use **paragraphs** to organize their ideas.

A paragraph should have **one main idea**, or **topic**. This idea is usually stated in a **topic sentence**, the first sentence in the paragraph.

The rest of the sentences, **supporting sentences,** should work together to tell about, or develop, the main idea.

   *Pierce eats a lot of vegetables. His mother told him that they are good for him. His favorite vegetables are carrots and tomatoes. Sometimes he eats carrots when he is hungry between meals.*

© McGraw-Hill School Division

---

## TEACHING TIP

To make sure students understand topic sentences, supporting sentences, and main ideas, refer to these concepts whenever you read stories or articles to the class. For example, if you read students a current event article from the newspaper, ask them to help you determine the topic sentence, the supporting details, and the main idea of one of the paragraphs. By incorporating these concepts and terms into regular curriculum work, students will be more prepared for these types of questions on the TerraNova.

© McGraw-Hill School Division

# ITBS Index

# SAT-9 Index

# TerraNova Index

© McGraw-Hill School Division

# TEACHER NOTES

# TEACHER NOTES

# TEACHER NOTES

# TEACHER NOTES

# TEACHER NOTES

# TEACHER NOTES

# TEACHER NOTES

# TEACHER NOTES

# TEACHER NOTES